Schema Therapy with Couples

"*Schema Therapy with Couples* is a very helpful addition to the clinical couples' therapy literature, integrating the individual challenges people face in their own growth with managing a relationship with someone else who also faces their own individual challenges. Drs. DiFrancesco, Roediger, and Stevens provide a guide through this very difficult but everyday terrain that every couples therapist must navigate."

John Gottman, PhD, Author of *The Seven Principles for Making Marriage Work*

"In 25 years of treating couples and closely following the literature, this is the most significant development I have seen. *Schema Therapy with Couples* provides a highly developed systems-oriented theoretical model. With its foundation in schema therapy, this approach can deftly deal with the most severely dysfunctional couples by focusing on personality dysfunction, change at a deep cognitive-emotional level, and potent emotive techniques. *Schema Therapy with Couples* is an extraordinary volume chock-full of figures, instructive clinical examples, and powerful clinical interventions. This innovative work will undoubtedly influence how you treat couples."

Lawrence P. Riso, PhD, Professor of Clinical Psychology, American School of Professional Psychology at Argosy University, Washington, DC

"Schema therapists working with couples bring to their work the insights of the schema therapy approach usually integrated with concepts and insights from couples therapy approaches such as those of Johnson (emotion-focused therapy), Gottman (Gottman couples therapy), Hendrix (Imago therapy), and cognitive-behavioural approaches. Their interest is in the more difficult cases where one or both parties have longstanding psychological problems, often due to significant trauma, abuse and instability in childhood: a personality disorder, a mood disorder (bipolar or chronic depression), addiction, and so on. For several years, the authors of this book have been active in a schema therapy for couples workgroup and share their own discoveries and insights and those of other workgroup colleagues. They show how the central concepts and approach to case formulation and intervention in schema therapy provide a coherent integrative framework. The authors offer a set of guiding and enabling principles as well as practical examples of how to implement specific schema therapy interventions such as mode clash analysis, the mode clash-card, differentiating needs from wants, and imagery and chair-work. The book is rich in clinical examples that will enable readers to encounter the distinctive contribution of the schema therapy approach to couples therapy."

David Edwards, Schema Therapy Institute of South Africa and Rhodes University

"This book teaches the basics of couples in conflicts and provides a deeper, need-based understanding of what goes wrong in relationships. Therapists are offered a toolkit to meet, understand, evaluate, handle, and help couples to stay together despite all interpersonal turmoil. Schema therapeutic couple therapy opens a new window of understanding and provides innovative ways to help."

Gerhard Zarbock, PhD, Clinical psychologist, Director of IVAH, a government approved CBT-training center, Hamburg, Germany, co-author of *Mindfulness for Therapists*

Schema Therapy with Couples

A Practitioner's Guide to Healing Relationships

Chiara Simeone-DiFrancesco, PhD
Counseling Psychologist

Eckhard Roediger, MD
Psychiatrist and Psychotherapist

Bruce A. Stevens, PhD
Clinical Psychologist

WILEY Blackwell

This edition first published 2015
© 2015 John Wiley & Sons, Ltd.

Registered Office
John Wiley & Sons Ltd, The Atrium, Southern Gate, Chichester, West Sussex,
PO19 8SQ, UK

Editorial Offices
350 Main Street, Malden, MA 02148-5020, USA
9600 Garsington Road, Oxford, OX4 2DQ, UK
The Atrium, Southern Gate, Chichester, West Sussex, PO19 8SQ, UK

For details of our global editorial offices, for customer services, and for information about
how to apply for permission to reuse the copyright material in this book please see our
website at www.wiley.com/wiley-blackwell.

The right of Chiara Simeone-DiFrancesco, Eckhard Roediger, and Bruce A. Stevens to be
identified as the authors of this work has been asserted in accordance with the UK
Copyright, Designs and Patents Act 1988.

Library of Congress Cataloging-in-Publication Data

Simeone-DiFrancesco, Chiara.
 Schema therapy with couples : a practitioner's guide to healing relationships / Chiara
Simeone-DiFrancesco, PhD, counseling psychologist, Eckhard Roediger, MD, psychiatrist
and psychotherapist, Bruce A. Stevens, PhD, clinical psychologist.
   pages   cm
 Includes bibliographical references and index.
 ISBN 978-1-118-97264-9 (hardback) – ISBN 978-1-118-97267-0 (paper)
1. Couples therapy. 2. Couples–Psychology. 3. Schema-focused cognitive
therapy. I. Roediger, Eckhard. II. Stevens, Bruce, 1950- III. Title.
 RC488.5.S537 2015
 616.89′1562–dc23

2015008534

A catalogue record for this book is available from the British Library.

Cover image: Cloudy sky with bright sunshine © TAGSTOCK1/Shutterstock Storm
Clouds Saskatchewan ominous wheat fields Saskatchewan © Pictureguy/Shutterstock

Set in 10/12.5pt Galliard Std by SPi Global, Pondicherry, India
Printed and bound in Malaysia by Vivar Printing Sdn Bhd

1   2015

Contents

List of Figures and Tables

Figures

Tables

About the Authors

Dr. Chiara Simeone-DiFrancesco (M.A./M.Ed. 1980/81 Columbia University, NY; Ph.D. 1990 U. of Mississippi), Counseling Psychologist. She founded Wisconsin Family Growth & Reconciliation Center LLC, working with couples for 25 years in private practice. Chiara now directs the Marriage & Family Schema Therapy Institute, a division of Healing International, Inc., a non-profit she co-founded in 1986. Training fellow schema therapists, she founded the ISST Special Interest Group on Couples Schema Therapy, and now chairs its international Subcommittee. Besides training and consulting, Chiara offers 3-day "Couples Intensives" in Wisconsin and Virginia, USA. She speaks and writes in the secular and Christian arena, with a special interest in marriage preparation, healing and support. Her website is www.SchemaTherapyforCouples.com and contact is SchemaHealing@gmail.com

Dr. Eckhard Roediger (MD, Frankfurt, Germany, 1986) is a neurologist, psychiatrist, and psychotherapist. He trained in psychodynamic and cognitive behavior therapy. Eckhard has been the director of the Psychosomatic Department of a clinic in Berlin, since 2007 working in private practice and as director of the Schema Therapy Training Center in Frankfurt. He is the author of a number of German books on schema therapy (www.schematherapie-roediger.de), currently ISST President.

Dr. Bruce A. Stevens (PhD, Boston University, 1987) was Associate Professor in Clinical Psychology at the University of Canberra, Australia. He is now Wicking Professor of Aging and Practical Theology at Charles Sturt University, Canberra. He also has a part-time private practice at Canberra Clinical and Forensic Psychology, a practice he founded in the early 1990s. Bruce was chair of the Canberra section of the Clinical

College of the Australian Psychological Society for four years (2009–2013). He gives many professional workshops on couple therapy throughout Australia. He has written five books, most recently a practitioner book with Dr. Malise Arnstein (*Happy Ever After? A Practical Guide to Relationship Counselling for Clinical Psychologists*, Australian Academic Press, Brisbane, Queensland, 2011), which is mostly from an emotion-focused therapy for couples perspective.

Preface

From all of us

In this book, we have cited many experts and authors, including colleagues, and have tried to convey their ideas accurately. Sometimes we have illustrated a range of opinion, and we do not necessarily agree with everything we have cited (it would not be good to cite only those we agree with, or only those whose work lacks any hint of controversy). In areas of disagreement, we must not overlook anything that could be useful or valuable. We can only take responsibility for expressing our own opinions in these pages.

The authors participate in the Couples/Marital Interest Group of the International Society of Schema Therapy (ISST) (chaired by Simeone-DiFrancesco). This is a group of experienced schema therapists who meet at least monthly to share ideas about treating difficult couples. Some of those ideas, not yet published in peer-reviewed papers, have informed this book. Where possible, we have tried to acknowledge and give credit for all contributions.

We would like to thank the many clients who have helped us to learn to be better therapists and to use ST more effectively.

Please note: All case examples have been made from a composite of clinical experiences, so any resemblance with any actual client is purely coincidental.

From Chiara Simeone-DiFrancesco, PhD

www.SchemaTherapywithCouples.com

This work is in itself an example of the united effort of three colleagues who have become good friends in the process of writing. While we support and agree with the principles we have put forward, we each apply them differently. We offer our written "jewel" to share, yet we each practice the dialogic attitude of acceptance, even where we may have serious issues of disagreement in working with actual cases. Such is the beauty of this work. We believe its principles are applicable to all cultures, faiths, and situations, but its application can take on individual variations in time, place, and culture. This is the beauty of schema therapy and Healthy Adult mode!

I have found our journey in writing together to be a learning experience on all levels, intellectually, emotionally, and spiritually. Through it, some of my own needs in all those areas have been met, and I am very grateful to my colleagues for this. As you read, I hope that you will be able to sense the spirit of humility and openness to learning that my two colleagues, Bruce and Eckhard, have modeled. It has been one of those blessed growth and transformational experiences in life to be part of this journey together. I hope and pray that you will be as inspired as each of us has been in discovering schema therapy for couples (ST-C).

Many possible research applications can stem from what we have presented here. It is a seedbed for further development. We stand with excitement to see how the minds and especially the hearts of our readers are opened to new possibilities of healing and connecting others. My vision is for ST-C, with its heart-changing possibilities, to have an effect on the worldwide divorce rate. If our collective lives can make an impact on that, then they will have been well spent, especially for the future of children who need their parents to be secure and well-connected in love.

We look forward to you, the therapist-reader, developing your own comfort with, and application of, ST-C. And we look forward to you, the seeking and perhaps hurting couple or individual, to perhaps gaining some hope and some strengthening and turning towards healthy ways. Together, we may dare to hope that we will all grow on the continuum towards the fulfillment of the Healthy Adult—with humility and openness, and much thankfulness for those who model for us the greatest virtues. "And the greatest of these is love which holds and binds everything together." (1 Corinthians 13:13)

We welcome your feedback through email, mail, or even phone calls, as we believe that ultimately we are better together!

From Eckhard Roediger, MD

Writing in English was a special challenge for me, but writing together with Chiara and Bruce made it surprisingly easy. We all enjoyed the mutual exchange and inspiration. I especially want to thank all members of the ISST Couples/Marital Special Interest Group initiated and conducted by

Chiara, for their creative and courageous input. They all contributed very much to this book, and we tried to cite them wherever we remembered their personal contributions. Besides that, looking at my own marriage through ST glasses and applying the model described in this book to ourselves helped my wife and I to deal with life challenges much better. So there were gains in many fields! I hope you, as the reader, feel the same.

From Bruce A. Stevens, PhD

bstevens@csu.edu.au
I feel profoundly grateful. I am approaching the age at which many people retire (or at least think about it), but I have found a life of continuing creativity and intellectual stimulation. I am delighted to be with Shayleen. I am surrounded by wonderful colleagues, graduate students and, of course, the courageous couples who challenge any ideas articulated here, saying, "It's all very well to say that in a book, but will it work with us?" I am very grateful for Chiara and Eckhard, two leading schema therapists whom I have found to be both generous and understanding. I have learned more from them than I can adequately acknowledge.

Acknowledgments

I dedicate this to the most glorious reality of marriage, a unity made in heaven. May all see the hope which is ours to share in Christ Jesus.
—Chiara Simeone-DiFrancesco

I dedicate this to my beloved wife, Andrea, who has shared my life for better or worse for more than 30 years now.
—Eckhard Roediger

To Rowena, Kym, Naomi, and Christopher—four wonderful children. And Shayleen, with thanks for the journey.
—Bruce A. Stevens

Abbreviations

BPD	borderline personality disorder
EFT	emotion-focused therapy
EFT-C	emotion-focused therapy for couples
ISST	International Society of Schema Therapy
SMI	Schema Mode Inventory
ST	schema therapy
ST-C	schema therapy for couples
SUDS	Subjective Units of Distress Scale
YPI	Young Parenting Inventory
YSQ-3	Young Schema Questionnaire, version 3

Introduction

First, a bold statement: There is an urgent need for yet another book on couple therapy.

It is time to bring a new perspective to persistent problems and seemingly irresolvable difficulties in relationships. We believe that schema therapy (ST) is a potentially more effective approach than what is currently available. This therapy can deal with problems largely ignored by mainstream cognitive therapy. This includes dysfunctional patterns in intimate relationships and changing troublesome memories from childhood (Arntz & Jacob, 2013). ST has established itself as an evidence-based therapy for treating the most difficult therapeutic problems, and this book explores ways to apply this "strong" therapy to work with couples in effective interventions.[1]

ST has easy-to-grasp concepts, such as schemas and modes, which make sense of the couple's past experiences, educate them, and open the door to allow them to speak freely about ways in which both can feel more connected. These concepts allow the therapist and couple to communicate about what is inside an individual's inner world—and give clearer explanations of what is experienced, such as bodily sensations, varied feelings, thoughts and beliefs, values, and much more. When an individual learns about the origins of dysfunctional patterns, life and relationships tend to

---

[1] It is interesting that some of the best therapy outcomes, with large effect sizes, also use group therapy. Couple therapy might be thought of as being somewhere on a continuum between individual and group therapy. For a review of the results of randomized controlled trials with ST, see Arntz (2012a), and for the cost-effectiveness and evidence of effectiveness see Arntz (2008), Bamelis (2011) and Bamelis et al. (2012). We postulate that it is precisely these "rough edges" of personality, even the "soft conflict" of detached and unaware couples, that require a similar therapeutic "touch." Kindel and Riso (2013) were the first to produce evidence-based research on the effectiveness of the treatment of couples with ST. Dr. Robert Brockman will facilitate further research through the ISST Couples/Marital Subcommittee.

make sense. Better yet, the process, mutually applied, progressively gives the couple effective tools to intercept habitual negative interactions and personality patterns. In the first publication we know in ST-C, Simeone-DiFrancesco (2010) stressed: "ST for Couples and Marriages is a consummate therapy of reality-based hope." This leads to dramatic changes. Few therapies can offer such potential for change, and at the same time create a culture of mutual acceptance and understanding.

Couple therapy has advanced on many fronts. It has been greatly informed by the research of John Gottman (1999, 2011). The effectiveness of emotion-focused therapy for couples (EFT-C) is now well established through clinical trials (Johnson, 2004). However, couples with traits of personality disorder present the greatest therapeutic challenge because of their typically volatile relationships and disordered thinking. This includes the emotional instability of those with borderline personality disorder, the withdrawal of the schizoid, the self-focus of the narcissist and the "moral insanity" of the psychopath. ST was developed to treat more difficult people who present for therapy with powerful interventions, including active re-parenting in imagery rescripting, chair-work dialogs, and behavioral pattern breaking. ST combines the depth and developmental theory of longer term treatments with the active, change-oriented approach of shorter term therapies (Young et al., 2003). We hope to build on the important contributions of Gottman and EFT-C, but highlight the unique contribution that ST can make to working with difficult relationships.

As authors, we bring two mental health disciplines to this book: psychiatry and clinical/counseling psychology. We have made contributions to the theory and practice of ST with "needs" and "wants" (i.e., re-parenting) (Simeone-DiFrancesco & Simeone, 2016ab); mode explication and stages of treatment (Simeone-DiFrancesco, 2011); understanding the schema–mode model in detail, mode cycles, methods of treatment (i.e., details of the imagery rescripting and chair-work techniques), and using clash-cards (Roediger & Jacob, 2010; Roediger, 2011; Roediger & Laireiter, 2013); and distinguishing infant modes from child, parent and compensatory modes (Stevens, 2012b). We hope that this book will not be read as a simplistic "how to" manual, but as a practical guide for clinical work.

We hope to offer the experienced practitioner a map for the rocky terrain of therapy with the most challenging couples. We have also found, through experience, that using ST for couples can lead to lasting change in relationships.

About the Companion Website

This book is accompanied by a companion website:

www.wiley.com/go/difrancesco/schematherapywithcouples

The website includes blank versions of forms in the book for your own use.

1

What Schema Therapy Offers

1.1 What is Hidden, What is Seen

For couples, the most common clashes are around the "rough edges" of personality. Indeed, there is a great silence in relationship therapy about the influence of personality disorders. Research has established that such traits are very common. Only 23 percent of the general population is relatively free of them; over 70 percent of people "have some degree of personality disturbance" (Yang et al., 2010).

It makes sense that character traits will cause relationship difficulties. We are attracted to a *personality* but live with a *character*. If there are long-term character problems, which is another way of describing personality vulnerability, then relationship difficulties are inevitable.

> Richard had a history of many short-term relationships, which were perhaps more sexual "flings" to avoid boredom. He would leave when lovers became more "needy". He had been sexually abused as a child and never experienced warmth or protection by a parent or step-parent. He knew only criticism. Eventually, he married Carol because he wanted a stable relationship to raise children. When he had an affair, it was devastating to his wife. It was hard to even talk issues through because Richard avoided conflict. A lot was happening in this relationship that was far from obvious.

Some couples deny any problems, even to the point of separation and divorce, but there is a long history of hidden clashes underlying the deterioration of their relationship.

Schema Therapy with Couples: A Practitioner's Guide to Healing Relationships, First Edition.
Chiara Simeone-DiFrancesco, Eckhard Roediger, and Bruce A. Stevens.
© 2015 John Wiley & Sons, Ltd. Published 2015 by John Wiley & Sons, Ltd.
Companion website: www.wiley.com/go/difrancesco/schematherapywithcouples

Reflect: What has been your most difficult couple to treat? Why? Do you recognize possible traits of personality disorder?

1.2   Listening to the Evidence

There is currently a crisis in relationships, and couples commonly present for therapy. So why not simply use the available evidence-based treatment for relationships? The answer is not straightforward. There is good research. John Gottman (1999) has contributed enormously to what we know through his "Love Lab." He has provided years of longitudinal data on couple processes. This includes easy-to-understand principles thoroughly grounded in extensive research. This can inform our practice. While Gottman and his colleagues have not yet produced randomized controlled trials, his work would meet the criteria of the American Psychological Association's policy statement on evidence-based practice in psychology: "the integration of the best available research with clinical expertise in the context of patient characteristics, culture, and preferences" (see APA, 2006).

Sexton and Gordon (2009) distinguished three levels of evidence:

1. evidence-informed interventions based on pre-existing evidence
2. promising interventions, but preliminary results not replicated
3. evidence-based treatments with systematic high-quality evidence demonstrating efficacy with clinical problems that the interventions are designed to address.

There is some Level 3 support for behavioral marital therapy (Jacobson & Margolin, 1979), cognitive behavioral marital therapy (Baucom & Epstein, 1990), integrative couple therapy (Jacobson & Christensen, 1996), and emotion-focused therapy for couples (EFT-C; Greenberg & Goldman, 2008).

In our experience, EFT-C works with many, and perhaps most, couples. But there is no specifically evidence-based therapy for couples with personality disorder (or for couples with strong traits, even if not diagnosed). What exists is evidence of the effectiveness of *individual* treatment for individuals with personality disorder, initially borderline personality disorder (BPD). It makes clinical sense that difficult couples may need an enhanced approach with ST or dialectical behavior therapy (Linehan, 1993). Both employ stronger interventions aimed at changing ingrained aspects of character. A 2010 review concluded that dialectical behavior therapy has Level 3 and ST has Level 2 evidence for effectiveness with adults diagnosed with BPD (APS, 2010, p. 112). A study of ST treatment of BPD inpatients using groups has reported large effect sizes (Farrell & Shaw, 2012), and a study has recently indicated the effectiveness of ST with other personality disorders (Bamelis et al., 2014).

We believe that ST has significant advantages over dialectical behavior therapy,[2] so applying ST to working with couples (schema therapy for couples, ST-C) is the focus of this book. We hope that it may prove to have some of the strengths already demonstrated by ST case conceptualization and interventions in individual and group therapy.

1.3   Beyond Just Cognitive Therapy

One of the strengths of ST is its origins in cognitive therapy, which has the advantage of conceptual clarity and ease of understanding. Now, in the twenty-first century, it incorporates a good deal more than talk. This includes both non-verbal cognitions (imagery) and embodiment techniques (Rosner et al., 2004). It is essentially integrative.

Aaron Beck (1963) initiated the "cognitive revolution" and developed what is now extensively researched cognitive behavioral therapy for the treatment of depression. This approach was then applied to the whole range of psychological disorders. But cognitive behavioral therapy did not prove as effective with the personality disordered, which led to "third wave" therapies, including dialectical behavior therapy and ST.

While Beck referred to schemas, it was more in the sense of clusters of negative beliefs about the self. A similar understanding of schemata is found in the work of Theodore Millon, in which patterns of dysfunction are foundational to personality disorder (Millon, 1990, p. 10). Jesse Wright and colleagues followed in this approach and noted that people typically have a mix of different kinds of schemas: "even patients with the most severe symptoms or profound despair have adaptive schemas that can help them cope ... efforts to uncover and strengthen positively oriented beliefs can be quite productive" (Wright et al., 2006, p. 174).

---

[2] Dialectical behavioral therapy, while effective, is essentially a "here and now" cognitive therapy. It also makes the assumption that a "wise mind" or "healthy adult" is always available, while ST deals with that not being the case. ST also goes to the developmental origins of adult problems, to effectively "repair" experiences of neglect and trauma through imagery work embedded in a re-parenting relationship.

1.4   Jeff Young and the Development of Schema Therapy

ST was developed from cognitive therapy as a means of treating difficult people. Jeffery Young et al. (2003) linked maladaptive schemas to neglect and toxic childhood experiences. They reflect the unfulfilled yet important needs of the child and represent adaptations to negative experiences, such as family quarrels, rejection, hostility, or aggression from parents, educators or peers, as well as inadequate parental care and support (van Genderen et al., 2012). This approach has more of an emotional focus and a willingness to explore the childhood/adolescent origins of psychological problems.

Young identified a comprehensive set of early maladaptive schemas, which were defined as "self-defeating emotional and cognitive patterns that begin early in our development and repeat throughout life" (Young et al., 2003, p. 7). Schemas are identified by clinical observation (Arntz & Jacob, 2013). The expression of such patterns has different levels of severity and pervasiveness. The idea of schema *activation* is fundamental to an understanding of Young's contribution. A more severe schema is distinguished by how readily it is activated, the intensity of affect and how long distress lasts (Young et al., 2003, p. 9).

ST provides a blueprint for the child and later adult's world. While schemas might have had some survival value for the child (Kellogg, 2004), by adulthood they are "inaccurate, dysfunctional, and limiting, although strongly held and frequently not in the person's conscious awareness" (Farrell & Shaw, 2012, p. 9).

Young et al.'s (2003) understanding of schemas drew on a variety of sources. Indeed, they outlined parallels and differences with major approaches, including Beck's "reformulated" model, psychoanalytic theory, Bowlby's attachment theory (especially internal working models), and emotion-focused therapy (EFT). ST has integrated techniques adapted from transactional analysis and gestalt therapy (Edwards & Arntz, 2012). Jeff Young (2012) also described ST as an individual therapy with systemic implications. There is a breadth, applicability and ease of understanding that encourages a broader application.

Young (1999, p. 20) also identified needs of childhood in five "domains," which can be seen as five tasks for therapy:

- connection and acceptance
- autonomy and performance
- realistic limits
- inner-directed ness and self-expression
- spontaneity and pleasure.

1.5 The Schema Model

Young identified the following 18 schemas: Abandonment (instability), Mistrust-Abuse, Emotional Deprivation, Defectiveness-Shame, Social Isolation (alienation), Dependence Incompetence, Vulnerability to Harm or Illness, Enmeshment (undeveloped self), Failure (to achieve), Entitlement Grandiosity, Insufficient Self-control (or self-discipline), Subjugation, Self-Sacrifice, Approval Seeking (recognition seeking), Negativity Pessimism, Emotional Inhibition, Unrelenting Standards (hyper-criticalness), and Punitiveness. Maladaptive schemas hinder people from recognizing, experiencing, and fulfilling their own needs (Arntz & Jacob, 2013).

Reflect: You can think about schemas as patterns of vulnerability, or as domains in which emotional learning took place in childhood.

Young also looked at patterns of response to schema vulnerability, including surrender, avoidance, and compensation leading to specific coping behavior. The 18 maladaptive schemas are very comprehensive, especially when coupled with three response patterns. However, there are potential treatment difficulties:

1. *Complexity.* The whole list of the schemas with response patterns is potentially 54 different schema–coping presentations. While most people may only have a few schemas with characteristic response patterns, more disturbed people, such as those with BPD, typically will be troubled by many schemas. This leads to considerable complexity.

2. *Instability.* The relative instability of low-functioning clients adds another layer to the difficulty. In a session, there may be frequent "flipping" between various schema activations and coping behaviors, which the therapist needs to track. These difficulties led to the development of *modes* to describe schema activation in the "here and now" of treatment.

3. *Couple interaction.* Volatile couples present in ways even more unstable than the same people in individual therapy. Thus the intensity of reactions, more frequent flipping in sessions and difficulty tracking changes make up a real therapeutic challenge. Since modes (defined in Section 1.6) are "what you see," the changing states can be seen and interventions used to target what is happening in the here and now of the session.

However, it is very useful for a therapist to keep thinking in terms of schemas. This provides a very useful clinical context. It is the "depth picture" behind the more obvious presentation of modes.

1.6   Introducing the Mode Model

When Young started working with severely disturbed lower functioning borderline clients he soon found that his schema model was too complicated, so he searched for a different conceptualization. He described the triggering of a schema—its activation, which he called a "mode" (initially called "modus" or "schema states"). So modes are the way schemas appear. A mode can also be the expression of multiple schemas and incorporate different coping styles (van Genderen et al., 2012). The number of possible reactions to schema activation is unlimited.

We do not actually see a schema, but only the activation in the here-and-now of experience (Kellogg & Young, 2006; Roediger, 2012b, p. 3). Recognizing modes helps a therapist to see the "action." Thus, a mode is a transient expression of schema vulnerability. This includes the emotional, cognitive, and behavioral dimensions of personality (which are further integrated in ST; Farrell & Shaw, 2012). While you *have* a schema; you *are in* a mode.

The major groups of modes are as follows (see Figure 1; for details of the mode model, see Section 6.2):

1. *child modes*, which are regarded as an activation of body systems, such as attachment and self-assertiveness leading to basic emotions

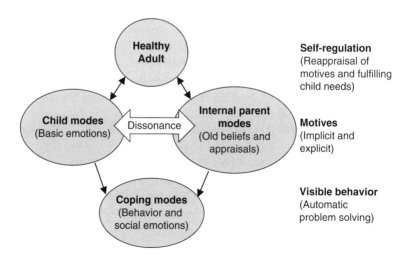

Figure 1   Basic mode model

2. *internalized parent modes*, which preserve the messages, beliefs and appraisals the child heard since infancy
3. *maladaptive coping modes*, which present as visible behaviors resulting from the interaction of child and parent modes, including social emotions
4. *healthy modes*, which are the integrative and adaptive modes "Healthy Adult" and "Happy Child."

ST sees adult interpersonal problems as the result of negative schemas fixed in childhood. The schemas remain more or less unchanged. Once triggered, they revive the same feelings, appraisals, and tendencies to react as in a distressed child. You might liken it to a person who steps into a time machine and then returns to childhood to a similar reaction. The adult becomes the child again. Hence, this state is called a *child mode*.

The activation of a child mode indicates that a core need has not been meet (The exception is the Happy Child mode). Usually, the person keeps seeking some fulfillment. In this way, child modes have a signal character.

Young proposed that a schema therapist respond with "limited re-parenting." This intervention may differ from what is proposed by therapies that discourage any dependence upon the therapist. But when the child's needs are more consistently met, first by our re-parenting and then by the client's own Healthy Adult mode, and possibly later by the Healthy Adult mode of their partner, the client will grow stronger. This is the result we seek through both individual and couples ST.

Reflect: Do you think this might parallel attachment theory? The assumption, from an attachment perspective, is that securely attached children become more autonomous.

Vera had a traumatic childhood in which she was neglected by an alcoholic single mother. An uncle repeatedly sexually abused her. She had a disturbed attachment with her mother, and her schema therapist identified a number of schemas, including Abandonment, Mistrust-Abuse, Emotional Deprivation, Dependence, Defectiveness- Shame and Subjugation. The therapist found her highly unstable in sessions. Vera kept changing between activated modes (what is called "flipping"), and it seemed at times that her distressed states were fed into by a number of schemas. So the therapist used a mode conceptualization to focus on the states that were being fed by the schemas. This made it simpler for her to keep track of how to relate to Vera and help, and also to help Vera understand herself. In early sessions, Vera was mostly in Vulnerable or Angry Child modes, and regardless of which schema or schemas were putting her in those modes, that was what needed to be attended to there and then. The therapist also tried to keep Vera more in the

Vulnerable Child mode so she could get at her unmet needs—reversing the emotional legacy of childhood. This also helped her to attach to the therapist as a parenting source. Later, this led to Vera being able to allow her partner to meet her needs in a healthy way.

Therapy Tip: Once a schema is activated, the person may be in a child mode. In this state, a client should be addressed gently, as we would speak with children. Child-related needs should be met through reassurance, affirmation, empathic limit-setting, blocking a parental mode, and so on.

In summary, a schema is a trait—a tendency to react. A mode is a mental state. As long as schemas are not activated, they remain in the background. Once activated, schemas appear as constantly changing states called modes. We cannot work directly with schemas, only with activated schemas, or modes. This helps case conceptualization because it integrates what is seen with potential interventions to enable an effective treatment plan (van Genderen, 2012). We introduce some helpful resources, such as the mode map in Section 8.2.

Therapy Tip: Try to introduce the mode model early in therapy, usually within the first two or three sessions (Arntz & Jacob, 2013).

1.7   The Challenge of Working with Couples

How does this help us to understand couple relationships? Schemas and modes help to provide a comprehensive framework for understanding relationship dynamics. If a person wants to understand their own relationship, or when we are working in individual therapy, then perhaps the complexity of focusing on individual schemas is less challenging than for a couple. Indeed, some schema problems are relatively straightforward (for example, working with Enmeshment, which might be focused on a single relationship). If this is the case, it might be easiest to work with a single schema related to a specific difficulty.

Natalie brought Sigmund to couple therapy. She had discovered an affair that he had kept hidden for over 12 months. She wanted to understand the vulnerability in their relationship: "Why did this happen?" Sig was contrite and wanted to recommit to his marriage. Through ST-C, Natalie faced her schema vulnerability of Emotional Inhibition and Unrelenting Standards. Sig saw his actions in terms of an Entitlement schema. Both had influential childhood experiences, which were addressed through re-parenting imagery. Behavioral pattern breaking was very important in rebuilding trust.

However, understanding modes enriches the entire experiential process for both individuals and couples in therapy. It reduces the complexity of the schema interactional cycles for couples. Working with modes is usually the most practical way to do ST-C, because it allows a here-and-now approach to the current interaction by demonstrating the clash between modes, sequencing the mode cycle and the common elements of unmet "needs" without being flooded by unnecessary detail early in therapy. Working with modes provides direction and immediate gains in couple sessions.

1.8   Limited Professional Literature

Not much has been published in relation to schema work with couples. A somewhat dated review of the cognitive literature was provided by Wisman and Uewbelacker (2007) in their chapter "Maladaptive schemas and core beliefs in treatment and research with couples." The focus on schemas was cognitive, at best providing a review of cognitive behavioral therapy and attachment with some cognitive measures, but there was almost nothing that could be considered creative or cutting edge in terms of treatment. The authors concluded that "no published studies to date have evaluated the efficacy of cognitive therapy specifically devoted to modifying maladaptive schemas or core beliefs" (Wisman & Uewbelacker, 2007, p. 216).

Travis Atkinson (2012) contributed a chapter in the more recently published *Wiley-Blackwell Handbook of Schema Therapy* (van Vreeswijk et al., 2012a). He argued that ST provides "an expansive compass to help the couple's therapist assess and differentiate core maladaptive themes underlying relationship distress" (Atkinson, 2012, p. 323).

Reflect: What have you always wanted in a therapy for couples?

ST offers the following:

1. *Language.* ST uses an easily understood language of patterns in the self and in relationships. Key concepts such as schemas, coping styles, and modes are easy to understand. Indeed, the ideas are close to a commonsense psychology. The concepts educate and make sense of past experiences for people—and open the door to allow them to speak freely about what they presently feel is relevant.
2. *A focus on the difficult.* Hard-to-treat personality disorders are the normal focus and are not treated as exceptional cases.
3. *Effective interventions.* There are powerful techniques, such as imagery work related to limited re-parenting, chair-work to address core beliefs

in an experiential way, and behavioral pattern breaking. There are important ideas about transforming schemas and strengthening the Healthy Adult mode, and guidance in how to more effectively communicate with a partner who is stuck in a child mode. In this way, ST can realistically address the most problematic aspects of interpersonal behavior and allow us to understand it in terms of prior interpersonal experiences.

4. *Influence of the past.* In ST, the therapist has techniques to counter the past when it intrudes on current relationships. This approach can enhance family-of-origin work, taking the burden off the present relationship so the couple can make a new start in therapy without the legacy of unresolved issues from childhood. You can find an effective balance of couple and individual sessions so that progress can be maintained.

5. *Progress with individuals.* It is even possible to do considerable work "solo" to improve the relationship without the participation of a partner. By including dialog and even limited schema/mode conceptualization about the absent partner in individual therapy, the scope is broadened beyond presenting problems. The therapist can work with the individual on all of their schema vulnerabilities, even those triggered by the relationship, and blind spots in therapy are reduced. Couples and marital work can even have significant accomplishments with this one-person scenario. Even one session with the unengaged partner can have benefit and provide a wealth of data for the therapist working with the other in the schema model.

    The relationship or marriage is a combination of two people. When one partner changes their behavior, the relationship changes. ST is not wasted work, even if the couple separate, because it can provide a more solid foundation for future relationships.

6. *Needs.* The therapist will fulfill core needs in counseling and provide a model for functional self-disclosure and the communication of needs. This modeling of a Healthy Adult can be learned by the couple.

7. *Integrative process.* The experiential techniques applied in ST integrate cognitive, emotional, and behavioral changes in one therapeutic process. Functional behavior is enhanced by healing early maladaptive schemas.

ST offers more than technical eclecticism. There is a deep "assimilative integration" (Messer, 2001) of different perspectives and insights from various schools into a system of therapy with a coherent, conceptually economic model that translates into a workable practice for the therapist (Edwards & Arntz, 2012, p. 20). This approach encourages a schema-based case conceptualization tied closely to treatment planning.

Reflect: Why are you reading this book? Have you used ST with individuals and now want to try it with couples? Are you new to ST and hope to find an effective therapy for working with traits of personality disorder?

1.9   Brief Outline of the Stages of Schema Therapy for Couples

The following is a suggested outline of treatment (unfamiliar terms and techniques are explained later in the book):

1. *Empathic engagement.* Make an emotional connection with the couple. The challenge in the first session is to see issues "through the eyes of both." Allow the couple to demonstrate their dysfunctional way of relating.
2. *Initial contract for alliance and therapy.* This can include the two commitments of working on the relationship and not deliberately behaving badly towards the partner (Hargrave, 2000).
3. *Assessment.* Possibly use a genogram. Use ST questionnaires and other resources. Focus on understanding the childhood origin of adult relationship problems. What issues belong where? Be guided by Young's five tasks. Try to conceptualize the information in a "mode map" for both partners as a reference point for your further work.
4. *Formulation.* Clarify an ST-C understanding of problems in terms of Young's schema chemistry, clashes, and locking. What are the dynamics of attraction? Put gridlocked problems and patterns into schema and mode conceptualizations. Use mode cycle clash-cards to identify how dysfunctional modes play out. Develop a comprehensive but focused treatment plan.
5. *Treatment interventions.* Base interventions primarily on mode maps, eventually including the most prominent schemas, to deal with the legacy from the family of origin. De-escalate mode clashes. Use ST interventions, including imagery, limited re-parenting, chair-work, strategies to strengthen Healthy Adult mode, and behavior pattern breaking. Find a balance of individual and couple sessions. Move from

dysfunctional modes to healthier coping modes. This includes coaching the couple to identify and de-escalate schema activations and mode clashes (using mode cycle clash-cards, mode dialogs, empathic confrontation, and empathic compassion). If possible, encourage couple interactions that enable a re-parenting of each other and dealing with bad memories. The couple learns to apply dialog tools and special techniques to enhance re-parenting.

6. *Building friendship.* Conduct connection exercises to build friendship (Gottman & Silver, 1999) and provide building blocks for more secure attachment (similar to emotion-focused therapy for couples) to increase positive behaviors. Encourage the couple to take responsibility for their own relationship. Strengthen Healthy Adult and Happy Child modes. Use new clashes for the couple to practice skills and to coach them in the use of those skills. Use the concept of bringing in the "A team" to resolve conflict.

7. *Termination and relapse prevention.* Work towards a successful end of therapy with periodic "relapse prevention" sessions. Help the couple to articulate a relationship story, incorporate the experience of therapy, learn how to anticipate future mode clashes, and create a plan for dealing with crises. Arrange periodic check-ups and readjustments. Perhaps the couple can make an agreement about being willing to return to therapy for a minimum of one session if problems reoccur.

Reflect: As you look over this outline of ST-C, what aspects do you think would be easy for you to put into practice? What would be very challenging? Think about making small steps to build up your skills and to gain confidence before attempting more advanced skills.

Summary

In this chapter we have introduced some of the defining characteristics of ST, including how it developed first with schemas and then with modes. The focus has always been on treating difficult people, and there is growing evidence of therapeutic effectiveness with individuals, especially in group treatment programs. ST-C is designed to use similar interventions in treating couples. This chapter has also outlined the stages of treatment with couples.

2

The Initial Contract and First Interview

In Genesis, the first book of the Bible, God created. We have a similar task in working with couples: to bring order out of chaos. Usually, the couple arrives in a crisis and very little is predictable except for the mutual blame of the other for problems in the relationship. There is an almost universal belief: "I would be happy if only my partner would change."

2.1 The Initial Interview

The first interview begins with initial contact. Generally, the more suffering (or anxious) person will ring and arrange the first session. An exception is when one of the two has already decided to leave the relationship and wants to leave the abandoned partner with a caretaker (the therapist). Such agendas are not always obvious. In another scenario, one person wants to save the relationship but the other refuses to come.

The first session will give a number of meaningful clues. How do they greet you? First name? Formally, with Mr., Ms., or Dr.? Or perhaps, "We're so desperate that we need to see a shrink." This will indicate something of the relationship expected and possibly provide your first indication of schemas or modes that might be present. Where do the couple choose to sit? Those in marital distress will tend to sit as far apart as the room allows! You may find that the one who arranged the interview will sit closer to you—implying that they believe they have found an ally.

Generally, one of the two is more reluctant to come. He or she may already be strongly retreating from the relationship. If there is to be any

Schema Therapy with Couples: A Practitioner's Guide to Healing Relationships, First Edition.
Chiara Simeone-DiFrancesco, Eckhard Roediger, and Bruce A. Stevens.

effective couple treatment, it is a matter of the highest priority for the therapist to engage that distancing person (Johnson, 2004). Make sure that you give that individual considerable attention, affirming their perspective, and try to be very empathic to what they have experienced. Only in this way can you achieve a working alliance with a couple. Also, listen and try to understand the partner as well, but you usually have more latitude with him or her. Only people who feel heard and understood will want to return for another session.

Sometimes it is helpful to bring your initial impression to the couple, in a self-disclosing way:

> It seems to me that you, Nancy, are more convinced that this therapy might be helpful. I'm afraid that you, Tom, are "half out of the door." So my first task is to find a way for this process to be useful to you as well. So initially I'll address myself more to you than to Nancy. I hope you, Nancy, can tolerate this for the sake of the relationship. Please give me a sign when you feel you're dropping out too much, OK?

Openly addressing the unwanted result (Tom leaving therapy) may seem confronting, but it increases the possibility of realistic engagement in therapy and demonstrates transparency as fundamental to ST-C.

2.2   Issues that Present

Usually the couple will have a few "target complaints." It is valuable to draw these out in a balanced way, trying to give more-or-less equal attention to both in the relationship, and then turn complaints into realistic goals.

First, try to achieve an initial understanding of the two perspectives. This can be challenging when the couple have come because of "bad behavior": perhaps an incident or pattern of violence, infidelity, financial irresponsibility, substance abuse, or criminal activity.

> Martius and Mary came for counseling after he was charged with accessing child pornography on a work computer. Mary was shocked, understandably, but wanted to preserve their marriage if at all possible.

You may feel judgmental, but to work well with a couple you need to empathically immerse yourself in how they see the world and each other. This is foundational to couple therapy. You will have achieved this when you can begin to understand why the bad behavior felt justified or even necessary. Indeed, with personality-disordered couples you can, more or less, be assured that there have been impulsive actions that may have damaged the relationship.

Therapy Tip: Try to gain some understanding of the needs behind maladaptive coping behavior ("needs" and "wants" are examined in detail in Chapter 11).

Occasionally, a couple will be equally motivated to work on difficulties. This is a good prognostic sign. Sometimes, a couple will both want to end their relationship, in which case it can be a worthwhile therapeutic goal to achieve this with a minimum of hurt to them, their children, and their wider families.

If possible, schedule 60–90 minutes for the first appointment with the couple. Some time is usually needed to make a preliminary assessment (described in Chapter 3). Towards the end of the first interview some therapists give a few minutes, others longer, for each person to talk with them alone so they can ask, "Is there anything that you can only say to me without your partner being here?" You may then be told about violence or alcohol abuse or some "dark secret." It is, of course, important to appear non-judgmental. Ask a specific question about whether there is a current affair. Usually this is answered truthfully, but not always. It is a powerful secret, which has an influence on the progress of therapy. Another useful question is, "Is there anything I should know in order to help you?"

There is some difference of opinion among experienced clinicians about whether you should know a secret that is not shared by the partner. Strong arguments have been made on both sides of this issue, and it is simply our preference to want to have the most accurate information possible to help the couple. At times, knowing a secret will put us in an awkward position. In ST, some individual work will usually be needed for family-of-origin issues. In this context, it is quite likely that sensitive material will emerge—so perhaps it is inevitable that a therapist will at times carry secrets.

Another, related, question is whether to encourage a person to disclose a past affair. It is wise to be cautious about this. Naturally, a present-tense affair will need to be addressed, but a past affair is another matter. Should you let sleeping dogs lie? One advantage of telling a partner about an affair is that this is easier to repair than damage from an affair discovered during the course of therapy (Atkinson, 2012). However, any disclosure will escalate the crisis for an already distressed couple, and possibly provide a terminal blow for the relationship. Equally, though, many couples seem willing to work on the relationship regardless, even strengthening their ties.

But it may be reckless to introduce anything into therapy when you cannot predict a favorable outcome.[3]

There is nothing more natural in the first session than for a couple to demonstrate their fighting style. This provides valuable information. Are they silent, passive, mutual in their blame, out of control, sarcastic, verging on violence? Sometimes there are clear roles: one may be submissive while the other is aggressive and overbearing.

> Libby had a scared look in her eyes, which darted around the room. Brad was definite, even dogmatic, about how easy their problems were to solve. He seemed to think that all Libby needed to do was obey him.

Any expression of conflict may be taboo, with the result that there is great reluctance to address an issue directly. It is informative to see what attempts are made to move from being stuck. This will usually reveal a limited range of coping styles and a restricted capacity to adapt. At this point, you will start to *see* what schemas become activated and what modes tend to dominate their interaction. Note the individuals' typical mode cycles. Is there any attempt to repair? Any signs of emotional maturity? Also note whether there is a "harsh start-up" (Gottman & Silver, 1999).

Another question to keep in mind is "Why now?" Usually, something has led to the decision to seek help. Has it been a severe fight, an affair, a decision to leave, financial problems, or suicidal thoughts? If there are significant co-morbid conditions, it may be wise to work in tandem with a psychiatrist, an outpatient unit or an agency (e.g., one specializing in alcohol or drug dependence). You also may need to delay couple therapy if you see unmanageable risks, such as violence, including a potential for homicide, suicide, rampant substance abuse, or criminal activity. Offering therapy after the completion of an anger management or alcohol program can be a strong inducement to address such an issue.

Therapy Tip: It is much easier to set conditions at the beginning of therapy than later.

---

[3]   There are also very complex ethical issues related to this. You may want to think about "release of information agreements" relating to individual sessions and the possible intrusion of a family law process on the confidentiality of individual sessions and note taking. Also, there is the issue of your therapeutic relationship with the partner who does not know and could feel betrayed by your withholding relevant information. A lot is at stake with such issues, and there is no risk-free approach.

2.3 Expectations

You will want to check with the couple about their expectations from treatment. How do they see counseling helping? What is your role? Are both partners willing to contribute actively? In this way, you can tailor what you do to their felt needs and what might be expected to work for them in their relationship. Some outcome research implies that this approach has the best treatment results (Hubble et al., 1999).

It is helpful to give some indication of how long treatment might take: "I would like to see you both for six sessions. You may well see some improvement by then and we can reassess." You may want to give an impression of how you see the problem and propose a way forward.

If there are clear indications of personality disorder, you will need to be far more cautious in your prognosis:

"It's good that you have come to me. You both feel that things are out of control. Because of the situation, you're both very reactive to each other and unsure of proceeding. I think we'll need to schedule some individual sessions, then when you're both ready and "positioned" for working together, some couple sessions—initially, say, six individual sessions each and then four tentative couple sessions. I can't guarantee that even then you'll see much improvement, but you'll have a better sense of whether this is a process that can help you."

It might be helpful to add that improvement is dependent upon the couple being active, for example by doing homework assignments, and taking risks to improve their relationship. There is only so much a therapist can do!

Therapy Tip: The act of coming to see a therapist can initially be reassuring and a source of hope, but progress needs to be made quickly if both people are to remain engaged in the work. Sometimes this will guide what to work on first, so if possible address an easier problem first, rather than a deeply entrenched one.

2.4 "Contracting" for Therapy

Hargrave (2000) stressed the need to address two issues with a couple. Both are about the couple being prepared to engage in therapy. It is useful for each partner to be willing to give up a position of "rightness" and to acknowledge some contribution to difficulties in the relationship—what Hargrave terms the "essential humility of marriage." This forms part of a foundational agreement, which provides a working stability in the relationship. The two requirements are:

1. *Commitment.* There is a need to commit to work on restoring the relationship—what has been called the "no escape clause" (Hendrix, 1988). This involves putting the relationship first and, if there is any affair, to at least put it on hold for an agreed period. In some instances, you may want to soften this to working on "a process of clarification for you as a couple" (but still no affairs—at least in general). At a deeper level, this allows for a reawakening of hope that the relationship may again meet emotional needs.

2. *Do no harm.* Agree to the medical principle of "First, do no harm" (*Primum non nocere*). This is applied to the relationship. You can ask the couple to restrain themselves from intentionally harming their partner. This includes both passive neglect and aggressive action (Hargrave, 2000). Rule out insults, yelling, and threats. If there is any history of physical assault, this principle should also be acknowledged and safety established to the satisfaction of both (and the therapist!). It is understandable to feel like retaliating, but the initial agreement is to act in a more civil manner. Simply give the respect that is due to any member of the human race.

It is best to pause until the couple agree to make this commitment. You can complete the assessment phase, and think about case formulation, but do not try to make progress beyond that point without some commitment.

Infidelity is a potential barrier to a commitment to work on the relationship. This can present in a variety of ways. If a person is currently in an affair without their partner's awareness, then the absolute minimum would be their commitment to put the affair on hold. The "deal" is absolutely no contact (including phone calls, text messages, and emails) for as long as therapy takes. If they are unable to "burn the bridge" to the lover, you may need to negotiate an agreed period (at least 10 weeks) of no contact. This allows the person to focus on the relationship and not take their pain to a "soothing other." Relationship needs should be met in the primary relationship. We would not insist on a disclosure to the partner unless they already suspect some kind of emotional or sexual involvement. In that case, the affair is intuitively known, and not to be transparent is to seriously impair the partner's "reality testing." You may want to insist that the person who has strayed sexually has a sexual check-up to limit any risk to an unsuspecting partner.

Therapy Tip: Sometimes an individual will continue to see the lover but make outright denials. Ask yourself whether there are any signs of grief and how actively that person engages in therapy.

Much of this discussion about dealing with affairs is contentious. There are many experienced couple therapists, indeed leading relationship researchers, who would advocate full disclosure.

It is necessary for the couple to behave in a more civil manner. Sadly, couples know each other's points of vulnerability, and they are often enraged for a variety of reasons, so it is tempting for them to lash out. This is understandable, but goodwill becomes precious if counseling is to hold any hope of repair. The term "goodwill" may sound lame, but it makes a huge difference. Compare the following two comments about a partner:

JOHN: "I know Claire is a really decent person. I was incredibly hurt when she had that affair, and lied about it, but I know she was desperately unhappy with my long hours at work. She's a good mother and I want to keep the family together if possible. I think we can work things out."

BETTY: "Marrying Bill was the worst decision of my life. I am stuck with him because of our religious and social beliefs, but I sometimes think of God as a cosmic sadist to have condemned me to be with such a person. I have to learn how to put up with this. There's no hope for happiness."

The difference is goodwill. With goodwill, the partner is seen as a good person with basically decent intentions. It is clearly related to trust and other relationship qualities, but, importantly, goodwill is like "oil" that makes the relationship "engine" run smoothly.

Therapy Tip: Gottman (1999) identified contempt as poison in relationships. It would be wise to address this if it becomes obvious in therapy.

An initial goal, then, is to quickly establish some stability, with commitment, reliability, and responsibility for the relationship. This can be strengthened by agreeing on "rules of conduct" and by considering a written contract. The parable of building a house on sand, rather than rock, is relevant (Matthew 7: 24–27).

Reflect: What do you do as a therapist to try to stabilize a couple in crisis? What successes can you identify in work over the past few years? What frustrations? What would you like to be able to do better?

2.5   Safety First

Initially, try to create a "secure base" in sessions (Johnson, 2005). From there, the couple can confront the ways in which dysfunction has previously defined their relationship and notice the exceptions when it worked better. Help to create safety rules for the couple, but be aware that moving towards greater safety is a process and not an easily attained goal. Good interventions for creating greater safety within a session include immediately stopping clashing, empathic reflection, validation, empathic inference (exploring and expanding their experience), and collaborative problem solving about safety issues (Johnson, 2005). The therapist tracks and identifies maladaptive mode cycles that maintain distress in the relationship. Try to develop concrete solutions for relevant issues.

> Brenda discovered that Merv had been making withdrawals from their bank account. He had a shopping addiction after he returned from war service overseas. The cycle was that Brenda would criticize him for petty things, and then he would get defensive and "shut down." This would infuriate her and she would go for "character assassination." He would then leave the house for intervals of up to days at a time. The couple therapist was able to draw their attention to how their needs were going unmet. The therapist encouraged the couple to make some changes to accessing credit cards and accounts at the bank, which addressed Brenda's immediate concerns, and Brenda agreed to attend a mindfulness group that met weekly at the psychology practice.

2.6   Additional Concerns

Relationship counseling will draw on all your skills, such as empathic listening and dealing with intense emotions by intervening straightforwardly. Being passive with couples will not work. ST-C is active: it involves stopping clashes, asking "inquisitive" questions, clarifying emotions, refereeing, giving rules, teaching communication skills, modeling functional behavior, and assigning homework tasks. Travis Atkinson (2012) has underlined the role of the therapist "catching bullets" in order to make the therapeutic space safer by doing everything possible to protect both in sessions. Emotional regulation can be challenging from the first session. Almost always, this need will be obvious for at least one person in the relationship. This is addressed in some depth (e.g. Section 7.1).

You may need to intervene with crisis management and initial skill building. Generally, there is a need for sufficient stability to do the work of therapy, so it might be necessary to start with a current clash and establish some safety building skills. This may "jump the line" before exploring current problems and relationship history. We describe this "quick" entry for high-conflict couples in the next section.

It is essential to deal with safety concerns because it is impossible to foster intimacy in an atmosphere of fear. If one partner has pressing mental health concerns, they may need to have a psychiatric consultation and you may need to wait until that partner is stronger and has sufficient containment of affect before bringing the two together as a couple. Essentially, do what needs to be done and, if necessary, make it a condition of therapy. But, as therapy progresses, encourage the couple to take increasing responsibility and affirm any useful initiatives they might undertake. You can model listening, interpersonal respect and limit setting, which demonstrates communication skills.

Gottman noted the difficulties in relationship counseling, including high relapse rates, but added, "Anything we do will work to some degree, as long as the therapist is highly active and the intervention has some clear rationale that is articulated ... otherwise, people will terminate against professional advice" (Gottman, 1999, p. 6).

Think about how you will plan the course of couple treatment. The question of whether or not to have individual sessions has been much discussed. Together with Jeff Young and Wendy Behary, we believe that you will be limited in doing ST-C without having individual sessions with each partner, addressing biographical material, as well as couple sessions to improve current functioning. Naturally, there are different aspects to consider when and how to intersperse individual sessions, but it is rare that one can do ST-C with just couple sessions. Sometimes the story will not make sense, perhaps suggesting secrets, which will need to be checked out in individual sessions. You might think about balancing the number of individual sessions for both partners. Trust issues may also push the couple therapist to have more extensive individual sessions with empathic validation and re-parenting. We do not recommend distributing sessions on a "fair" basis, but offering the "needy" partner as many individual sessions as they need to cope successfully with their schema activations, as long as the other partner can accept this. Progress counts, not formal justice. Ultimately, both will benefit.

2.7 Beginning with a Crisis Intervention

We ask much of couples in therapy. Often they will reveal difficult and even "stubborn" problems. Just coming is an admission that things are not working. Difficult relationships typically have a high level of clashing based on rigid thinking, so there needs to be a quick start. It is the responsibility of the therapist to get immediate gains if at all possible. Give both the chance to briefly tell their side of the story. This is balanced with a limit on destructive interactions which "throw dirt in the water." Low-functioning couples will immediately display "out of control" conflict. The therapist must take control or therapy will become an "unsafe" place. Assist them by focusing on a relevant current problem. Do what it takes!

Unproductive fighting has to stop. You may have to say "Stop" with a firm and rather sharp voice to wake up Healthy Adult mode for each. In rare circumstances, touch may help—putting a hand on the forearm. Work with what happens in the here and now. As the therapist, you see the patterns "in the present tense": they are not just something recounted to you second hand. Focusing on the here-and-now interaction can also avoid conflict about who is telling the "right" story. The coping modes are the target, not the content.

Both partners need to commit to trying to limit hostile interactions. This includes the time outside sessions. It may be helpful to use a "stop sign" to interrupt the cycle without any further comment. Whoever is the first to notice that a new clash is getting started shows the sign (e.g., raising the hand of form a T, like the sign to interrupt a basketball match). Then both partners are "committed" to stopping instantly without further comment. You can advise the couple to retire to separate rooms. This eliminates any triggering cues and allows time for both to return to Healthy Adult functioning again. This can be set as initial homework.

2.8   Ending the First Session

You might think about an ST intervention at the end of the first session. A good metaphor is to "press the pause button of the video" or to "rewind" to a significant interaction. You can then take a close look and analyze what happened in slow motion, based on the presenting coping mode cycle.

THERAPIST: "The more Susan attacks, the more Tom avoids. The more Tom avoids, the more Susan will attack to get closer to him. This is a cycle that cannot work. You need to stop immediately. We'll work towards a deeper understanding of why you do that in the following sessions."

You may want to use a mode cycle clash-card (see Chapter 8) as a joint referencing point early in therapy, even if the couple is not familiar with the model yet. This works because the clash-card works with what you see or can access in the here and now of the session and does not require any further knowledge. The card takes attention away from the partner and examines the process. It is helpful to interrupt the couple's activated pattern and guide them into a more adult and cooperative pathway. If the couple starts clashing again, stop immediately, as described above, and label the mode:

> Did you realize how quickly you lapse into these mode cycles? You both contribute. No one can fight alone. It takes two to tango. Neither of you is fully to blame for the cycle. You both contribute. The cycle is the problem. No cycle—no hurting. This is our common enemy!

This joint perspective removes the "guilt" question for both partners and lays a path to reconnection. It may be helpful to end the first session with the stop commitment described above.

In the second session, give a brief summary and then introduce the schema and mode model to increase mutual understanding. You might make up a handout or give them a photocopy of pages from this book. This provides some "common ground" understanding.

2.9 Starting with One Partner First

It is possible to work with one partner in individual sessions and have an effect on the couple relationship. From a systemic perspective, there is no doubt that behavior change in one partner induces changes in the other partner as well. Systems tend to stabilize themselves in a given way (Maturana & Varela, 1998). The other partner will consciously or unconsciously counteract changes because those changes challenge the current balance in the system. The mode cycle model helps the client understand their partner's reactions and underlying basic emotions. Anticipating the effects of the new behavior on the partner's basic emotions helps to include their responses into the therapy. Respecting the partner's core emotional needs and including them in the new behavior prevents frustration. Chair-work with the absent partner is a helpful tool (stepping into the partner's shoes). Sometimes the partner can be indirectly involved or gradually challenged to contribute to the therapeutic process. Looking at it that way, individual therapy has the potential to influence the couple in a strategic way and in that way can be regarded as "couple therapy." This broadens the scope of this book. Here are some ideas about how this can happen:

1. *including a partner* by thinking and talking about an absent partner in mode cycle terms
2. *inviting* the partner into an individual session for diagnostic reasons to provide a wider perspective
3. *explaining* the client's mode model (using with the mode map) to the partner (initially through handouts)
4. *asking* the partner to support the person's change from therapy outside the session
5. *developing a mode cycle* for the couple's interaction, with both partners involved.

Including a partner is not a yes-or-no question. Try various things. Very often, the previously skeptical partner (usually the male) will become more open after grasping the rationale of ST. It is different from what he or she might have expected of couple therapy.

A final thought: therapy can help the engaged person to feel more empowered, calm and confident—useful qualities regardless of the course of the relationship. Sometimes just one person who learns how to be more consistently in Healthy Adult mode can make a difference in the relationship. Simeone-DiFrancesco has had some people thank her for saving the marriage, even when the partner never came in! Such is the potential power of ST-C.

2.10   How Many Therapists?

Schema therapists usually work with both partners, not only in conjoint sessions but in parallel individual sessions as well. But this is not the norm in the profession, and we expect that some therapists will have objections to this way of proceeding. One of the strengths of ST, at least from our vantage point, is that it is questioning of what is, perhaps, routine in a search for what might be best for our clients. We would like to argue for what might be a single schema therapist working in different ways with clients.

ST often combines conjoint and individual sessions. Many relationship therapists work with the couple, and refer to a different therapist if individual sessions or an individual therapy seems necessary. While this can seem justified, as it preserves the couple-therapist role, there are some problems. As a therapist, you will bond emotionally with your client. This establishes a good working alliance, but you also get confidential and even biased information. Seeing the partner either individually or in a conjoint sessions will provide a more "objective" picture, or at least a more balanced one.

Given all this, having two therapists involved with a couple in a crisis may tend to separate the couple. Adding separate couple therapy to two individual therapies will not solve the problem. There will be an unavoidable information gap between three therapists. And all this is compounded when the therapies are based on different conceptual models.

Also, collaboration is not easy. Communication between professionals can quickly become messy or competitive. Yet the success of treatment for the couple often depends on effective cooperation. So we will try to provide some ideas on how to best work it out. Stick to your conceptualization, be patient with the other therapist, and remain open to reality testing. Difference in perspective is often helpful. Consider the following:

- Be careful not to undermine each other. Alternatively, avoid going into Compliant Surrender mode.
- You will need to have an agreement with the couple to charge for time spent in collaboration. Without proper reimbursement, the process can become too burdensome in your practice and you may begin to unconsciously avoid spending sufficient time collaborating or develop underlying anger towards the couple.
- Discuss and adjust the pace of the collaboration as you go along.
- Have signed informed consent to disclose information between all parties.
- Do identify troublesome coping behaviors and recognize that the other therapist may not know what their client is actually doing, but only what the client is able to articulate and report about themselves.

Usually, the couple therapist will proceed in a more "detached" way using mode maps and clash-cards, while the individual therapist strives to keep parental modes at bay, but both try to meet the needs of the child modes.

Therapy Tip: We think it is best to have a single schema therapist involved at all levels of working with a couple. One approach has the best chance of shifting child, parent, and coping modes into Healthy Adult.

2.11   With the Individual or Couple?

Usually it is best to see the couple together. Initially, you will probably ask them fill out informed consent documents. You may need to inform them (in writing) that if they meet with you as a couple, they may not be able to see you for individual therapy at a later date if the relationship severs. This will be solely at your discretion. Make sure that you have signed releases of information between the partners which allow you to get the information needed to treat them. This still allows you to withhold damaging material, but it leaves that to your discretion.

If you want to deliver inventory results, schema profiles, schema mode inventories or similar results, we suggest that you meet individually first with the person who has taken the test. Let the person absorb the results, and check whether they are ready to share their results with the partner.

Caution: Watch out for making one party vulnerable when the other person has yet to learn empathy.

Therapy should not be so overwhelmingly adverse because of abusive interactions or unrestrained rage that one of the couple does not want to return. So, when there are significant rough edges of personality traits, meet individually with the person until you have a solid re-parenting relationship, a good case conceptualization, and some understanding about how you will proceed in therapy. You might then decide how useful the partner is able to be at that point. Prepare the partner individually for a role in re-parenting, or even prepare them both individually to be able to empathize (as opposed to condemning the partner for bad behavior).

Reflect: In the case of infidelity, you might consider more joint sessions to encourage a sense of transparency and trust.

Sometimes there is a need to separate a couple who have had a serious and life-threatening history of domestic violence. Treat each individually while still addressing the cycle. Conceptualize. Work to heal the trauma. Treat the mode of the perpetrator. Do your best to ensure safety. Judge when the victim is ready to reinvest in couple therapy.

Often, one partner will call about relationship issues, but their partner may not be willing to come. Sometimes they want to get a perspective in first. It may be wise to try to understand the agenda of the caller. Some education about what you do in ST-C may change the situation. During the first visit, formulate your own opinion about whether it is a good idea for the partner to come in soon. Sometimes it is clear that the first party needs to deal with something first, and for the partner to remain open and trusting about joining up later. This is usually a good indicator for a positive outcome.

At the point when it becomes clear that you can work with the couple on their relationship with sufficient safety, you can shift to couple work.

Lastly, we tend to do what is necessary to balance cost-effectiveness and efficacy. Some couples will want mode work and imagery shared in a session with their partner. This can be a powerful source of emotional reconnection. Others feel too vulnerable and need the safety of an individual session to reveal their basic emotions and core needs. So it is best to go slowly and with caution. The session must remain safe. Work from your case conceptualization. Ultimately, this will assist each to feel more secure and hopeful, and lead to more effective treatment.

Warning: Some clients are so overcompensating that they refuse to give the therapist permission to work in a flexible way.

At times, it is not practical to have one partner sit through a session when 99 percent of your attention is focused on the partner. At other times, it is useful to develop empathy by having one partner relive as you do trauma work with the other, and the partner may actually help out, come into an imagery scene, and comfort and protect. Make these therapeutic judgments as you plan the next session or two, and then you can schedule accordingly. Sometimes it is helpful to have the partner on hand, in the waiting room, so you can bring them into a session if needed. Some people will not mind being available in this way.

The goal is not keeping the couple together at any price, because the bottom-line principle relates to human worth. People cannot allow themselves to be dehumanized and destroyed. This is everyone's basic human right. We try to help the couple to look at their relationship from the emotionally cooler Healthy Adult point of view and then take action instead of clinging on to the partner or forcing them to "freeze" a state that no longer exists, or surrender to harm. Allowing harm to continue cannot possibly be healthy or moral. This is where Simeone-DiFrancesco, who works with many Christian churches, challenges marriages, saying: "The morality point is what you do, and what you don't do about it, and if you are free to remarry. It is never a 'sin' to stand for justice and healing. Use every point of leverage to shake up or change a harmful relationship." It is a point of culpability to avoid the issues, passively settle, or exit in a worse way as the "victimized" party. Although the path is complex, many harmful states can be abated and healed, given goodwill and effort. This, in fact, is the power of ST-C—to potentially turn harmful and hurtful relationships into ones that are edifying and meet the deepest of human needs. The attitude of "Don't give up" needs to be "coupled" with "And don't give in" to the mode cycle, which is the true enemy!

Summary

In this chapter we have explored what might happen in a first interview. Some challenging issues can present, such as an affair, different motivations to engage in therapy, and unrealistic expectations. If you are working with the couple, then some basic commitments that prioritize the relationship and limit destructive interactions are important. Sometimes you will only have one person presenting to address couple issues, and therapy will have to adapt. It is important to adopt an ST perspective from the start of couple therapy and to begin to notice what you will need to develop a case conceptualization. And it is helpful to include the "couple-interpersonal" perspective into an individual ST as well.

3

Relationship Assessment

Assessment is foundational to couple therapy. It provides the first lines on a map of the relationship. Think about where you live. Can you think of different vantage points in your town or city, where you can look over the terrain that is familiar to you from driving or walking around? In a similar way, looking at a relationship from a number of perspectives gives a more encompassing view of what is happening with a couple. This chapter has a number of useful tools for assessment, including designing your own questionnaire, using genograms and autobiographies of relationships, and understanding couple dynamics in terms of schemas.

3.1 A Questionnaire

You can design a personal questionnaire for couples. Write it to reflect your approach. Put some thought into what questions might inform your therapy. Hargrave (2000, p. 68) had questions about descriptions of parental discipline, how and when there was teaching about sexuality, and descriptions of relationships in the family of origin. He also included the following questions:

* As a result of growing up in your family, what did you learn about how lovable or important you are?
* In your family what was the most important thing to do or be?
* How did you know you were loved?
* What was the most important thing about being a family?

Schema Therapy with Couples: A Practitioner's Guide to Healing Relationships, First Edition.
Chiara Simeone-DiFrancesco, Eckhard Roediger, and Bruce A. Stevens.
© 2015 John Wiley & Sons, Ltd. Published 2015 by John Wiley & Sons, Ltd.
Companion website: www.wiley.com/go/difrancesco/schematherapywithcouples

- How did you feel among your siblings?
- What did you learn about being a man or a woman?
- What are your expectations for the relationship?

What questions most interest you?

Reflect: Think about your forms, including informed consent forms. Would there be some benefit in a general questionnaire? What about one or more focused schema inventories?

3.2   The Genogram

The genogram is a simple way of organizing information about families over three generations. It provides symbols for a kind of "family tree." This visual map was developed in family therapy but is now far more widely used. Many therapists find it useful for assessment. You can keep track of family members and maintain an intergenerational systems perspective. Perhaps, if it is not familiar to you, it is worth trying with a couple.

The following details can be included on the diagram:

1. *significant people:* name, age, highest level of education, occupation, and significant problems
2. *times:* dates of birth, death, marriages, divorces, separations (anniversaries tend to raise anxiety or cause sadness); any other significant stressors or transitions (accidents, illness, change of job, moving house)—especially if any occurred just before a legally relevant event, such as work-related stress, separation, or an injury
3. *locations:* geographical locations of parents and other family members; patterns of migration
4. *ethnic and religious affiliations.*

Then add indications of psychopathology, including alcohol abuse, genetic defects, suicide, violence, accidents, job instability, problems with gambling, sexual abuse, criminal behavior, drug addiction, other addictions, and mental illness. It is easy to have short-hand symbols, such as @ for alcoholism, but make up your own for any theme that you find significant. If all this provides the bones, then the flesh is the emotional patterns. Who are the success stories in the family? What are the criteria (business, academic, sport, or financial success)? Are there clear gender roles? How important are sibling positions? Who are the "black sheep" or "scapegoats"? What are the family rules, taboos, hot issues, secrets, and family scripts—or anything that interests you.

The wider context can also be considered. What are the historical forces that shaped each generation? What wars, economic conditions, birth-rate changes, cultural forces, and new technologies were influential? Have notions about gender changed or remained the same? If there was a migration, what differences in culture were introduced? One cultural value that influences self-care is selflessness versus self-consideration. Did this change in the family? How has the meaning of work changed through the generations? Note that the genogram is a tool in which you can create your own symbols to track what you want in a clinical history.

While all this is very comprehensive, it is possible to sketch out the genogram and include enough relevant details to inform your assessment in 10–15 minutes. It need not "have everything" but can be a sketch for later additions.

The genogram in Figure 2 records clinically significant information. Tom and Nancy grew up in alcoholic homes. Tom had a previous marriage to Jane, which ended in divorce; she later died of breast cancer. Nancy lives much closer to her immediate family and tends to get involved in their dramas. In 1986, a year after the stillbirth of her daughter Ann, she experienced multiple stresses following the death of her mother: her father increased his drinking and her younger brother was admitted to hospital with a diagnosis of schizophrenia. This might explain her need for

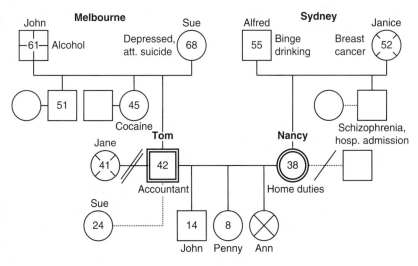

Figure 2 Genogram of Tom and Nancy

additional support, which she sought in the brief affair with Joe. Tom and Nancy are now presenting for relationship counseling because Tom is "having feelings" for Sue, a temporary administration assistant in his accountancy firm. Nancy complains that Tom works long hours, neglecting his family and household tasks.

3.3   Why do a Genogram?

The advantages of a genogram include the following:

1. *Visualization.* The genogram helps to keep track of people, the situation, and the context of the relationship. It is easier to focus on a visual diagram (and return to a point where everything is summarized) than on scribbled notes. You can put dot points for a treatment plan and interventions on the same page.
2. *The symptom is in context.* We can see the family history. This is a good way to incorporate historical elements into a diagnosis. It might also be important for differential diagnosis, such as distinguishing a biological from a reactive depression. Antisocial behavior, violence, and addictions often run through families. Doing a genogram reminds you to ask the right questions.
3. *Personality disorder.* It helps to diagnose this. There are usually intergenerational patterns of neglect, trauma, abuse, and relationship instability. This is a good early warning that progress will be slow and that you should expect surprises!
4. *Context.* Problems can be seen in a larger context. With complex families with strong intergenerational themes, you can assume that recovery will take longer. This is also true for relationship difficulties.
5. *Emotions.* You can track emotional patterns. What emotions were expressed, what were repressed?
6. *Parental models.* Think about what parents modeled to children and consider patterns of nurture.
7. *Attachment.* You can begin to identify attachment patterns and schema transmission through the generations. Perhaps put the shorthand "AB" for Abandonment, and so on, on the genogram to indicate which schemas or modes were dominant for people in the family and in previous generations. You will soon see intergenerational patterns of schemas.
8. *Flexibility.* It is a flexible tool, and you can create your own symbols for whatever interests you.

It is important to be emotionally "clean" in our work. Having worked on our own family-of-origin themes and dealing with emotional issues in personal therapy helps us, as relationship therapists, to achieve greater objectivity in the assessment and treatment of couples.

Monica McGoldrick and Randy Gerson's book *Genograms in Family Assessment* (1985) is now slightly dated, but it is very comprehensive and can add to your understanding of this useful tool.

To Do: Draw your own genogram and reflect upon family themes. When you consider your family, think about interviewing the elders in your family. They may be the keepers of the oral history and will help you to understand themes and patterns that have shaped the family over the generations.

3.4   Autobiography of Relationships

People mostly "live" their relationships, gaining the experience but missing the meaning. You might consider recommending the following exercise as homework for individuals and couples: "Write an autobiography of your relationships. This can begin with early experiences of your parents, the foundational relationship, but include experiences of 'first love' or early attraction, group dating, pairing off, first kiss, first committed relationship, de facto or formal marriage experiences. Write it with a focus on the emotional highs and lows and try to get a sense of repeating patterns."

> Darren wrote about his history of relationships. He was able to track through his relationships how characteristic ways he reacted to people, such as being suspicious, had contributed to unresolved problems. He also considered his emotional reactivity and how it dominated some relationships that ended badly for him.

3.5   Schema Identification

It is important to appreciate that ST involves a shift from current problems to whole-of-life patterns. Jeff Young and his colleagues (2003) identified a number of maladaptive schemas. These are templates from childhood for styles of thinking and emotional responses. This typically leads to schema-driven behavior. Schemas include beliefs about the self, the world and other people, which result from unmet childhood needs, innate temperament, and early environmental influences. They are composed of memories, body sensations, emotions, and thoughts that originate in childhood but are elaborated through an individual's life.

Reflect: Consider the following people with relationship problems:

> Nellie cannot bear the absence of her boyfriend. She constantly rings and texts Paul at work. He complains about her expectation that he instantly respond to her "constant demands" or she will get angry and "pout for a day or two."
>
> Michael is very self-important. He does have a high-status job but constantly reminds everyone of his successes. He expects full support from his "trophy wife," who now feels an afterthought to what is important to him in terms of his ambition.
>
> Betty still lives at home with her aging mother. She said, "I meet eligible people; that part is easy enough. But then they'll realize that I have to care for my mother. That's almost a 24/7 responsibility. And she never seems to approve of anyone I bring home."
>
> Les is almost savage in his put-downs and criticism of his de facto spouse. This harshness is often expressed in front of Mandy's family and is very embarrassing. Her mother said, "Les is actually emotionally abusive; you must do something about it."

What patterns of behavior would you identify?

The list of schemas has been revised over the past two decades, and the following is the most recent. We have also included brief summaries, which we have drawn largely from Young et al. (2003) and Arntz & van Genderen (2010). The schemas are grouped into five categories, which Young called "domains." Each domain represents schemas deriving from the same unmet core need, such as for attachment, autonomy, limit setting, adequate self-centeredness, and playfulness.

3.5.1   Disconnection and rejection

This domain is characterized by attachment difficulties related to a lack of safety in interpersonal relationships (Arntz & Jacob, 2013). An individual who scores highly on these schemas cannot depend on the security or reliability of others. There is an assumed lack of reliability, support, empathy, and respect. They may come from a family in which they were treated in a cold, rejecting manner. Emotional support may have been lacking, perhaps even basic care. Caregivers were unpredictable, uninterested, or abusive.[4]

---

[4]   We alternate grammatical gender for reasons of inclusiveness. The choice does not to identify a schema or mode as more male or female.

- *Abandonment (instability)*. He expects to lose anyone with whom there is an emotional attachment. Important others are seen as unreliable and unpredictable in their ability or willingness to offer nurture. All intimate relationships will eventually end. His partner will leave or die.
- *Mistrust-Abuse*. She is convinced that others will, in one way or another, eventually take advantage of her. What is expected is hurt, being cheated on, manipulation, or humiliation.
- *Emotional Deprivation*. He believes that his primary needs will be either not met or inadequately met by others. This includes physical care, empathy, affection, protection, companionship, and emotional care. The most common kinds of feared deprivation are of nurturance, empathy, and protection.
- *Defectiveness-Shame*. She feels intrinsically incomplete and bad. As others get to know her, her defects will be discovered. Then they will want nothing to do with her. No one will find her worthy of love. There is an over-concern with the judgment of others. A sense of shame is always present.
- *Social Isolation (alienation)*. He has the feeling that he is isolated from the rest of the world, is different from others, and does not fit in anywhere.

3.5.2 Impaired autonomy and performance

This individual believes that they are incapable of functioning and performing independently. There are problems with autonomy and achieving full potential. They may be fearful that making decisions will damage important relationships. They may come from a clinging family, from which they could not break free and in which they were overprotected. In this way, the person learned the schema from childhood models. Sometimes the child experienced neglect (Arntz & Jacob, 2013).

- *Dependence-Incompetence*. She is not capable of taking on normal responsibilities and cannot function independently. She feels dependent on others in a variety of situations. She may lack confidence to make decisions about simple problems or to attempt anything new. The feeling is one of complete helplessness.
- *Vulnerability to Harm or Illness*. He is convinced that, at any moment, something terrible might happen and there is no protection. Both medical and psychological catastrophes are feared. He takes extraordinary precautions.

- *Enmeshment (undeveloped self)*. She is over-involved with one or more of her parents. Because of this symbiotic relationship, she is unable to develop her own identity. At times, she has the idea that she does not exist without the other person. She may feel empty and without goals. However, she will report having a very close and supportive relationship with the person with whom she is enmeshed (Arntz & Jacob, 2013).
- *Failure (to achieve)*. He is convinced that he is not capable of performing at the same level as his peers in his career, education, sport, or whatever is valued. He feels stupid, foolish, ignorant, and without talent. He does not even attempt to succeed because of an abiding conviction that the attempt will lead to nothing.

3.5.3　Impaired limits

This individual has inadequate boundaries, lacks a sense of responsibility, and has poor frustration tolerance. They are not good at setting realistic long-range goals and have difficulty working with others. Perhaps they came from a family that offered little direction or gave them the feeling of being superior to the world.

- *Entitlement-Grandiosity*. She thinks that she is superior to others and has special rights. There is no need to follow the normal rules or expectations of society. She can get away with what she wants without taking others into consideration. The main theme here is power and control over situations and individuals. Rarely is there any empathy.
- *Insufficient Self-control (or self-discipline)*. He cannot tolerate any frustration in achieving his goals. There is no capacity to suppress feelings or impulses. It is possible that he is attempting to avoid being uncomfortable in any way.

3.5.4　Other directedness

This individual always takes the needs of others into consideration to gain attachment and represses their own needs for self-assertiveness. They do this in order to receive love and approval and avoid activations of the first category. The family background is often one of conditional love. The needs and status of the parents took priority over what was important to the child.

- *Subjugation*. She gives herself over to the will of others to avoid negative consequences. This can include the denial of all her emotional needs. She thinks that her desires, opinions, and feelings will not be important to others. This often leads to pent-up rage, which is then expressed in an inadequate manner (i.e., passive–aggressive or psycho-somatic symptoms).

- *Self-sacrifice.* He voluntarily and regularly sacrifices his needs for others whom he views as weaker. If he does attend to personal needs, he is likely to feel guilty about doing so. Being oversensitive to the pain of others is part of the presentation. In the long term, he may feel some resentment towards those for whom he has sacrificially cared.
- *Approval Seeking (recognition seeking).* She searches for approval, appreciation, acknowledgment, or admiration. This is at the cost of her personal needs. Sometimes this results in an excessive desire for status, beauty, and social approval.

3.5.5   Over-vigilance and inhibition

At the cost of self-expression and self-care, this individual suppresses their spontaneous feelings and needs and follows their own strict set of rules and values to avoid harm by activations of schemas from the second category. It is likely that their family emphasized achievement, perfectionism, and the repression of emotions. Caregivers were critical, pessimistic, and moralistic, while at the same time expecting an unreasonably high standard of achievement.

- *Negativity-Pessimism.* He always sees the negative side of things while ignoring the positive. Eventually, everything will go wrong, even if it is currently going well. He may be constantly worried and hyper-alert. He often complains and does not dare to make decisions.
- *Emotional Inhibition.* She holds tight control over her emotions and impulses, as she thinks that expressing them will damage others and lead to feelings of shame, abandonment, or loss of self-worth. This leads to the avoidance of all spontaneous expressions of emotions, such as anger, sadness, and joy. It also involves avoiding conflict. Often, she will present as very detached and overly rational.
- *Unrelenting Standards (hyper-criticalness).* He believes that he will never be good enough and must try harder. He will try to satisfy unusually high personal standards to avoid criticism. He is critical of himself as well as of those around him. This results in perfectionism, rigid rules, and sometimes a preoccupation with time and efficiency. He does this at the cost of enjoying himself, relaxing, and maintaining social contacts.

- *Punitiveness.* She feels that individuals must be severely punished for their mistakes. She is aggressive, intolerant, and impatient. There is no forgiveness for her own—or others'—mistakes. Individual circumstances or feelings are not taken into account.

The Young Schema Questionnaire version 3 (YSQ-3) is often used to assess the most relevant schemas for treatment. It exists in a long (232-item) and a short (90-item) form. Social Undesirability, a 19th schema, has been suggested (Lockwood & Perris, 2012) but only the 18 listed above are currently assessed by YSQ-3, and it is generally agreed that at least 15 have good research support.[5]

ST-C has a focus both on both individual ST for each partner and on joint couple sessions. An individual ST work-up, with an individual attachment to the therapist, is essential. This includes the standard inventories—the YSQ-3, YPI (Young Parenting Inventory), SMI (Schema Mode Inventory) and Multimodal Life History Inventory—plus the therapist performing a detailed conceptualization for each partner.

Reflect: Can you use the above list to identify any schemas that might be operating for Nellie, Michael, Betty, and Les (who are described at the beginning of Section 3.5)?

The following schemas are found in the examples:

Nellie has an Abandonment schema. She has to stay in emotional touch with her partner, seeking reassurance and emotional comfort, fundamentally because she has no confidence in being able to meet her own emotional needs.

Michael has an Entitlement-Grandiosity schema. He has to be important and be constantly recognized for his achievements. There are limits in the way he connects with others—it is based only on receiving recognition and affirmation.

Betty has Enmeshment and Self-sacrifice schemas operating in her relationship with her mother, and possibly also Subjugation if she allows her mother to veto her relationships.

Les has Punitiveness and Insufficient Self-control and possibly Unrelenting Standards schemas.

It is easy to see how these patterns in relationships would undermine stability and satisfaction—if not for the person then certainly for the partner.

---

[5]   See www.schematherapy.com for inventories that are currently available for health professionals. Consider joining the ISST and getting access to the full range of resources.

Therapy Tip: ST now works mainly with modes because modes are what we see. However, you may convey to couples at least the general idea about how schemas work. It is helpful to understand that current feelings may be driven by schemas rather than by the environment. Schemas ground the modes. Without an understanding of schemas as persisting patterns, working in the background of our personality, modes remain arbitrary. The modes are explained in Chapter 6. It is enough, at present, to simply note that the above schemas originate in childhood through patterns of experiences that are adverse or simply insufficient to meet needs, regardless of the person's appraisal of specific situations. Consciousness associated with an individual's activated schema is determined by developmental factors. In this way, ST is based on a unified theory (Farrell & Shaw, 2012).

3.6 Core and Compensatory Schemas

An understanding of core and compensatory schemas is important. Young distinguished "unconditional" and "conditional" (Young et al., 2003, pp. 22–23). This allows for a dynamic sense of development with schemas. The core schemas are those that result from damage done to an individual's self-concept during development (listed in Domains 1 to 3), while compensatory schemas (listed in Domains 4 and 5) are developed in order to cope with or avoid activation of the primary schema. So there exists a kind of coping already, on the level of schemas, besides the coping styles described in Section 3.7.

> Ricky had a troubled childhood marked by inconsistent parenting from her mostly single mother and later her abusive stepfather. At an early age she developed Abandonment and Emotional Deprivation schemas; later she found ways to cope by pleasing others through Subjugation and Self-sacrifice. Essentially, these masked the earlier schemas ("I can cope as long as I put others first.").

With time, the compensatory schemas will become more rigid and maladaptive and, perversely, end up reinforcing the original schemas (Sheffield & Waller, 2012).

3.7 Schema Coping Styles

There are three ways to respond to a schema. Young called these *coping reactions.* When they are used frequently, they turn to pervasive personal *coping styles.* Just for clarification: schema coping describes how an individual deals with their own schemas. Thus, it cannot be compared with the animal behavior of fight, flight or freeze because that describes behavior towards an external enemy. But a schema is an "enemy within." Coping styles are relevant for the integrated concept of coping modes. In a nutshell, surrendering to a schema means continuously suffering from it. Avoiding means trying to keep away from triggering circumstances, and compensation describes a contradictory behavior to the original schema.

> Linda had a significant abuse history. Her father and older brothers took advantage of her sexually. She was date-raped when she was 16. Understandably, she has a Mistrust-Abuse schema that she responds to in different ways. At times she withdraws from men, suspecting even the most innocent of malicious intent. She will often use cannabis or binge drink. Recently, she began dating a man who was recently paroled from prison for violent offences.
>
> Linda illustrates all three of the potential coping reactions to Mistrust-Abuse schema activation. When she engages in reckless one-night stands (or is in a relationship with a high-risk male), she is surrendering (because she behaves in such a way as to repeat the schema). When she is over-suspicious and maybe engages in a women's rights campaign, she acts against the schema, which is compensation. When she just goes off by herself and drinks, watching football in the sports bar, she is avoidant.

In summary, coping styles include:

1. **Surrender.** The person gives into the schema:
   - *Behavior.* This is seen in repeating behavioral patterns from childhood by looking for people and situations that are similar to what led to the formation of the schema.
   - *Thoughts.* Information is processed selectively (seeing only what confirms the schema, not what counters it).
   - *Feelings.* The emotional pain of the schema is directly experienced.
2. **Avoidance.** The person avoids activities that trigger the schema and emotional reactions. The result is that the schema is not engaged. There is no access to the schema to change or revise it.
   - *Behavior.* This includes both active and passive avoidance of all kinds of situations that might trigger the schema.
   - *Thoughts.* This can be seen in the denial of events or traumatic memories. This also includes psychological defenses such as dissociation (emotional detachment).

- *Feelings.* This includes smoothing over feelings or escape into numbness.
3. **Compensation.** The person behaves in the opposite direction from the schema. This results in underestimating the strength or influence of the schema. You can recognize this with aggressively independent behavior, often with a fragile veneer.
- *Behavior.* This can be identified by exaggerated behavior that is opposite to the schema.
- *Thoughts.* These are opposite to the content of the schema, with opposite feelings. The person denies the presence of the schema.
- *Feelings.* The person feels uncomfortable with feelings associated with the schema. The feelings may return if the overcompensation fails.

Consider the following examples:

Brian had an easily activated Defectiveness-Shame schema. As an adolescent, he was ashamed of his body and joined a gym to bodybuild. Gradually he developed his physique to the extent that he entered body-building competitions. He used steroids to add muscle mass. This was an obvious compensation for the way he felt about his body. But if he did not perform well in the competitions he would be flooded by the original feelings of being defective and not measuring up. This would trigger surrender to the schema. At times, Brian would also abuse cannabis as a way of avoidance.

Michelle had a very strong Self-sacrifice schema, but by surrendering to it she was often exhausted by the demands of others. She would avoid by binge eating, and this led her to return to therapy.

Therapy Tip: It may be that the coping styles are not stable. Try to look at coping styles in a longitudinal perspective, over time, and see a possible variety in relation to a schema (van Genderen, 2012). Table 1 gives some examples of the different ways of coping with a schema.

Reflect: Think about some of the most difficult couples you treat. Can you recognize schema patterns and characteristic ways of coping?

3.8 Schema Chemistry in Therapy

Transference is a familiar therapeutic idea. The concept is closely aligned with Freud. He first articulated the concept in *Studies in Hysteria* (1893–1895) and further explored it through the failed case of Dora: "A whole

Table 1   Examples of schema coping behaviors

Schema	Surrender	Avoidance	Compensation
Mistrust-Abuse	Allowing others to abuse you	Not starting a close relationship	Abusing others, persecuting abusers
Defectiveness-Shame	Excusing yourself instantly when getting blamed	Saying nothing and going away when being criticized	Working hard to get "perfect" so no one can criticize you
Self-sacrifice	"Bleeding out" for others	Giving excuses why you can't engage in something	Aggressive protection against (anticipated) expectations
Unrelenting standards	Trying always to be the best	Not participating so you can't fail	Apologizing that your talents are just a gift

series of psychological experiences are revived, not as belonging to the past, but as applying to the person of the physician at the present moment" ([1905]1963, p. 138). Transference became central in classical psychoanalytic treatment, providing both a window to the past and a present reality. But if transference is the transferring of feelings about a previously significant person on to the person of the therapist, then counter-transference was the same dynamic but from the therapist's perspective.

Freud's negative evaluation of counter-transference prevailed until Dr. Paula Heimann's important 1950 paper led to a reassessment in psychoanalytic circles. She argued, "My thesis is that the analyst's emotional response to his patient within the analytic situation represents one of the most important tools for his work … This is the most dynamic way in which his patient's voice reaches him" (Heimann, 1950). In this way, counter-transference became central to a process of assessment and treatment (see also Arntz & Jacob, 2013, pp. 58–59). More recently, Solomon and Siegel (1997) edited a book of papers on counter-transference in couple therapy.

ST allows a more contemporary understanding of these dynamics in terms of "schema chemistry" (or mutually triggering schemas). It describes what happens emotionally between the partners or between the individual or couple and the therapist. It is a process in which schemas are activated by memory-based likenesses, which in turn distort a healthy reception of the current dyadic relationship. We need to have a high level of awareness about our own schema vulnerabilities to transcend and be able to rise above them. It is only natural that early maladaptive schemas will be activated in therapy (Weertman, 2012).

A schema-based supervision model has recently been published (Roediger & Laireiter, 2013). It prompts us to look at the therapist's schema activations and vulnerability to end up in mode cycles with clients. Leahy (2001) detected typical schemas among therapists. The most relevant ones are Emotional Deprivation, Self-sacrifice, and Unrelenting Standards. When a therapist works with couples, failure to place proper limits on the demands of a client is a major pitfall. It is also important to remain aware of personal resonances, which allow the therapist to express vicarious feelings as a "loudspeaker" for the clients. A couple schema therapist takes his or her own schema activations and turns them into therapeutic tools. This might lead, for example, to getting in touch with unexpressed or repressed feelings of a subjugating partner and creating a safe space for exchanging and reflecting feelings. Alternatively, awareness of one's own activation or the client's or couples' activation with the therapist might become an avenue leading to a more detached appraisal in chair-work, which we cover in Chapter 9.

To Do: If you have not done the YSQ-3, this would be a good time. Watch out for coping with compensation for underlying schemas, such as Self-sacrificing, offsetting a deeper Failure schema, for example. Check out the various aspects of Domain 2 to see whether they apply.

Therapy Tip: Be careful: many therapists have underlying schemas in Domain 2 but learned to compensate them through achieving in a career. Achieving a medical or psychology degree is a proof of academic success, but can be based on schema compensation. So eventually ask your friends how they perceive you.

Examine your results in the YSQ. What does this tell you about your vulnerability with certain couples? Where could you expect interlocking schemas with your clients? Think of your last few difficult couples and consider, in terms of schemas, why you struggled.

> Nathan, a young psychologist, was seeing a couple in which the man had an extensive criminal history, including incarceration. He had significant anti-social attitudes. His de facto partner was diagnosed with borderline personality disorder. She struggled with drug dependency and self-mutilating behaviors. Nathan found his Unrelenting Standards schema challenged by a lack of progress with this couple. He talked this over with his ST supervisor: "I think I expect to see almost instant results. This insight reassures me that I'm a competent therapist."

In the clinical setting, we only have direct first-hand access to two sources of data: *mental status*, which includes the observation of actual behavior shown in the session, and *schema chemistry* triggered within ourselves.

While there may be some report from third parties or data from psychological testing, most of what is said in a clinical setting is self-reported or anecdotal. The challenge of assessment is to integrate a whole range of data into a coherent understanding of the case.

Summary

In this chapter we have discussed the process of assessment. This includes the use of questionnaires, including those that you might design. The genogram is a useful assessment tool. You can also use the journal exercise of an autobiography of relationships. Then we explored how people develop a range of schemas, how the various coping styles develop, and the idea of "schema chemistry" in relationships. The focus in Chapter 4 is on understanding unresolved issues brought by the couple from their respective families of origin. How do we begin to bring that important information to bear on the couple relationship and, of course, how do we most effectively intervene?

4

Understanding the Origins of Relational Styles

In a marriage service, two people stand before family, friends, and perhaps God to make "lifelong" vows. Such a commitment conveys what is consciously intended "for better or for worse," but—and it is a big *but*—there are agendas from the edge of awareness that will profoundly influence the chances of success in the relationship.

If there are highly unrealistic expectations, they will fester and ultimately poison the couple's life together.

4.1 Healthy and Unhealthy Co-functioning

Everyone enters a relationship with agendas. This is hardly surprising. Healthy couples can have non-conscious agendas, usually around complementary functioning: Martin is good with keeping track of money and paying the bills; Sally takes the initiative to book weekends away to enliven the relationship. This happens at various levels: Don is rational to a fault, but his male partner Bobby is emotionally intense and somewhat dramatic. There is a balance of thinking and feeling in the relationship. Or Nicola plans everything to the last dot point, but Kenny values being spontaneous. Both partners contribute in different fields in a complementary way. Such differences may increase conflict, but can also lead to enhanced couple functioning. As long as such differences are balanced, this can work well, and children benefit from a wider range of experiences with parents.

Schema Therapy with Couples: A Practitioner's Guide to Healing Relationships, First Edition.
Chiara Simeone-DiFrancesco, Eckhard Roediger, and Bruce A. Stevens.
© 2015 John Wiley & Sons, Ltd. Published 2015 by John Wiley & Sons, Ltd.
Companion website: www.wiley.com/go/difrancesco/schematherapywithcouples

Emotional legacies, however, can cause problems. Early emotional damage from a disturbed childhood can last a lifetime. This can be with or without awareness.

> Tommy entered adulthood knowing that he was failed by his family. Not even basic needs were adequately met. He received love only with "strings attached," but mostly neglect. His single mother failed to protect him from sexual abuse from one of her boyfriends. He saw his mother caught up in mutual domestic violence. As a teenager, he was left to his own resources, without discipline or guidance, and left home at 14. He recalled a reversal of roles: "I had to comfort Mom when a boyfriend dumped her."

This results in what has been called the "parentified child."[6] The cost is high: the loss of a normal childhood. Some parents will even blame their child when their own needs are not met. Such experiences add up to a loss of safety, security, and self-esteem. The inevitable result is adults with emotional deficits and a sense of violation. Tommy experienced a compulsion to meet his intense personal needs.

> Mandy and Vince were madly in love. Attraction was instant and the resulting bliss lasted three or four months, until some cracks appeared in their relationship. Mandy had been sexually abused by an uncle when she was 8 years old and her first relationship was marked by violence, including forced sex. It is hardly surprising that she began to have sexual difficulties with Vince: "I find it hard to relax and enjoy being with him. I keep expecting terrible things to happen." Vince brought his own problems to the relationship as well. His mother was single and a chronic alcoholic who neglected her children. Vince was the oldest and took responsibility for raising his younger siblings. He did this, but resented the loss of a normal childhood. When it came to Mandy's difficulties, he was impatient: "Why can't she get her shit together!"

This couple has brought "baggage" into the relationship. Everyone does, but some legacies make the new relationship almost doomed from the start. It is important to recognize this and to clarify what is at stake and "what belongs where," or confusion will result. If the past is confused with the present, it will be nearly impossible to find a healthy way forward.

> Mandy needed therapy to work through issues of sexual abuse and violence. She had specialized trauma therapy to deal with intrusive thoughts

---

[6]   This is a widely discussed term—see "Parentification" in Wikipedia.

and images. Gradually, she was able to create a "safe place" for a different sexual experience with Vince. While Vince had his legacy, he was able to talk about this experience with his younger brother, now a social worker, and through his journal he revisited his childhood experiences and found he could better leave it behind. He still felt resentment about what he missed out on, but he was able to distinguish it from the support Mandy needed in her journey of recovery from trauma. This mutual understanding drew them closer together.

4.2   A Dark Legacy

Hargrave (2000) noted that, after neglect or abuse, a child may grow up with either rage or a sense of entitlement—or possibly both. This makes psychological sense because adults can remain still emotionally stuck in childhood and acting out unconscious needs. Such a damaged person, when in a relationship, will take almost any action to secure the nurture and care needed. This leads to destructive behavior, including manipulation, threats and abuse. It has been called "destructive entitlement" (Boszormenyi-Nagy & Krasner, 1986).

Scott had an abusive childhood. His father left when he was still in the womb. His mother was mostly single but had periodic turbulent and often violent relationships. When violence was in the house, he was often fearful for his life. He became a disturbed child, stealing cars when he was in early adolescence and binge drinking from his late teens. When he got out of prison, he was puzzled about his relationships: "I have no trouble with meeting women. Everything is fine for a few weeks, maybe a month or so but then … I don't know."

Kylie had a horrific childhood. She was taken into foster care when her single father could not adequately care for her. She was severely bullied at school because she was "different." She was smoking heroin by age 15, but later went into a residential drug program led by Teen Challenge, a Christian organization, and became clean. She said, "That program really saved my life. It helped me take responsibility for my life and not blame others. I wasn't 'lucky' as a child, but I can now see how this has made it difficult for me to have stable relationships. It helps if I take it one step at a time and keep my expectations low. I keep asking myself, is my reaction to my partner Tim or from my past? That helps a bit but I often get it wrong because, well, reactions always feel justified."

In these examples, Scott has no insight into his problems but Kylie has begun to understand "what belongs where."

The real question is about how to deal with this history. Think about what is *on stage* and what is *backstage*. The actors, now adults, in the relationship dramas play out destructive behaviors through manipulative acts, threats, abuse, and acting out sexually. The dysfunctional behavior is obvious. But the real clue is that often the person will feel justified. Why? Emotionally, the adult is a child trapped in family dynamics and can only see through a child's eyes. Naturally, the result is profound instability in adult relationships.

Now to address both. Rage may be externalized with verbal abuse, threats, and/or violence. It may also be internalized by being locked in dark depression or self-destructive acts such as cutting, binge eating, or suicide attempts. Clearly, this is very stressful in relationships and must be addressed. Perhaps equally destructive in a relationship is a sense of entitlement. This is expressed in the maxim, "What's mine is mine and what's yours is mine as well!" Entitlement tends to be narcissistic. Nevertheless, there may also be a feeling of shame in the background, with an assumption that "I was unworthy of love" (possibly reflecting a Defectiveness-Shame schema). It can be helpful to go "backstage" to biographical history to understand the current behavior and resolve it effectively.

4.3   Unconditional Love?

The expectation of "unconditional" love may indicate an additional script being acted out on that stage. This is like a stereotypical Hollywood romance: "My partner will love me unconditionally" only works out well in the movies (which last less than two hours!). In real-life relationships, reality eventually intrudes.

A moment's thought about "Love needs to be unconditional" will reveal the unreality of that statement. Adult romantic relationships are always conditional (e.g., Thou shalt not have affairs, Thou shalt not be violent, Thou shalt be responsible and help to meet household duties and/or expenses, etc.). There is a symmetrical give and take in all adult relationships. Both have to make deposits into the "relationship account" (Covey, 1997).

The closest we get to unconditional love is that of a parent for her child (or maybe of an adult child for an aged parent needing deep emotional care). Now we can highlight the essence of the dysfunctional script being played out in many relationships. The expectation is that: "My partner will love me unconditionally and will give me what my parents failed to provide." It is hardly surprising that things begin to go terribly wrong with unexpressed expectations to repair my psychological history, be my therapist, and love me without limits. And usually there is an additional expectation of "mind-reading" as well. While ST will coach couples to be sensitive to each other's childhood needs, we need preparatory work, especially with couples who had very dysfunctional childhoods.

This explains some aspects of relationships that can be puzzling. Since the unmet needs originated in childhood, they are almost impossible to satisfy in adult relationships with a natural assumption of reciprocity. Inevitably, this leads to a partner's feelings of being a "dry well" with no more "water" to give in the relationship. It also explains why people behave so badly *and feel totally justified*. A child will have a tantrum if his needs go unmet.

Reflect: What needs did you have as a child that were not met? Do you think this contributes to any adult problems you may have faced? Is it possible that such experiences have shaped the kind of therapist you have become?

4.4   Dealing with the Past

The schema therapist will need to listen to the story of violation and possibly neglect from the family of origin. This can be done in individual sessions, but also consider couple sessions where sharing the story can build mutual understanding. In this process, identify what drives the damaged partner and explain what was not provided in childhood. It was natural to expect more then, but not now. The therapeutic goal is to first highlight and then deal with that injury (Hargrave, 2000).

You may need to provide some psycho-education about childhood needs. This will include what should have happened in an appropriately protective and nurturing family. Explain the lasting damage to a child and later adult from such failures in parenting. This can be compared with what is reasonable to expect in adult relationships. It is only when we appreciate the backstage dynamics that the play begins to make sense. Many relationship problems masquerade as adult issues when resolution can only be achieved by addressing childhood origins. This distinction can make a contribution to enhancing relationship stability.

Jezz had an intense look when she said, "But I just want to be able to love him freely. It's so frustrating that he won't respond. I know I shouldn't hit him, but I lose it and it's just to get his attention."

Anthony remarked, "Bel sometimes refuses me sexually. Mostly she is willing, but then if I'm frustrated and at the club, what's a man supposed to do? There's always someone willing."

Jezz and Anthony, in different ways, are responding to a sense of unmet need with entitlement: "I must be happy." There seems to be minimal awareness of the cost to be in a "committed" relationship.

There are many conceptualizations of childhood needs. One of the most helpful for therapy is Jeff Young's five primary tasks of childhood: connection and acceptance; autonomy and performance; realistic limits; inner-directedness and self-expression; and spontaneity and pleasure. With optimal development, a child will develop in a balanced way in all five areas.

Failure to meet these needs can be linked to dysfunctional schemas:

- Basic safety and stability (schemas: Abandonment, Mistrust-Abuse, Vulnerability to Harm)
- Close connection to another (Emotional Deprivation of nurture, empathy, protection; Social Isolation)
- Self-determination and self-expression (Enmeshment, Subjugation, Dependence, Failure)
- Self-actualization (Unrelenting Standards, Enmeshment, Approval-Seeking, and maybe Negativity, Self-sacrifice)
- Acceptance and self-esteem (Defectiveness-Shame, Punitiveness)
- Realistic limits and concern for others (Entitlement, Insufficient Self-control).

Couple Homework Exercise: Rate your childhood experience on a scale of 1/10 to 10/10 for each of these domains: connection and acceptance, autonomy and performance, realistic limits, inner-directedness and self-expression, and spontaneity and pleasure. (1/10 would be the result of abuse and/or neglect, 5/10 would be an average meeting of needs as compared to peers, and 10/10 would indicate a sensitive, child-focused environment in which needs were fully met). Discuss as a couple.

In ST, the past is not over. There is a range of powerful experiential techniques to change the "grip" of past emotional deficits, traumatic experiences, and behavior patterns. Consider, as an example, behaviors that include extremes of being over-controlling or chaotic, which both have origins in childhood. Such behaviors might have made sense in dysfunctional families but become problematic in adult relationships. A later chapter explains specific ST-C interventions.

4.5 A Note on Attraction

What does Kylie see in Justin? This question is often asked but, as everyone who has friend knows, it is hard to answer. Attraction is no less difficult for a therapist to understand.

Harville Hendrix (1988) thought about attraction as one of a number of non-conscious factors in a relationship. Young has talked about "schema chemistry." He thought that this was influenced by passionate love versus companionate love, healthy attraction, idealization of the partner, and the unavailability of a desired partner. This chemistry is also generated by the activation of core schemas. Indeed, couples often choose each other on the basis of their schemas, often by re-experiencing familiar childhood emotions or recalling situations that were distressing. As a result, a person may remain in an unhealthy relationship.

> Victor knew that he had a distant father who mostly ignored him. He was attracted to "macho" males. He would go to gay bars and enjoyed the attention of the men. But sometimes he would find himself in dangerous situations: "I seem to pick guys that can't accept their orientation. I've been assaulted, once ending up in intensive care in the hospital." He would react to his Mistrust-Abuse schema, choosing to put himself in risky situations. He also had a pattern of Subjugation. This would be a "perfect match" for someone with a lot of aggression, with underlying Entitlement and Punitiveness schemas.

It is helpful for the therapist to carefully explore the biographical history to better understand such dynamics.

Therapy Tip: When attraction seems even more irrational than usual, it is a good idea to think about schema vulnerability and consider it a signal to do work on the family of origin.

4.6 Brain "Chemistry" linked to Schemas

"Chemistry" is often seen as a proof of love: if it feels right, it must be right! But what is this "emotional" reasoning based on? At one level, feelings are based on neural activation. One result of getting in touch with prior experiences is to experience feelings—sometimes intensely. There are stimuli or triggers. Current stimuli are continuously compared with prior experiences and their outcomes. The neural system develops in a balance between self-contained stabilization and being open to new experiences ("broaden and built-theory," Frederickson, 2003). The self-organization procedure has been described from a constructivist perspective by Maturana and Varela (1998).

A system organizes itself out of chaos around so-called "attractors." External influences interfere with the attractors, creating a differentiated energetic "attractor landscape" with hills and valleys. The system tries to stabilize itself in the valleys, just as water runs downhill. In this context, learning can be viewed as building up new attractors and thereby creating alternative states. This is a way of understanding how schemas are built up. You can understand schemas as "neural attractors" guiding the neural activation into pre-existing pathways based on prior learning experiences (Grawe, 2004). But moving from one attractor to another needs energy to overcome the "energetic hills" between two attractors. The "energy" a therapist brings into therapy supports attractor state changes within the client, which they would not be able to manage by themselves.

Schemas bias our perception, appraisal, and reactions: we see what we know, and do what we can. When we choose a partner who is similar to significant others, it gives us a familiar feeling and a latent sense of "knowing the game." Based on character traits and attachment style, some people tend to explore new and maybe strange partners, but insecurely attached people prefer taking on what they already know. The schemas and the neural pathways make the partner attractive. If the chemistry does not fulfill the core needs of the partners, they might feel trapped in their pre-existing schemas. They fit well, but there is no development, no escape.

Reflect: Can you draw a picture that shows your neural attractors in relationships?

4.7   An Interlocking Schema Perspective

There is a concept of interlocking schemas in ST. Couples can have joint schemas that might be *dysfunctional* but *compatible*.

Think about Mistrust-Abuse combining with Punitiveness:

> Mike was raised in an abusive home. His father abused alcohol and was violent to all the children. His mother was passive and unable to protect them. Mike found Angie, who was intense, lively, and warm. She also had "dark moods" in which she could lash out in uncontrolled fury at the slightest provocation. She was emotionally abusive, and afterwards rarely if ever apologized.

Mike has Mistrust-Abuse, almost expecting abusive behavior, which with Angie's Punitiveness is virtually guaranteed. Both schemas have their origins in childhood but tend to "fit" in familiar adult patterns. We can understand schema chemistry as the compatibility of what feels familiar to both, and perhaps the attraction as a non-conscious knowing that their relationship will involve interlocking schemas.

There are potentially many possible interlocking schemas. The following examples give an indication of possible combinations.

Danny had a history of unreliable parenting through being in care with various families. He was acutely sensitive to abandonment and tended to be very controlling in relationships. This usually pushed partners away until he met Betty, who thrived on his dependence on her. They were inseparable. Danny has a compensated Abandonment schema and Betty has Enmeshment. The result, for different reasons, is that they are always together.

Ben was a successful lawyer. He wanted the best of everything and felt it was his due. It was his optimism that attracted Suzzi, who said, "I always expect everything to go wrong." She was raised caring for younger siblings. Ben has Entitlement and Unrelenting Standards schemas, which fit in with her general Negativity-Pessimism, Subjugation and Self-sacrifice schemas.

Amanda did not get her needs met as a child. She was a forgotten child in every family and social context. As an adult she was a bottomless pit of need, but generally acted as if she needed nothing from anyone. She felt at ease with Ned, who had "something of a gambling problem," but she was less happy when she found out he was having affairs. Amanda had an Emotional Deprivation schema, which at times she surrendered to and at times over-compensated for. Ned had an Insufficient Self-control schema.

Kylie developed an eating disorder in her early adolescence. She remained obsessed about her body image even though she was slim to the envy of her friends. Her negative view of her body was reinforced by the hypercritical attitude of Larry, who constantly pointed to imaginary faults and was relentless in his pressure for her to resume dieting. He could also be harsh when angry, and was easily angered. Kylie has a partly compensated Defectiveness-Shame schema, which has dominated her self-image and which ties in with Larry's Unrelenting Standards and Punitiveness schemas.

Charles was "hopelessly neurotic." He was on a disability pension after developing a multi-point pain disorder for vague work-related reasons. It was as if he needed a full-time carer, whom he found in Bridget. She was highly attentive to his physical needs. Charles had a Vulnerability to Harm schema, which fit in well with Bridget's Self-sacrifice schema.

These examples illustrate how schemas can match and interlock.

Young's idea of schema chemistry is that this can explain some of the dynamics of attraction in a couple's relationship. It also provides some understanding of psychological compatibility in longer-term relationships. Of course, such schema compatibility might not be a healthy match. There can be underlying pathology, but the relationship can nevertheless be stable and satisfying for the couple if there is a good fit of underlying needs.

4.8 Drawing the Threads Together in Case Formulation

A good case formulation includes such information as initial impressions, presenting problems, the history of the difficulty, previous therapies and solutions attempted, changes sought by the couple, any recent stressors or life changes, possibly a genogram, a prognosis and an expected length of treatment, including an appropriate treatment plan. While there has been some bias against the use of diagnosis in marital and family therapy, it is important to be aware of any individual psychopathology that can affect the couple relationship as well as the individuals.

While we use general terms such as "relationship therapist" in this book, the authors come from disciplines with a strong emphasis on assessment. We encourage all therapists, regardless of professional identity, to remember their training and bring those skills to couple counseling.

Relationship issues are often (but not always) related to psychological disorders and co-morbid conditions. Consider the following:

> Mary has brought Mark into counseling because of concerns about his gambling and how much it is costing the family. Mark recently returned from war service in Afghanistan. She wonders whether this might have some role to play in the increase in his gambling.
>
> Kylie has a problem with her anger. Brett is threatening to leave if her aggression is not better contained. Is her irritability that of an untreated depression or perhaps the brooding anger of borderline personality disorder?
>
> Bettina has just come out of hospital after a two-week admission related to her anorexia, and there is a need to closely monitor her weight. Natalie, her partner, is feeling highly stressed: "I love Bet, but what can I do? I can't take responsibility to keep her alive! I know she's unwell. I need some support and guidance for what I should be doing." Natalie is taking lithium for bipolar disorder.

It is clear that there are relationship issues with these three couples, but also psychological disorders, which add to their complex clinical presentations. It is important to have a good understanding of disorders such as addiction, PTSD, depression, borderline personality disorder, anorexia, and bipolar disorder. We can also think about how such disorders might affect an intimate relationship. Perhaps this is stating the obvious, but such potential complexity demands greater clinical training—not less!

There is a need to include early history, when the patterns of relating have been formed. This family-of-origin work helps people in relationships to recognize the influence of prior hurts, to understand "automatic responses," and (we hope) to interrupt dysfunctional processes. In all this, using analysis based on identifying schemas and their interactions makes a very important contribution to case formulation, especially in couple work. This will later be expanded using modes.

While the medical model is not especially in vogue with many couple therapists, we can learn a lot from its emphasis on assessment and formulation being foundational to an effective treatment plan. Formulation introduces the need for a theoretical perspective.

To Do: Think about a couple you have been seeing and know well. How would you formulate their relationship in terms of schema vulnerability? What modes do you see in the sessions? How do you plan to address their needs? Perhaps it is best to think *schemas* but to intervene focused on *modes.*

4.9   But why Theory?

Why theory? We think that the answer is obvious. When you are in the room with a distressed couple, there is an abundance of issues to address. You might take note of developmental stages, presenting symptoms, degree of cohesion, communication, sense of reality, affect, boundaries, and attitudes. Clifford Sager (1981) listed dependence, passivity, distance, abuse of power, dominance or submission, fear of abandonment, need to possess or control, level of anxiety, mechanisms of defense, understanding of love, gender identity, sexual expectations, cognitive style, and self-acceptance. It is also important to understand couple issues, such as deficits in communication, conflict resolution skills, emotional contracts, interlocking cognitive distortions, and inappropriate or blocked emotions (Weeks & Treat, 1992, pp. 10–18).

Nothing mentioned here is unimportant and many factors are vital to understanding a couple's relationship. But to address everything would take something like the stereotype of psychoanalysis—five times a week over 20 years!

It is as if the room is full of rabbits, hopping around, twitching their ears, landing in your lap, each saying "Follow me!" A good theory will tell you which rabbit to chase and how to prioritize a few of the others. There are plenty of rabbits that will not initially be especially noticed. In this way, the therapist will not be so distracted by the weekly crises and have more sense of direction in treatment.

Experience also teaches us to see patterns in a typical "problem list." This is encouraged in ST because schemas result in patterns of behavior. Hence we can develop our case formulation based on maladaptive schemas inducing current mode activation. It is helpful to use the idea of collaborative case formulation from cognitive behavioral therapy in this area as well, since it also encourages the couple to take more responsibility for progress in therapy (Grant et al., 2009, p. 136). How do they understand their relationship difficulties? While some people are unrealistic or blaming, there can be surprising insights—after all, they tend to know each other very well!

Summary

In this chapter we have looked at the origins of a couple's attraction, patterns of reciprocity, the influence of needs not being met in childhood, and the legacy of abuse and neglect. This was understood in terms of interlocking schemas in relationships. We re-emphasized the need for case formulation.

In Chapter 5 we look at the foundations of evidence-based couple therapy in Gottman's research and emotion-focused therapy for couples, and see some of their contributions to theory and intervention.

5

Foundations for Evidence-Based Practice in Couple Therapy

Two therapeutic streams flow into ST-C. Both have a strong evidence base for "normal" couple difficulties. The first is the extensive research of John Gottman on relationships (1999, 2011; Gottman & Schwartz Gottman, 2009). He has carried out important longitudinal studies through his "Love Lab." This work has important practical implications for couple therapy. The second is emotion-focused therapy for couples (EFT-C), which has proved its effectiveness in clinical trials. This chapter features an extended case study of William and Betty and illustrates how both approaches can offer theoretical contributions and methods of intervention that can contribute in practical ways.

5.1 Case Study: Bill and Betty

Bill and his wife, Betty, were both in their late 50s. For one session in the therapist's office, Bill wore his "old school tie," which did not match the color of the rest of his clothes. His wife, Betty, followed him into the office. She strode in with determination.

BILL EXPLAINED THE PROBLEM: "I've been offered a temporary promotion to our branch office in Rome. It's a wonderful opportunity that I won't see again before I retire. It's only for nine months ..."

BETTY INTERRUPTED: "But he'll be leaving me behind for that time! It's just like when he works late and goes on all those trips interstate. I never see him."

Schema Therapy with Couples: A Practitioner's Guide to Healing Relationships, First Edition.
Chiara Simeone-DiFrancesco, Eckhard Roediger, and Bruce A. Stevens.
© 2015 John Wiley & Sons, Ltd. Published 2015 by John Wiley & Sons, Ltd.
Companion website: www.wiley.com/go/difrancesco/schematherapywithcouples

THERAPIST TO BETTY:	"That would be frustrating?"
BETTY:	"I've given up on expecting him to care. I raised the children and this is the thanks I get!"
THERAPIST:	"You're angry about how he's treated you? But maybe also you feel neglected and lonely."

Betty nodded and was unable to speak.

The therapist encouraged the exploration of emotions in the couple relationship: "Emotion binds couples together, but it is also what rips them apart" (Greenberg & Goldman, 2008, p. 20). No couple therapist will go too far astray following the "hot spots" of emotional processing in working with couples. It always *feels* relevant.

There was exploration of the reason for Bill wanting to take the overseas position and how exciting he thought living briefly in Italy might be. Then he continued:

BILL:	"I just feel overwhelmed, almost smothered by Betty's demands. She's constantly negative and criticizing, when I'm lucky [with sarcasm]. Mostly it's blame and barely contained rage."
THERAPIST:	"You feel overwhelmed. It's just too much." [The hostility is noted but left to be challenged later; see Gottman, 1999.]
BILL SAID QUIETLY:	"I've been thinking about leaving. I know it's a big step after 30 years of marriage, but I thought that I could use the months in Rome as a trial to see how I got on alone."
BETTY:	"So that's why you want to leave me behind? It's not just the inadequate living allowance? You bastard! I suspected as much!"

Bill and Betty had an imbalance in their "relational dance." The underlying emotional turmoil was also obvious and had led to mutual pain, resentment, and even despair. In an individual session, Bill was able to express his anger over what he considered were excessive demands and lack of recognition of the effort he had made to be a "good provider." Betty had a couple of individual sessions and was able to acknowledge her level of dependence in the relationship and to see that her anger was pushing Bill away—now and perhaps through the years of their marriage. The prospect of the end of the marriage was very frightening to her: "How will I be able to manage? The children are grown up. Who would want me?"

These interactions in EFT-C can be understood as offer and counteroffer. This can assist the therapist in analyzing sequences in the couple relationship. Understanding the sequences is part of EFT-C theory that guides the focus on to this "rabbit." The couple sees the identification and labeling of the sequence as a useful intervention that helps to bring mutual empathy. With empathy there is an emotional softening. Positive outcomes for couples have been related to softening the couple's interaction.

How might this develop through the EFT-C method?

> Bill comes home late from work. Betty says, "Late again! What was so important at work?" She is proposing in this interaction that she become the prosecutor and he the defendant in the ensuing interaction. This may also confirm dominance and submission.
>
> Bill might be submissive: "Yes, you're right. There's nothing happening at work that's more important than you. I'm sorry, it won't happen again."
>
> Or Bill can adopt an attack strategy: "I work to keep you in the manner that you've been accustomed to. How can you take the high moral ground when you laze around all day, waiting for me to come home so you can find something to criticize?"

Of course, these scenes are also replayed in therapy, but it is helpful to slow down the interaction and help the couple to understand what cycle is being played out. This is one of the core strategies in ST-C, too.

5.2   Repair Attempts

Gottman and Schwartz Gottman (2009) helped us to understand "repair attempts." It is too easy to focus on an external factor ("Late again!") when the feeling mix for Betty is loneliness, fear of abandonment, and grief. Betty initially denies her inner state, becomes focused on an external, usually with projection, and finally blames Bill. The painful change for Betty must begin with her acknowledging the emotions underlying her attack in order to recognize her underlying vulnerabilities and powerlessness, rather than resorting to attempts to control. In all this, Bill's response can be helpful or unhelpful, and the extremes of submission or counterattack tend to "lock in" the familiar cycle.

We can contrast the different types of invalidation:

- *Ignoring.* Bill leaves the room for his study without saying anything.
- *Criticizing.* Bill to his wife: "Why are you dressed in the same clothes you wore yesterday?"

- *Dominant defining.* Bill: "You have no right to resent me coming home at 8 pm; you should be grateful that I work so hard."
- *Misunderstanding.* Bill: "You're just bitter because I forgot your birthday last week."

And validation:

- *Understanding.* Bill: "You expected me home a lot earlier and it's natural to be upset."
- *Confirming.* Bill: "I can see how upset you are. It was thoughtless of me."
- *Respect.* Bill: "I can see how upset you are. I should have rung you when I realized that I'd be late."
- *Attunement.* Bill: "It's understandable that you're so upset. You expected me home at 6 pm and you might have been worried that something bad might have happened."

Gottman (1999) has observed that couples rarely relate to each other with active listening. Once negative emotions enter, everyone responds in kind—even in happy marriages! Ultimately, happiness in a relationship is more about the capacity for solving conflicts effectively rather than pursuing an ideal of mechanically trained "good communication." Gottman identified "Four Horsemen of the Apocalypse" that can accurately predict relationship failure:

1. *Criticism.* There will always be complaints in a relationship, but criticism is personal: "*You* always … *you* never …," and a range of questions that aren't really questions, but more insults. The criticism is an attack on the personality or character of the partner.
2. *Contempt.* This conveys an ugliness in a relationship and is associated with cynicism, sarcasm, eye-rolling, hostile humor, and mockery. The contemptuous person assumes the "higher ground." It is toxic and is virtually absent in happy relationships.
3. *Defensiveness.* While this can be understandable, it is blaming ("You are the problem") and rarely helps because the partner may "turn up the heat" in order to be heard.
4. *Stonewalling.* This involves tuning out or not hearing the partner. It is a protection against feeling flooded.

Such interactional styles are destructive, and it is useful to limit them with an ST approach as well. The Gottmans advise reducing these harmful interactions in order to build the "sound relationship house" (Gottman & Schwartz Gottman, 2009). The elimination of such negatives and building up the friendship base of the relationship will be the precipitators for forming a lasting and satisfying relationship. In ST-C, we differ in seeing the "house" as a "hospital," where both normal people and "abnormal" people need the healing of internal schema-driven patterns through the identification of past memory-driven learning and through limited re-parenting. Both are discussed in Sections 9.2 and 9.3.

Gottman and Schwartz Gottman (2009) have described a "bid for connection" when one partner "turns towards the other." These bids happen many times in even small segments of time. It perhaps surprises us when we consider how often we are distracted by life events and how infrequently we are actually in a mood to emotionally connect and engage. Perhaps we should be amazed that people are sometimes able to match up their emotional availability at the same time! The reality of frequent failed bids for connection is not a judgment on whether two people love each other or even on the quality of their relationship. A couple needs to learn how to "make repair attempts." The Gottmans have listed a range of such attempts in their training materials. In Chapter 8 of this book (on mode maps), we also illustrate what some repair attempts look like in the Healthy Adult mode. Repair attempts as identified by the Gottmans tend to be more general. However, many of these phrases can be incorporated well in our ST-C efforts.

Many of the repair attempts modeled by the Gottmans work well, such as: "Oops, I'm sorry, I missed what you were trying to do," "Forgive me, I was tuned out," "Oh, did that ever come out of my mouth wrong; let's start over." Or add a schema perspective to the language of a couple: "Oh no, it's just one of my schemas!"

In Chapter 9 we outline the "rewind the video" technique as a repair attempt. We ask couples to use the bid for connection that works. Encourage them to try and try again.

Bids can miss the target. This can be easily modeled in sessions, when the therapist can admit missing something and then model the repair attempt. We can also coach the couple when the bid fails in a session: "Wait a minute, I don't get what just happened here. What are you really feeling? Tell me about it." Since not all failed bids for connection are "created equal," not all repair attempts are equally effective. It will often take an extended dialog to explore underlying needs and hurts.

The ST-C model is based on these useful developments but goes beyond them. What sets ST-C apart in both theory and practice is the added intricacy of our case conceptualization, the precise re-parenting targeting unmet needs, physiological interceptions of triggered modes through mindfulness techniques, the rescripting detail of healing the activated memories, and the offsetting of the *artifacts* of the entire continuum from major trauma to everyday life expectations coming from unmet needs and unhealthy experiences. These artifacts include the resultant internalized parent mode, the sensation state of the lingering child modes, and the habitually activated coping modes, which can be dislodged when identified and parceled out. Hence, the healing goes more deeply—although perhaps never deep enough, as we always struggle to develop it even further.

Our hospital imagery is apt, as this is indeed surgery, but surgery that operates on the psychological remnants of childhood experiences and allows us to hold on to the healing and positive experiences of loving and stable connection.

5.3   Accessing the Full Spectrum of Basic Emotions

Differentiating the involved emotions is an important contribution of EFT, along with heightening those feelings in order to get them resolved and clarified and allow for softening and reconnection. Back to Bill and Betty for an illustration of this technique:

BILL: "I feel blamed about everything associated with my work. Betty seems irritable and impatient with me—I just can't do a thing right!"

THERAPIST: "You want her to see the 'gift' that you bring through your work, and perhaps also to see you as a competent provider?"

BILL: "Yes, I really feel that I put myself out. Her comments are cutting."

THERAPIST: "Is it your self-esteem that's cut?"

BILL: "I feel hurt and wounded ... bleeding, in fact!"

THERAPIST: "Maybe also humiliation?"

BILL: "Yes, I feel small and exposed to her comments ..."

The psychologist went on to explore the effects of shame and anger at what was experienced as a violation. Later in the session:

BETTY: "I know I'm quick to anger."

BILL: "Damned right!"

THERAPIST, IGNORING BILL'S COMMENT: "But is that all you feel?" [It is important that the therapist support

	the person making therapeutic progress, not the partner who is taking a "shot" at her.]
BETTY (MORE REFLECTIVE):	"I'm not sure."
THERAPIST, A MOMENT LATER:	"I'm sure there are some softer emotions …"
BETTY:	"Maybe I'm sad. I really miss Bill through the day and I look forward to him coming home. When he comes back late, without even a comment except being caught at work, it's as if I don't exist."
THERAPIST:	"You feel invisible?"
BETTY:	"More like I don't deserve to exist."

Later the therapist observed:

"When Bill comes home late, a dysfunctional pattern gets played out. Sometimes, maybe often, Betty, you express anger and resentment as part of your overcompensatory coping, but maybe beside that you feel sadness, in effect missing Bill, which underlies the importance of emotional connection.

"Bill, you often feel criticized, as if your efforts mean nothing, but it wounds you deeply in relation to feeling exposed and found wanting. Perhaps we can think together about how the pattern is preventing you both getting what you need.

"We need to look at the neglected or blocked basic emotions behind the obvious emotions related to the superficial coping behavior. Perhaps creatively, together, we can construct some opportunities for a healthier interaction?"

While the EFT model distinguishes between primary and secondary emotions in the sense of chronological sequence (Greenberg & Goldman, 2008), our approach is influenced by Ekman's model of basic emotions versus social emotions (Ekman, 1993):

1. *Basic emotions* are the person's most fundamental and original reaction to a situation. They are pre-cognitive "embodied" physiological expressions of survival patterns. Basic emotions indicate that core needs are hurt or not met. This includes sadness in relation to loss, anger in response to violation, and fear in response to threat or abandonment. These emotions cover the whole spectrum between attachment and assertiveness-orientation, and they enhance the self and intimate bonds.

2. *Social emotions* are emotional reactions, including internalized appraisals and beliefs induced by significant others, and part of

the resulting coping behavior (Leary, 2000). Examples include embarrassment in response to being hurt, envy after being set back, hopelessness following several fruitless attempts to fight for one's rights, guilt after being shut off, and shame following harsh criticism. This understanding is closer to the cognitive model, in which thoughts and beliefs influence the post-cognitive emotions.

This approach helps the couple to become more emotionally aware, especially of the softer basic emotions underlying the need of attachment. The superficial anger feelings result from an activation of the self-assertiveness system. This activation overrides the attachment system. Being in this angry attractor state blocks other basic emotions, leading to a dichotomy of coping behavior between one pole of striving for dominance and control and another of trying to maintain or regain attachment by being more-or-less submissive, or at least cooperative. Look for the signs when the tension seems to drain from the session, to be replaced by an emotional softening in the couple interaction. This gives space to look at the previously blocked attachment system. The threat to the attachment system leads to the basic emotion of sadness or fear that has previously been dominated by the anger. This attunement to the blocked basic emotion clears the way to be less polarized and to find more integrative adult solutions.

We show (e.g. in Sections 6.3 and 8.2) how the ST-C model helps us to see distortions coming from the memory-driven parental modes, which put a cognitive spin on our perceptions and emotions by inducing social emotions and drive negative cycles. That awareness of what is driving negative cycles can lead to more realistic choices to possibly change dysfunctional patterns.

There is also an appreciation of emotional style. Some people are over-regulated or shut-down in their emotional expression, whereas others are under-regulated and over-expressive, especially of negative emotions. You can use cognitive behavioral therapy, dialectical behavior therapy and mindfulness techniques to assist in emotional regulation. This can help the over-regulated to be more emotionally aware, say by using a mindfulness of emotion exercise, and, for example, breathing or "urge surfing" anger to gain a "soft start-up" (Gottman & Silver, 1999).

5.4   A Dead End?

Gottman has argued that "most marital arguments cannot be resolved." This is part of his conceptualization and also affects how he handles (or in some cases is unable to address) couples with severe personality disorders or even strong ambivalence about staying in a relationship. Gottman and Silver note that couples spend years trying to change each other's mind or way of seeing an issue (1999, p. 23).

Couples have both soluble and gridlocked problems. Soluble problems find practical resolution and perpetual ones can be managed in more constructive ways. Gottman has argued that it is better to understand the bottom line of what is hard to change and learn how to live with difference by honoring and respecting each other. Marsha Linehan (1993) also advised that people need to accept the unchangeable and work on the changeable. Only then can the couple build a shared sense of meaning and purpose.

The conflict between Bill and Betty about his work focus has been chronic and might be considered unresolvable until he finally retires. And even then he will probably find some interests to absorb him, to the dissatisfaction of Betty.

In ST-C, we tend to look at things from a different perspective that allows for deep personality change. Some ST-C practitioners, such as Simeone-DiFrancesco, maintain that when a couple understands the difference between *needs* and *wants* they are able to communicate at a new level that evokes empathy. From there, creative options to recast *wishes* into more mutually acceptable *wants* emerge. This can help to avoid stalemates and lead to "win–win" agreements. The distinction between soluble and persistent problems need not be static. ST-C includes the option to work on the schema background of both partners. In this way, the underlying bedrock of personality can be changed, which might result in some persistent problems becoming soluble. We discuss this further in Chapter 11.

Therapy Tip: Simeone-DiFrancesco has offered a straightforward way to differentiate between the neglected core need and the negotiable wish. Think in terms of the word *universal*. Is this need something you think everybody has? Everybody, whether they realize it or not, draws from the same set of emotional core needs, such as those listed by Young. Think about this in a global way. For example, instead of "My need is for you to straighten out your sister Suzie!" you say instead, "My need is for acceptance." Then put any specific thoughts about Suzie in the wish category. This will also help you to understand why the relationship with Suzie is painful. The wish could be: "For you to affirm me to Aunt Mary, and tell her that you will not accept her putting me down any longer."

Now to return to Betty and Bill. Eventually, Betty was to see the progress they had made as a couple:

"I suppose we have been more or less stable in 30 years of marriage. The children were wonderful but the empty nest meant my life felt empty. I was unable to manage this and began to be more critical and less appreciative of Bill. The unhappiness was buried by both of us, but came to a crisis with Bill's promotion to Rome.

"It was a crisis we had to have. It made me realize that I need to learn to be vulnerable again with Bill, and let him in on my thoughts, needs and dreams. I had essentially adopted my 'role' as a mom as my identity, and no wonder there wasn't much of me to even connect to. I've come to realize I surrendered in the early part of our marriage, then got resentful and avoided through the typical child-focused household.

"Instead of blaming him and feeling that he never really cared enough and was just insensitive, I've begun to open up and even challenge him with what I need. To my surprise, Bill likes this new me, and he feels less bored with our life at home. We've found intimacy in our companionship and I'm confident we can build a more satisfying life together. This crisis has been the break to make the bond stronger."

This shows the potential for the creation of a narrative that the couple can take from therapy.

5.5 Additional Thoughts

There is a very simple, maybe simplistic, understanding of how therapy progresses. A therapist will do three things in a typical session (not in any particular order, and often cycling between them):

- *deepen* emotional experience (or emotional activation)
- offer a *theoretical understanding* of the experience (clarification with a model)
- do an *intervention* (e.g. problem solving).

In relation to these three therapist activities, EFT-C has a clear focus on the emotions in the relationship. This is its greatest strength. The theory, based on attachment theory, has a base in extensive research but generally should be updated with Patricia Crittenden's (2000) dynamic-maturational model, which delineates an adult attachment model. The theoretical base for Gottman's work and treatment model is also extensive. It is also practical and effective in treating most couples.

However, we think that ST-C has a more nuanced developmental model leading to what Young called a "limited re-parenting" relationship and is more comprehensive with its schema and mode conceptualizations. There are also sophisticated experiential techniques. They provide not only strong interventions for activation, but also powerful techniques for healing emotional wounds. Being "skillful on all three instruments" permits changes even in the most disturbed individuals and couples. We consider the full scope of ST contributions in the following chapters.

Summary

In this chapter we briefly considered the contribution of both John Gottman's research and EFT-C. This was illustrated by an extended case study of Bill and Betty, which illustrated important therapeutic concepts, such as the nature of emotions, including those most damaging for the relationship. The need for repair and effective interventions was given priority.

Now our attention will shift to the unique contribution of ST.

6

Schemas and Modes

"The map is not the territory," Gregory Bateson (1972) observed. But as therapists we are guided by our theoretical perspectives, and we work blind without clinically relevant maps. We believe ST has added some lines to the maps.

6.1 From Schemas to Modes

Difficult couples present the greatest challenge for relationship therapy and stronger interventions alone are not the answer. We need an enhanced case formulation, which ST can provide, integrated with treatment. While this is often ignored in couple counseling, the coherence of an understanding based on theory, leading to effective interventions, is the only hope to provide what is ultimately necessary to help challenging couples. The need to tie case conceptualization with treatment planning is well argued by Pearl Berman (2010). ST-C provides a rich perspective for clinical understanding.

> Kylie had a history of child sexual abuse by two of her older brothers. Her self-esteem was poor and she believed that she deserved to be treated badly. There were easily activated schemas of Mistrust-Abuse and Emotional Deprivation.
>
> There was instant attraction when she met Brett. He had an overconfidence that was quite grandiose, with Entitlement and Unrelenting Standards schemas in the background. Kylie was attracted to his strength, and offered a pattern of Subjugation.

Schema Therapy with Couples: A Practitioner's Guide to Healing Relationships, First Edition.
Chiara Simeone-DiFrancesco, Eckhard Roediger, and Bruce A. Stevens.
© 2015 John Wiley & Sons, Ltd. Published 2015 by John Wiley & Sons, Ltd.
Companion website: www.wiley.com/go/difrancesco/schematherapywithcouples

Eventually, problems resulted from his punitive and controlling relationship style (schema of Punitiveness). They became locked in her sense of neediness (Emotional Deprivation) and his inability to respond (Emotional Inhibition).

This case example illustrates how ST-C, using a schema-based conceptualization, can be used to track what brings a couple together and also what will ultimately cause profound difficulties. We note that a schema perspective can be applied to marriage preparation courses, which are often sponsored by churches.

What evokes what? You can track sequences of schema activation in the couple relationship. There are also potential compensating schemas; for example, a person with Abandonment may have a compensating Self-sacrifice schema, which is then played out in the couple relationship with patterns of de-selfing.

An initial step, from an ST perspective, is trying to identify "trigger points" leading to an intense emotional reaction. This is a good indication that a schema may have been activated. The dialectical behavioral therapy skill of chain-analysis might be useful in tracking what happened before a reported relationship incident. You may want to give them the YSQ-3 and the SMI 1.1 and explain the results, at first individually. Identify and explore typical schema vulnerabilities. Try to understand the dynamic interaction of schemas, including "schema chemistry," "schema clashes" and being "locked in schemas." Gridlocked problems (Gottman, 1999) can be understood in a schema conceptualization as strong schema chemistry.

Remember that schema work can be quite complex, with 18 schemas and three ways of reacting to each: surrender, avoidance or compensation. This leads to 54 possible schema responses. This may potentially provide a more comprehensive framework than modes but can quickly become impossibly complex even with high-functioning couples. There is the additional difficulty that multiple schemas can activate at the same time (Atkinson, 2012). The problems associated with working with schemas led Jeff Young to a focus on modes. The mode model describes how underlying schemas are played out at a certain moment.

6.2   The Mode Model in Detail

Working with modes has proved to be an important therapeutic advance. Modes, being what you see, are the visible expressions of inner states. Dysfunctional mode states are obvious when working with unstable couples. This includes traits from the range of personality disorders.

Modes are user-friendly. Working with the mode map (covered in Section 8.2) allows a limited focus on four or five modes in treatment with an individual (Farrell & Shaw, 2012) and possibly fewer than seven or eight in total for a couple. It also leads to potential exactitude and comprehensibility. And it is a reliable guide to the therapist response required (such as validation or limit setting). A mode case conceptualization is much easier to oversee and handle for both the therapist and the couple.

The *child modes* are early survival-based responses. The child needed to find a way of coping when needs were not met (Farrell & Shaw, 2012). These modes represent basic emotions such as anger, fear, disgust, loss, and happiness, and are closely related to body sensations. Their appearance indicates that emotional core needs are not met or are threatened.

The *dysfunctional parent modes* are internalized attributions of significant others, including core beliefs and reoccurring negative automatic thoughts. These might be seen as toxic parental introjects (Freud, 1917), which are experienced as negative "voices inside the head."

The *maladaptive coping modes* are interpersonal coping reactions based on early childhood experiences in an environment that lacked an appropriate child focus, and the experiences often included social emotions such as shame, guilt, or feeling superior. This includes behavioral reactions on a spectrum between submission and dominance. It is fed by both basic emotions (from child modes) and appraisals (parent modes).

Further striving to fulfill our core needs, we eventually unconsciously "define" our interpersonal relationship to the other person: either "I am on top" (overcompensation striving for control and assertiveness) or "I surrender" (to gain attachment). In between these poles is a third option, as variations of avoidance or "flight" behavior: "I withdraw

Table 2   The most important modes

Child modes	Internal parent modes	Maladaptive coping modes	Integrative adaptive modes
Vulnerable Child	Punitive Parent	Compliant Surrender	Healthy Adult
Angry Child	Demanding Parent	Detached Protector	Happy Child
Enraged Child		Detached Self-soother	
Impulsive Child		Self-aggrandizer	
Undisciplined Child		Bully and attack	

from a relationship" passively (Detached Protector, as "freezing" behavior to avoid harm) or actively (Detached Self-soother, as "flight" reaction to protect myself). The child will have made a choice—possibly adaptive at the time—of the best way to handle the situation. With each similar situation, the child followed the pattern. Unfortunately, this coping style became more and more rigid through repetition (because the attractor became stronger). This was repeated and became more maladaptive over time. Naturally, as a child grows up there should be other age-appropriate ways of coping that are not fixed in maladaptive modes.

All four relational definitions are elaborated variations of the innate biological interactional patterns of surrender–freeze–flight–fight. We regard it as important to relate submissive behavior with surrender and not with freezing. A "frozen" rabbit (or a dissociative person) is not surrendering (to gain attachment), but trying to avoid harm through withdrawal. So freezing is an example of coping through passive flight, and not surrendering. Speaking about a triad of fight, flight and freeze is insufficient, because we have to differentiate four major coping directions represented in the coping modes of Compliant Surrender (surrender), Detached Protector (freeze), Detached Self-soother (flight), and overcompensation (fight). The selection of coping mode depends on the current internal activation of the child and parent modes.

> Nardi had an anxious child mode, Vulnerable Child, with a dominating Demanding Parent, so she reacted with a Compliant Surrender. This was repeated in unsatisfactory romantic relationships.
> Brett was being treated for alcohol dependence. He had an Angry Child, but this was blocked from expressing anger by his Punitive Parent, so he characteristically resorted to alcohol in Detached Self-soother.

It is precisely the blocking of underlying child modes that undermines further attempts to cope in a healthy way. As we note in our explanation of the mode map, the identification of the blocked child mode, versus the activated child mode, is critical. The coping mode is not always maladaptive, but pathways can be too rigid, alternatives are lacking, or changing strategies appear in a "flipping" way.

The Healthy Adult mode is the adaptive self-regulating aspect of a person. Roediger (2012b) outlined three major processes of Healthy Adult functioning: mindful self-reflection, detached reappraisal, and functional self-instruction. Naturally, this integrates reasonable thoughts and self-reflection, leading to problem solving. The therapist can assist the Healthy Adult of the person to reappraise automatic thoughts and core beliefs, replace them with adequate thoughts about the self or others, and disempower or "impeach" dysfunctional parent modes. All this leads to the important question: what does the child need? Healthy Adult is the hope for positive change.

The following is a list of the 14 most accepted schema modes. Modes describe what we see. Compared with a camera lens, we decide how closely we want to look at an object. Through a wide-angle lens, there are only three (or four) major groups of modes; through a close-up lens, we could distinguish an almost endless number of modes, depending on how closely we look at them. It makes sense, for therapeutic and scientific reasons, to identify modes related to the different personality disorders. Listing them in a mode inventory and making them measurable can help us link the presentation of specific modes with a personality disorder diagnosis. When working with people individually in a practical way, it is more fruitful to choose a moderate scope, with an overseeable number of modes represented in the dimensional mode map, and relate the presented modes to the client's difficulties. Hence, in our listing, we have chosen the more common modes found in the spectrum of normal experience. All presented modes can be placed somewhere in this dimensional construct. This is the reason why we focus on the most representative modes in the listing, which is adapted from Young et al. (2007).[7]

1. **Child modes**
   1.1 **Vulnerability**
       1.1.1 *Vulnerable Child* feels like a lonely child that is valued only insofar as he can aggrandize his parents. Because the most important emotional needs of the child have generally not been met, they usually feel empty, alone, socially unacceptable, undeserving of love, unloved, and unlovable.
   1.2 **Anger**
       1.2.1 *Angry child* feels intensely angry, enraged, infuriated, frustrated, or inpatient because the core emotional (or physical) needs of the vulnerable child are not being met. She will vent her suppressed anger in inappropriate ways. She may make demands that make her seem "entitled" or "spoiled" and that alienate others.

---

[7] We alternate grammatical gender in describing the modes, but there is no implication that a particular mode is more common in males or females.

      1.2.2   *Enraged Child* experiences intense feelings of anger that result in his hurting or damaging people or objects. This displayed anger is out of control and has the goal of destroying the aggressor, sometimes literally. This can be seen as the child screaming or acting out impulsively.

1.3 **Lack of discipline**

      1.3.1   *Impulsive Child* acts on non-core desires or impulses from moment to moment in a selfish or uncontrolled manner to get his own way, without regard to possible consequences for himself or others. He often has difficulty delaying short-time gratification and may appear "spoiled."

      1.3.2   *Undisciplined Child* cannot force herself to finish routine or boring tasks, gets frustrated quickly, and gives up.

2. **Maladaptive coping modes**

2.1 **Surrender**

      2.1.1   *Compliant Surrender* acts in a passive, subservient, submissive, reassurance-seeking, or self-deprecating way towards others out of fear of conflict or rejection. He passively allows himself to be mistreated, or does not take steps to get healthy needs met. He selects people or engages in other behavior that directly maintains the self-defeating schema-driven pattern. He may feel a lot of resentment.

2.2 **Avoidance**

      2.2.1   *Detached Protector* withdraws psychologically from the pain of the schemas by emotionally detaching. She shuts off all emotions, disconnects from others and rejects their help, and functions in an almost robotic manner. Signs and symptoms include depersonalization, emptiness, boredom, substance abuse, bingeing, self-mutilation, psychosomatic complaints, and "blankness." She shuts off from inner needs, emotions, and thoughts. This person feels empty (Arntz, 2012b).

      2.2.2   *Detached Self-soother* shuts off his emotions by engaging in activities that will somehow soothe, stimulate, or distract from feeling. These behaviors are usually undertaken in an addictive or compulsive way, and can include "workaholism," gambling, dangerous sports, promiscuous sex, or drug abuse. Another group of people in treatment compulsively engage in solitary interests that are more self-soothing than self-stimulating, such as playing computer games, overeating, watching television, or fantasizing.

2.3 **Overcompensation**

    2.3.1 *Self-aggrandizer* behaves in an entitled, competitive, grandiose, abusive, or status-seeking way in order to have whatever she wants. She is almost completely self-absorbed, and shows little empathy for the needs or feelings of others. She will demonstrate superiority, will expect to be treated as special, and does not believe she should have to follow the rules that apply to everyone else. She craves for admiration and frequently brags or behaves in a self-aggrandizing manner to inflate her sense of self. This compensates for inner feelings of inferiority, inadequacy, or doubt (Arntz, 2012b).

    2.3.2 *Bully and Attack* directly harms other people in a controlled and strategic way emotionally, physically, sexually, verbally, or through antisocial or criminal acts. His motivation may be to overcompensate for or prevent abuse or humiliation. He has sadistic properties.

3. **Dysfunctional parent modes**

    3.1 **Punitive Parent** is the internalized voice of the parent, criticizing and punishing the person. PP becomes angry with herself and feels that she deserves punishment for having or showing normal needs that their parents did not allow her to express. The tone of this mode is harsh, critical, and unforgiving. Signs and symptoms include self-loathing, self-criticism, self-denial, self-mutilation, suicidal fantasies, and self-destructive behavior.

    3.2 **Demanding Parent** continually pushes and pressures the child to meet excessively high standards. He feels that the "right" way to be is to be perfect or achieve at a very high level, to keep everything in order, to strive for high status, to be humble, to put other needs before his own or to be efficient or avoid wasting time. He feels that it is wrong to express feelings or to act spontaneously.

4. **Integrative adaptive modes**

    4.1 **Healthy Adult** performs appropriate adult functions, such as working, parenting, taking responsibility, and committing. She pursues pleasurable adult activities, such as sex; intellectual, esthetical, and cultural interests; health maintenance; and athletic activities. There is a good balance of her own and others' needs (Arntz, 2012b).

4.2   **Happy Child** feels at peace because his core emotional needs are currently met. He feels loved, contented, connected, satisfied, fulfilled, protected, praised, worthwhile, nurtured, guided, understood, validated, self-confident, competent, appropriately autonomous or self-reliant, safe, resilient, strong, in control, adaptable, optimistic, and spontaneous.

These modes correspond to the SMI 1.1 mode inventory.[8]

Reflect: Do you find it easier to see schema vulnerability or modes? Can you recognize changing schema activation or mode states? Can you readily name what you see in terms of either schemas or modes?

Therapy Tip: Most experienced schema therapists find it easier to work with modes.

Another Tip: We suggest focusing on a few main schemas and linking them right away with the mode explanations and the results shown from the SMI 1.1. Linking presented modes with some representative underlying schemas makes the client more sensitive to the childhood origins of their present experience. But, to avoid getting bogged down, do not try to be too much of a perfectionist. You can always bring in details later. Some partners prefer to hear the results alone in an individual session, since they are not sure how the other person will take or "use" the information. You may also be uncertain. We rarely risk identifying specific schemas for the first time with the couple together. The partners need to come to some understanding for themselves and then be positioned to be empathic towards self and other about these schemas.

Generally, the intensity of a couple's interaction will activate modes. If schemas are readily activated, what you will see are the modes they are played out in. Also, if the couple is unstable, there will be considerable "flipping" between modes, depending on changing underlying schema activations. It is generally best to act with a focus on modes because they are easier to detect and their interaction is following rather simple rules.

Note: Couples will often interact at a lower level of functioning than they might present as individuals, so appearing even more unstable. Additionally, borderline clients will activate most of the schemas, so it is easier to track modes. If there is any doubt, lean towards modes because any initial stability might be brief until the next crisis.

---

[8]   To access the SMI 1.1, go to www.schematherapy.com. As mentioned, the SMI is still under revision and further development.

Reflect: Think about how you might use the SMI 1.1 with couples.

Advanced Advice: Sometimes we may need to jump in quickly, bypass the schema explanation altogether, and initially map out a mode cycle. This may give the couple hope. They can begin to see that there is something to be gained by this process, ignoring all the current issues and schema detail for the moment as described in Section 2.8. This requires some confidence in the couple therapist. As therapists, we tend to range on a continuum of caution about "jumping in," but with experience our confidence and mastery over the session dynamics grow, and grabbing the couples' attention gets easier. The therapist needs to be able to intervene as a *very* Healthy Adult, and not be easily waylaid or redirected!

Couple Exercise: As homework, have each draw a pie chart in terms of modes. The size of each piece of the pie shows how much of adult life is spent in that state. Include only the most common modes. This exercise increases awareness of the different modes. Then have each draw a similar pie chart for their partner. The couple can compare and discuss how they see themselves and the other differently. Does this exercise suggest dynamics in the relationship? (c.f. Farrell & Shaw, 2012, pp. 140–1).

Reflect: Do the couple exercise yourself, if you are in a relationship.

When you explain modes to a couple, begin with the child modes (especially Vulnerable Child) and the core needs, and then the parent modes (labeled as "voices in the head"), but explain that the dysfunctional parent modes are not necessarily identical with the real parents (instead, they are the introjects of parents and authority figures from childhood).

Therapy Tip: How do you distinguish Detached Protector mode from Healthy Adult mode? Both can appear quite reasonable, but the core difference is that the Healthy Adult is always in touch with the basic emotions. The Healthy Adult neither shuts down nor gets trapped in social emotions.

6.3 Additional Modes

The "canon" of modes has not been settled. Additional modes are continually being suggested and debated in ST circles. See Figure 3 for a diagram of generally accepted modes (including some suggested modes).

In addition to those listed on SMI 1 in the first list, the following might be considered:

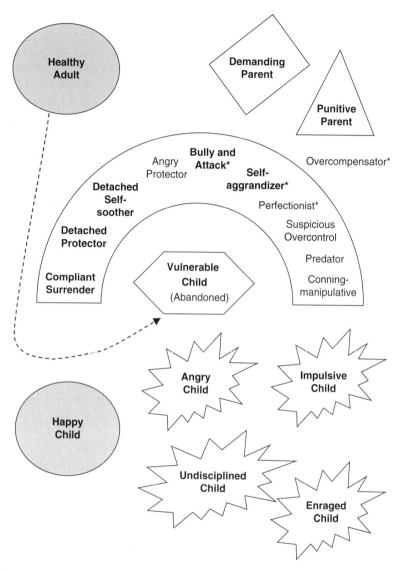

Figure 3   Diagram of generally accepted modes
Note: Modes in bold are in SMI 1.1.

- *Child modes.* David Edwards (ISST Marital/Couples Special Interest Group) has identified the Protector Child mode (which combines some childlike features with a protective role). Susan Simpson (2012) suggested Shamed/Deprived and "Needy" child modes. A Playful/

Exuberant child mode has been proposed (Lockwood & Shaw, 2012). Arntz (2012b) has distinguished subgroups of Vulnerable Child in Abandoned-Abused Child, Lonely-Inferior and Dependent Child, more or less related to different personality disorders.

Therapy Tip: You may wish to find out the "age" the child mode feels to the client. Remember: Clients in a coping mode usually feel "adult" and are not in touch with their persisting underlying childlike emotional underpinnings.

- *Coping modes.* Outside of Healthy Adult, the coping modes we have listed are all more or less maladaptive. It is useful to list a few other variants of the maladaptive coping modes. The Angry Protector is a very useful concept. Anger is expressed to protect the Vulnerable Child (Van Genderen et al., 2012). Anger may also be expressed indirectly through irritation, sulking, pouting, complaining, withdrawal, and oppositional behavior (Bernstein et al., 2012a). In this instance, it is a socially reinforced and not a basic emotion because it has been used effectively by significant others. This is also described in the groups of Farrell and Shaw (2012). The therapist is kept at a distance (Arntz & Jacob, 2013). Arntz (2012b) has argued for an Avoidant Protector mode, which uses situational avoidance as a survival strategy. A Self-stimulator mode has been suggested (Kersten, 2012). A Detached Imaginative World mode has also been described (Lockwood & Shaw, 2012).

Therapy Tip: Try playing with your own imaginative label of the craziness you tend to see. If this allows you to label and identify a pattern, it may help.

- *Overcompensation modes.* These are modes that also attempt to protect the Vulnerable Child. Young has identified an Attention Seeking mode (Arntz & Jacob, 2013). Another example of this is the hyper-vigilant Paranoid Over-controller (Bernstein et al., 2012a). This mode uses excessive control and perfectionism to avoid mistakes and feelings of guilt (Arntz, 2012b). Some modes, such as the Predator mode, are seen in antisocial groups. We can see how victims become offenders: they switch off their internal representations and turn punitive voices outwards. There may also be a Conning-Manipulative mode, which presents a "false self" by lying to achieve a goal (with Predator, applicable to forensic populations). Sadism–masochism might be the internal–external expression of a single mode.

- *Parent modes.* Parent modes present themselves with many facets, such as demanding, punitive, critical, cynical, negativistic, invalidating, and blaming, but they might also include some realistic aspects, such as moral or value consciousness. This can be healthy. An individual may want to attribute an appreciative value to a "parent" but may be blocked by a therapeutic focus on the negative internalized parent mode. To get them out of this loop, a therapist can make it a property of their Healthy Adult (which is built up by positive influences of parents and other significant others). Clients have to learn to modify Demanding Parent and "impeach" Punitive Parent because parental modes can limit and undermine their personal growth.

It is important to further explore the developmental spectrum in the modes. Re-examine Figure 3 and look at the extended mode model or the mode map (Figures 7 and 8 in Chapter 8), which lays out and positions each of the modes. This will provide a general orientation. The distinction between child and infant modes is explored in Section 6.4.2.

Therapy Tip: It may be very helpful to assign descriptive names to the modes, such as "Lonely Peter" or "Angry Debbie." This makes linking modes with everyday life easier and helps clients to identify the modes when they are activated.

Advanced Skill: Diagnostic imagery exercises can be used to further understand the biographical origins of current emotional problems (Arntz & Jacob, 2013) and to help us assess the mode.

> Mark was asked by his therapist to visualize a typical problem at work, and then associate to childhood memories. This visualization brought to mind memories about his authoritarian father. The therapist was able to identify Dominated Mark, who felt and behaved like a 10-year-old.
>
> To be able to conceptualize this Compliant Surrender mode, the therapist asked Mark to bring in a photograph of himself at that age. When he brought in the photo, discussion around 10-year-old Mark deepened his understanding and "feeling" of the Vulnerable Child mode behind it, and informed a clinical understanding of his tendency to still surrender today.

6.4   The Infant Mode Concept

6.4.1   General characteristics of infant modes

The idea of a developmental understanding of modes is inherent in ST. We propose a further elaboration using the concept of infant modes and possibly adolescent modes. Schemas are probably built up or developed from birth or even before. The earlier the imprint, the "rougher," more isolated, more extreme the schema will probably be—comparable with trauma schemas. The later the onset, the more the schema will be embedded in a moderating neuronal environment.

Modes have a developmental trajectory extending back to infantile self-awareness, with the possibility of an arrested development associated with experiences of trauma. Infant modes are a strong "bottom-up" activation. Early emotional experiences provide an "old" feeling.

A discussion of infant modes is important at this point. You may have found that some couples do not readily respond to ST. Behavior may be more irrational or need-driven than is normally expected. To extend the dynamic mode model, we suggest considering the following conceptualization of infant modes.

There are characteristics of infant modes in affect, cognition, and behavior:

1. *Affect.* Infant affect tends to be flooding, unstable or labile and less subject to emotional regulation involving global body states. This might be described as "early levels of emotional awareness" (Farrell & Shaw, 2012, p. 2). At this developmental level, an infant is reactive to external stimuli because of a very permeable "stimulus barrier." Emotions tend to be nine primary affects present from birth (Tomkins, 1962–1963). Note these are primary, not secondary (as distinguished by emotion-focused therapy). Infantile affects are largely undifferentiated. There is a developmental trajectory from body sensations into subjective states that can gradually be articulated as distinct feelings (Stolorow & Atwood, 1992, p. 42), but if this process is derailed expression can be blocked with *anhedonia* (dissociated or "dispersed"; McDougall, 1985). There is less cohesion of self (perhaps with a greater vulnerability to fragmentation and dissociation).

2. *Cognition.* The dimension of preverbal cognitions might be explored (sense of agency, physical and mental cohesion, affectivity, continuity in time, transmitting meaning, having intentions in mind, and sense of self that can enter into inter-subjective relationship; Stern, 1985). Indeed, a lack of verbalization might be an important indicator of early infantile states. Infantile consciousness has the least "reality testing" and may at times be "psychotic-like" (though usually transitory, as seen in the borderline). Generally, infant cognitions tend to be egocentric and rigid and lack insight, and there is minimal capacity to see future consequences. An important indicator might be a lack of mentalization, both with self (Fonagy et al., 2004) and others.

Thought is more concrete and literal rather than abstract and symbolic. A moral sense is primitive at best, with no evidence of a developed conscience. What is emerging is the capacity for narrative, but it will not necessarily be either accurate in a historical sense or cohesive in terms of meaning.

3. *Behaviors.* The earliest indicators of autonomy are found in infantile gaze aversion, gestures such as shaking the head, running away, and, gradually, language by about 2 years old. Possible indicators of infant mode activation could be an observable startle response or becoming "frozen" (Mary Giuffra, ISST Special Interest Group, see Giuffra, 2012). But, generally, infantile behaviors tend to be highly impulsive, at times compulsive, and thoughtless, without regard for consequences. Restraint from executive functions is absent or relatively lacking. A secondary compensating infantile reaction could be robotic movement.

It is possible to speak of infantile qualities in *all the modes*, including parental and protective or compensating modes.

In the following listing, 14 schema modes are modified to reflect characteristics of infant modes).

Vulnerable Child: Infant mode (IM). Crying out for physical comfort, distress is signaled by sobbing (or gestures rather than words), possibly food sought as nurture, needs are experienced as urgent and all important, and primitive idealizing of parents that is not reality tested. There may be a primitive terror of being alone and defenseless. If trauma related, may be more rigidly protected with easily triggered protective modes.

Angry Child: IM. Anger floods the self and executive thought becomes impossible. The anger is related to frustration of basic needs, more tantrum-like and easily erupting, lacking self-awareness and control. Needs are more concrete and related to early experiences of nurture (e.g., for food, comfort, or protection). The sense of entitlement is even more unreasonable compared to child mode, perhaps outrageous and highly egocentric.

Enraged Child: IM. The anger tends to be sudden, even instant, and explosive. This can be an uncontrollable tantrum or be described as a "dummy spit." Aggression tends to be impulsive, with "lashing out" to hurt. There is no awareness of other people beyond an impersonal presence. Such infantile rage may be self-directed, driving adult suicidal or other self-destructive behavior. States related to the Enraged Infant may relate to primitive narcissistic injury and threats to the cohesion of the self.

Impulsive Child: IM. Possibly this child mode should be located more in the infant realm. A distinction is possibly made on the level of concrete nurturance-related needs and even less considered action or consequences. Acting out is primarily physical.

Undisciplined Child: IM. The Undisciplined Child may be the appropriate child mode, with the Impulsive Child more an infant mode. If a distinction is to be made, possibly even shorter attention span and need for hyper-stimulation in activities.

Happy Child: IM. This is a case of "all of the above," but at an earlier developmental stage. The contentment is about more basic needs being met, such as being well fed or warm or comfortable—possibly in response to physical touch, such as being cuddled. Additional happy infant experiences may relate to curiosity and awe.

Compliant Surrender: IM. The dynamic is the same as in the child mode but expressed more with physical and outward compliance. Early child-like expressions include a tendency to sulk or be coy in relating to others seen as more powerful. Cognitions in response to outward submission tend to be more primitive, with revenge and destructive images.

Detached Protector: IM. There is an infant mode expression of detachment, which may be more pervasive, amorphous, rigid in response to triggers, seemingly with an "on/off switch" and withdrawn, with an absolute belief ("You can't touch me").

Detached Self-soother: IM. Addictions are more likely to be somatic, related more to food or drugs. This may be expressed as thumb-sucking in adults. Maybe smoking? If sexual activity, then most likely self-stimulation. Maybe self-soothing by engaging in a rocking motion. If engaging in risk taking, little or no consideration of consequences. Activity at this level tends to be "thoughtless." It may be possible to make a distinction between child and infant levels with Detached Self-soother.

Self-aggrandizer: IM. This may include exaggerated pleasure in the mastery of basic functions, such as bowel control or continence. In adults, cognitions have more of a magical quality, indeed, even less realistic grandiosity. There is a triumphant "King of the World" quality. There may be distinctions in the quality of grandiosity characterized by child and infant levels, with the latter more primitive and less based in reality.

Bully and Attack: IM. Less planned and more physical "striking out." There is a possible externalizing of self-hate or primitive Punitive Parent. If sadistic, more primitive, delighting in raw emotions associated with attacking the other, rather than pleasure in the pain of the other (which requires a perverted empathy). The intention is not so much to intimidate but to overwhelm and exert will, since the former is dependent on a minimal "theory of mind").

Punitive Parent: IM. This is probably developmentally determined at the age that the parental introject was received. If at the infantile level, the voice is more black (not even black and white), and absolute in demand or rejection. Self-descriptions in this mode are made with single words such as "dirty" (soiled nappy?), "bad," or "evil." Condemnation is more whole-of-self, not a specific accusation; possibly more related to shame rather than guilt. There is probably a clear link to self-injury, such as cutting. Commands tend to be self-destructive in a holistic way: "Die!"

Demanding Parent: IM. This mode is more childlike and related to appearances ("I must eat or dress in a proper way"). Possibly, the infant level is captured more in the Punitive Parent mode.

Healthy Adult mode: There is no IM associated with Healthy Adult.

These modes correspond to the SMI 1.1 mode inventory (Young et al., 2008).

6.4.2   Assessing and working with infant modes with couples

If it is clinically useful to think about modes on the developmental spectrum from infant to child to adolescent, how do we go about making such an assessment?

This can be achieved by the following means:

1. *Family history.* Note in the family history any indications of early trauma. What was the age this person was affected? Amanda has issues around abandonment. She had a history of being removed into foster care. If this disruption was at age 4 it might suggest infant mode(s), or at age 8 child mode(s). Additionally, there may be reports of sexual abuse, violence or neglect associated with certain ages. It is also important to consider the impact of cumulative traumas because at a certain age it may have become overwhelming.

2. *Early trauma.* Investigate the earliest trauma-related memory. This might be clearly associated with a traumatic event and relatively encapsulated. However, there may be a sense that the activated schema or mode has "prehistory," with perhaps earlier fragmented memories, dissociation, and trauma-related body sensations (Ogden et al., 2006). Maybe affect or somatic bridging can be used, but note when you are faced with a preverbal "wall." There may also be selectivity about what is heard (for example, saying something affirming but in a loud voice

when the person can only hear "loud," not the compliment). Noise stimulus can then be used for affect identification and bridging to childhood (Graham Taylor, ISST Special Interest Group). Such fragmentation is suggestive of adverse experiences as a young child.

3. *Context.* There may be contextual cues from a current triggering event. These may suggest an activating age, especially when linked to family history (Graham Taylor). In a time of crisis, Bobby reported thumb-sucking to help him get to sleep. His family said that his father left on a military posting when Bobby was 8, which was when they sought help for his thumb-sucking.

4. *Body.* Do not forget to include body awareness in your assessment. Look for infantile somatic organization, which is most obvious with aspects of a fetal posture, but indicators may be more subtle: head to one side, orienting downward in a helpless posture, or looking "up" at the therapist with idealization (Ogden et al., 2006, p. 178). You can mindfully explore the body memory and then at an appropriate time give that part of the body "voice" (Graham Taylor).

5. *Schema activation.* There are useful indications when you notice your own schema activation. Ask yourself what you feel drawn to provide.

6. *Indication of age:* When the person has an activated schema or is in a mode, think of the "age" that they seem to be, in that state. Hetty was in a wild-eyed panic as she thought about the time her family had to flee their home as refugees. She seemed like a "little girl," and the therapist thought about the anxiety of her own daughter going to pre-school. This may seem very subjective, but it is a useful indicator when balanced with other data. Or, more generally, you can try to locate the schema or mode developmentally in the range of infant–child–adolescent. In general terms, think about an infant mode from ages 0–4, child mode 5–11 and adolescent mode 12–18. Obviously this is not clear cut, but more a "center of gravity."

Dave Edwards (ISST Special Interest Group) advised therapists to consider "the developmental story of that mode." Stay with the phenomenological experience of the mode.

Kelly visited her mother for a brief holiday. She knew that Mistrust-Abuse was a powerful schema for her. As she prepared to visit, she went to the supermarket and bought a lot of provisions. As she drove to her mother's house, she asked herself, "Why did I buy so much for a three-day stay? It's as if I don't trust my mother to feed me." She realized that trust in relation to feeding is something established or broken in infancy. She also thought about related modes. She had an eating disorder related to binge eating in Detached Self-soother mode. She realized that this also had an infant mode quality.

Couple Exercise: As homework, a couple might be encouraged to look at albums of family photos and to look closely at photos in the infant ages of 1–4. Can the couple report back any vague memories or even a sense of something? This may be a physical sensation. What thoughts followed? This may help to explore possible infant modes.

6.4.3   *A note about treating infant modes*

An infant mode can be understood as being stuck at early developmental levels. This can guide treatment. Try to match communication and meet infant needs. Psychologist Mary Giuffra noted that "You don't need to talk" but maintain "baby resonance" (ISST Special Interest Group). In general, repeat slowly and, keep words simple. And Carolee Kallmann (ISST Special Interest Group) advised, "Look in my eyes, breathe with me, ground with me now." Sometimes it is best to talk to a mode in a "child voice" (Young, 2003). There is no progress to be made in trying to reason with an infant mode. The therapist needs to see and soothe. Maybe give them a soft toy like a big bear to hug, or let them imagine the therapist giving them a hug. In couple counseling, you might consider taking the attention off the partner who might be arousing intense emotional activation and focusing on the resulting mode effect on the other partner.

This also raises questions about which therapeutic interventions might be appropriate. The following example illustrates this:

Bettina had a Vulnerable Child infant mode of about 2–3 years old. This was obvious in her "little girl lost" quality and incomprehension that anyone would expect her to care for herself. She reached out to her therapist with constant phone calls in a highly dependent way, even about the most basic decisions she faced.

The therapist, speaking to the Vulnerable Child in child mode said, "Bettina, I know you feel lost and confused, just like a little girl [matching communication]. It's hard to know what's best for you. I'll give you some guidance about money [meeting her immediate need]. I want you to wrap yourself in that blanket; I can't hug you in the way you feel you need, but you can use the blanket."

The therapist also made up an "audio flash card," which was recorded on Bettina's smartphone to be played back whenever she felt distressed. The soothing quality of the therapist's voice was comforting.

The blanket is used by Farrell and Shaw in group therapy (2012). It is a good infant-level soothing strategy. If Bettina were simply in any type of child mode, this might not be as effective (since children resist being put to bed), but it was the vulnerability of the child mode that "called out" for some re-parenting soothing.

Of course, evaluate similar suggestions in light of what is ethically appropriate. "Wise-mind" psychotherapeutic manner involves the context of the therapist's cultural norm of peers local to his or her licensing juris-diction, as there are places where simple (non-sexual) touch is acceptable, and places where it is not. Here, your self-care needs to be placed ahead of what may instinctively feel useful for the unmet need of the mode, lest the final outcome be no re-parenting available from you whatsoever!

Nonetheless, the blanket is "concrete" and can provide object con-stancy. You can introduce other creative interventions with more cognitive complexity as needed for child modes. Paper tends to be one of our most useful and also most conservative transitional objects. The paper records of our in-session formation of mode maps or mode cycle clash-cards (covered in Chapter 8), are great tools for clients to take you "home" with them as a re-parenting figure and model of Healthy Adult.

George Lockwood noted that there are two primary modes through which core needs are met (Lockwood & Perris, 2012):

- The *maternal* involves experiencing the young child as an extension of oneself and responding to needs with direct soothing and nurturing. The focus is on connecting, mutual empathy, and ongoing availability. It is primarily based on the mother's attachment system and mutually supports the child's attachment system.
- The *paternal* mode involves experiencing the child as separate, feeling less inclined to respond with direct soothing and being less likely to believe that the child will benefit from an immediate gratification of needs. It is based on, and supports, the development of the self-assertiveness system. The child learns to deal with distress on their own. The focus of this mode is on separateness and independence.

Naturally, both genders have these two responses available (Lockwood & Perris, 2012, p. 47). Both pathways to meeting core needs are important for both child and infant modes, but each one needs to be accurately matched in terms of developmental level.

Simeone-DiFrancesco related an experience of treating an infant mode. She noticed when working with a young man that the usual ST interventions worked briefly but did not "stick." She understood that this suggested that this individual was in an infant mode. In visualization, the person went back to a feeling of rejection in the womb: "My mother didn't want me."

Simeone-DiFrancesco gave him a blanket to wrap around himself in session and then said, "You are safe. You are wanted." The man visibly relaxed. This degree of relaxation was not attained by doing the normal chair-work of standing together above the Vulnerable Child (with the young man "floating" above the mode, yet keeping in touch with the feelings of Vulnerable Child) and attempting to re-parent the child.

When the treatment focus switched to the more age-related mode, the symptoms of fear and distress evaporated. Impeaching the parent mode and simply allying with, and supporting, the needs of the child mode did not accomplish what resonating with the emotions of the infant mode did almost instantly. Once the young man's wife understood what was going on, she was able to comfort the infant mode of her husband, and received a similar and rather startling positive result.

Infant modes add another dimension to understanding couple interaction. Commonly, couples will activate at this level. Since these states are less available to reason, less articulate, and more flooded by feelings, the couple has to be coached to deal with such activation and not simply react. Progress can be made in trying to quickly recognize the rupture, learning to give a soothing response, and reassuring ("I don't want to hurt you."). Dave Edwards (ISST Marital/Couples Special Interest Group) stressed the need for the therapist to contain the couple at such times. Be vigilant to risks. For example, if one is in the infant mode of Vulnerable Child and the other is in a hostile parental or compensating mode (Punitive Parent or Bully and Attack), then the therapist needs to separate them until the damaging partner calms first, or actually intervene to protect, but also empathize, perhaps with the feelings of frustration the attacker might have. One cannot be passive and just allow damage to occur, as the couple may be too fragile to withstand this and still wish to continue therapy.

Generally, re-parenting as a strategy increases in importance with infant and child modes. Begin with internal feeling states. Feel these "in the body" and then talk about it, using Healthy Adult if this can be accessed. Farrell and Shaw noted that the parental role changes over the course of therapy, from meeting childhood needs to meeting adolescent needs in building Healthy Adult (see 2012, p. 39, matching p. 166). This can be extended to early childhood deficits as well. Also, think about therapeutic interventions that might be appropriate. Some compulsive sexual activity might be the result of infant self-soothing needs that have become confused in the process of psychosexual development.

Reflect: How would you as a therapist encourage a person in an infant mode, such as Impulsive Child, to distance from spontaneous impulses? How would you deal with Punitive Parent and Demanding Parent messages that have an infant mode quality? Since the infant mode is so vulnerable, you might want to "impeach" the Punitive Parent messages. The therapist is a substitute to deal with Punitive Parent until the person develops enough Healthy Adult to battle the internalized messages.

The therapist might encourage exercises to address infant mode activation in couples. For example, a couple may hug closely, cradle a head in a lap, or stroke the forehead of the partner. This can meet infant mode needs (movement interventions are explored in Solomon & Tatkin, 2011, chap. 6).

Thinking about infant modes is a work in progress and will need further development. It is possible that some of the child modes should be located in the infant realm. For example, Enraged Child may be an infant mode but Angry Child a child mode. The Suspicious/Over-control mode in the infant range might have a paranoid quality. The infant mode of Detached Self-soother might be seen in binge eating, and that of Self-aggrandizer may have a quality of magical control. We can also extend the child modes by thinking in a similar way about adolescent modes. Indeed, all of the 18 schemas could be reconsidered in a similar developmental framework. There is also the challenge of adapting interventions to better match the developmental level of presentation.

6.5 Some Additional Aspects Dealing with Child Modes

It is important to encourage clients to express needs. This is not easy if childhood needs were not met in a reliable way. Borderline personality disordered clients are often highly avoidant of their own needs because acknowledging any childhood need can be dangerous to a child in an abusive environment. But this is the way Vulnerable Child changes and Healthy Adult can be built up (Farrell & Shaw, 2012, p. 64).

> Nino was encouraged to say that he wanted Maria to listen when he was upset. They were able to negotiate that Maria would stop what she was doing and listen for a minimum of five minutes when he asked in a clear and assertive way, without any "attitude" or tone of aggression.

We need to match not only the mode in treatment (Farrell & Shaw, 2012, p. 16), but also the developmental level of the mode. Note that if there is a developmental age to the modes, it will affect how we dialog with and approach the mode, or help the person to understand why the mode might be feeling that way and why it might be a skewed perspective based on age. Maybe age-related memories can activate the mode corresponding to them. It is possible for us to fix an age of the child mode based on their history and how old the "child" feels to be in treatment. Often, it is connected with the painful memories of that period of their life. Sometimes you can ask clients to bring in a childhood picture, so they can relate to the child at that age, and in therapy find a way to meet their needs.

David Edwards (ISST Special Interest Group) also addressed the challenge in therapy:

> So when we do inner child work, the vulnerable child we work with has a history, including a history of coping, that goes back to the beginning. (Whenever that is! When does the attachment system start forming attachments?) That is why when we work with a Vulnerable Child we may find ourselves taken back to toddlerhood or infancy, and if we encounter a Protector Child (who rejects the Vulnerable Child) that also has a history and emerged as a way of coping.

Judy Margolin (ISST Special Interest Group) added some ideas as well:

> I imagine that there is a relationship between the longevity, quality and degree of injury (lack of need satisfaction) a person experiences and the rigidity in patterns of responding (schema) and ways of coping (modes) to that injury. These probably interact with the individual's temperament and biological disposition. We often see this in individuals who have experienced chronic trauma. It is interesting to consider a developmental spectrum of child modes, whether there is a qualitative difference in the presentation, and if it would affect the base treatment.

Reflect: Are mode states developmentally set or fixed by trauma?

There is a rich therapeutic and theoretical potential in considering the modes developmentally—not just the child-related ages but earlier—as some self-states reflecting infant self-awareness. The naming of a mode helps the person gain some distance from a negative part of the self, question the messages and fight back (Kellogg & Young, 2006, p. 449).

Modes have a lot of power, but the good news is that ST provides resources to reduce the strength of modes and to introduce ways of regaining control. The possibility of choice is important (Farrell & Shaw, 2012, p. 122).

6.6   Mode Cycles in Couples

Coping modes can be broadly categorized in the following terms:

- *Compliant Surrender:* A partner just absorbs the words of the parent mode, often coupled with the partner's words, believes them, and acts in ways that maintain that belief, even if the effort is to offset it. For example, a wife believing she is unworthy of love and attention acts in a schema coping style of overcompensation by being a "super mom," taking the kids to every activity their hearts desire. However, she is in Compliant Surrender coping mode to the internalized parent voice/mode, which tells her he would never want to spend special time with her, and together with this her child mode feels "not-special" and "un-lovable." She is also in Compliant Surrender to the husband who does not give her focus or attention, which she feels deeply, but she believes it would be useless to expect him to change.
- *Detached Protector:* Coping in a way in which the partners try to pro-tect themselves from further intensity of schema activation, such as by keeping busy, playing computer games, or focusing on the children rather than themselves.
- *Detached Self-soother:* Not dealing with the issue or each other and just going for soothing, such as through eating, impersonalized sex (regardless of emotional connection present), and so on.
- *Overcompensation:* Acting in a self-aggrandizing, controlling, bullying, attacking or fighting, or argumentative manner. This includes yelling and high-pitched, stressed-out voice tones, as well as stubborn ignoring, low-pitched mumbles and other passive-aggressive acts, such as con-temptuous eye-rolls, shoulder shrugs, statements of "Whatever," and the like. Overcompensators always strive for control.

These modes lead to possible dyadic interactions: each interaction becomes a loop or a cycle because it perpetuates the use of the maladap-tive coping mechanisms. Although we demonstrate here with a two-part pattern, at times there are variations of multiple coping modes, such as a partner going from Compliant Surrender to Detached Protector and finally to Overcompensator as the child mode changes, together with the introjects of the parent voice. This might lead to chains of coping mode changes. Below, however, are the basic five two-phase coping cycle pat-terns. Just think of them as being elongated, with other dyadic interac-tions tacked into, or onto, their cycle. Although this can get complex, it is usually a progression of left to right in the bottom boxes of the mode map (covered in Chapter 8), from the affiliation-seeking part of the nervous sensory activation to the more aggressive fighting activation. With couples who start with one partner in Overcompensation, the cycle does not usually progress to the overcompensating partner becoming soft and affiliation-seeking into Compliant Surrender (while the schema is intensely activated). Afterwards, when there is a cooling down (yes, with remorse, etc.), he or she can swing to Compliant Surrender—groveling, fearful clinging, and so on.

Think about the following styles of interaction:

a. *Overcompensator—Overcompensator cycle:* Both Lee and Stacey get into overcompensation to attack each other over an unexpected bill (highly unstable).

b. *Overcompensator—Detached Self-soother cycle:* Hetty criticizes Paul (in an overcompensating way) for not talking to her over dinner; he withdraws to his study to play computer games (moderately unstable).

c. *Overcompensator—Detached Protector cycle:* Jane (an Overcompensator acting out of her internalized parent mode) criticizes Andrew for being late from work, which he passively accepts while remaining emotionally detached in his Detached Protector, which in turn makes her feel entitled to be more critical and him feel all the more reason to be detached (this might be stable but is not satisfying for either partner).

d. *Detached—Detached cycle:* (with variations in types of detachment, such as simple avoidance or with the utilization of some sort of soothing): Sandy and Cici live parallel lives under the same roof in a more or less detached way. Sandy spends most of her free time playing computer games, and Cici reads voraciously (probably stable unless one partner finds an alternative, but sometimes stable as "living together apart"; c.f. Atkinson, 2012). If one starts to go on long bike trips, it might get unstable!

e. *Overcompensator—Compliant Surrender cycle:* This complementary cycle stabilizes a relationship unless the submissive partner withdraws (back to c) or starts to fight back (back to a), or the dominant partner gets bored and leaves the relationship.

Reflect: Think about the basic markers of progress in therapy with modes. Are you able to conceptualize your couples in terms of their mode cycles? Try writing some of them out and see what you come up with. What would it take to change these cycles? How does this direct you in your individual and couple work with them? How would it effect whether you see them jointly or together? Are you seeing the need for the Vulnerable Child to get soothed and the Angry Child to get guidance to grow? Dysfunctional parent modes in the background should have less "voice." They should weaken. Hopefully, less time will be spent in such modes. And maladaptive coping modes should become more flexible (Arntz & Jacob, 2013).

Reflect: What words would you use to empathically confront the following behaviors in the couple coping modes of Overcompensator: self-aggrandizing? perfectionism? bullying and attacking?

Becoming aware of being activated by specific modes can help a couple to distance from the emotional triggers and regard their problem not as personal but resulting from a "third party"—the mode cycle they are both engaged in. Switching into this "joint referencing perspective" (Siegel, 1999) helps the couple to slow down the clash and create some space for calm and an opportunity to rework it. Partners can see the patterns that create a break in their connection, and it helps them to take things less personally. The interactions can then become significantly more positive and less prone to schema traps. Later in therapy, for those who are self- and couple-aware, this conceptualization pinpoints where the communication went wrong and the schemas erupted.

> Cindy was astonished with the progress she made when she understood how negative comments from her family of origin had damaged her. She said, "I no longer need to absorb such a message!" Unfortunately, she still felt lacerated by the Punitive Parent voice in her head. When frustrated, she kept up a negative self-commentary. Cindy was able to take her new empowered sense of validation about the origin of such messages and say to herself, "You're making a comment and you had better stop!"

We observe that couple therapy with a primary emphasis on communication skills tends to drop off in effectiveness over time. Perhaps this is because cognitive awareness alone is stored in a rational part of the brain. Sometimes principles are hard to remember and continue to use unless they are experienced and practiced in new way. Gottman thought that the average couple therapy is only 70–75 percent effective for up to three years after the therapy, when effectiveness tends to drop off (Gottman & Schwartz Gottman, 2009). We hope that ST-C, when combined with experiential learning and changes in behavior, might be longer lasting.

Summary

This chapter has identified some of the advantages of using ST. You can begin by noting the trigger points in the couple relationship. This leads to the importance of working with modes in therapy. This includes both the standard list and other proposed modes. The idea of infant modes was introduced and related to therapeutic interventions. Also included was the idea of activating reciprocal mode cycles, including Compliant Surrender, Avoidance (Detached Protector and Detached Self-soother) and Overcompensator. In Chapter 7, couple interventions come more into focus.

7

Approaching Schema Therapy for Couples

What has ST to offer in treating couples? This unique approach to therapy, with a focus on relationship issues, is the primary focus of this chapter. In later chapters, we address specific interventions.

7.1 Practical Tips for Making Therapy a Safe Place for the Couple

The idea of a therapeutic "working place" is essential. The chairs should form a triangle that allows flexibility to change the focus. The couple should be able to talk to each other and the therapist to communicate directly with both.

The therapist "takes charge" of the session. The pilot has responsibility for the journey. There are times when the therapist will function as an intermediary. It may be necessary for the couple to talk to each other through you. If you need to strongly structure a session, instruct the listening partner to remain silent until you invite them into the conversation. If you encounter a highly reactive couple, direct communication between them should be minimized, if not actively avoided, to limit destructive interaction. If the listening partner interrupts, gently remind them to hold back for a few more moments. Do not "punish" the interfering partner or reward the person by focusing immediately on them. It is better to "mirror" the impatient partner and show understanding:

> "I see that you're very emotionally engaged and it's hard for you to hold your emotions back. I appreciate that you're so engaged. Of course,

Schema Therapy with Couples: A Practitioner's Guide to Healing Relationships, First Edition.
Chiara Simeone-DiFrancesco, Eckhard Roediger, and Bruce A. Stevens.
© 2015 John Wiley & Sons, Ltd. Published 2015 by John Wiley & Sons, Ltd.
Companion website: www.wiley.com/go/difrancesco/schematherapywithcouples

I'm eager to know more from your perspective, which we'll get to in a few moments. [Avoid naming an exact number of minutes, because the partner may call you to account!] Is this OK for you? If you can't wait, you're free to give me a sign. Thank you for your patience and cooperation."

Don't "torture" the impatient partner, but hear from them as soon as possible.

It is best to have the *couple* in therapy (Kanfer & Schefft, 1988), so encourage both to come. Joan Farrell and Ida Shaw (2012) have observed that in their group approach it is important to maintain an eye on both partners. Note signs of distraction by the passive partner, such as looking out of the window or at your paintings on the wall, checking their nails or, worse, pulling out their smartphone! Address this behavior immediately in a friendly way and ask whether they are still fine: "I noticed that you've been looking out of the window for a while. Can you listen a bit more?" If one partner is lashing out, the therapist instantly interrupts, "catches the bullet" (Atkinson 2012) and labels it: "Well, I'm aware that you're emotionally very engaged, but this has to be a safe place, so shouting this way is unhelpful in the session and probably elsewhere. So please stop!"

To Do: Role play dealing with a distracted partner with a colleague. Get feedback on how you intervened.

7.2   Balanced Attention Instead of Staying Neutral

It is not generally helpful to think in terms of dividing the time equally. More importantly, convey to both the sense that they are seen and understood equally. It is more a matter of connection. Sometimes the therapist grasps a meaning instantly; sometimes they have to take an "inquisitive stance" (Fonagy et al., 2004) and keep asking until the implicit meaning or message is revealed: "I don't really understand you, but I want to. So can you please explain it again? What exactly does it mean if you say that your husband doesn't love you anymore?" If the process is meaningful, the "passive" partner might listen for half an hour with great interest and emotional participation without being involved actively. This can continue to the extent that you have almost an individual session in the presence of the partner, which can be very helpful for understanding and emotional reconnection. But it is important to monitor the listening partner from time to time and keep in eye contact so that they still feel part of the process.

7.3 Thinking about Language, Tonal Regulation and the Use of Words

Language is central to the couple relationship. Words matter. In fact, words are an action in and of themselves. The childhood ditty of "Sticks and stones will break my bones but words will never hurt me" is not true. In ST, couples learn to identify loaded words. The couple becomes able to pause and create "space to calm." This is when they realize that a word may have become the trigger for a quick and unexpected clash. Just allowing for that possibility can lead to some clarifying questions and a few guesses about what was so upsetting. This will set the couple on a path to a simple "repair attempt" with a rephrasing and clarifying, plus an invitation for sharing about the memory that may have been triggered. It is also important to find positive words—with their partner's assistance—that are meaningful and meet deep needs.

Another aspect of sensitivity to language is the use of tone. The ISST Marital/Couples Special Interest Group had a meeting that discussed the use of tonal regulation in the context of infant modes. Mary Giuffra made the point that at times the words need to be very soft and even just emotive "holding" sorts of sounds, especially when a person is in an infant mode. The right words with the wrong tone will derail the communication. Less triggering words, with a soft or understanding tone, will frequently have a de-escalating effect and potentially a healing effect. The topic of communication is explored more fully in Section 7.8.

The inadvertent use of words can occur in therapy sessions. It may then trigger a disjunction between an individual and therapist. While this can breach the relationship, often the therapeutic alliance will strengthen after repair. A kindly and open exploration of what happened can lead to a deeper connection. The way the therapist deals with irritations or ruptures in therapy provides a model the couple can use outside the sessions.

Reflect: Ask colleagues for feedback about your voice tone in different settings.

To Do: Video record a session with a couple and, in supervision, ask for feedback about how your tone of voice comes across.

7.4   Using Self-Disclosure and Healthy Family Models, Heroes, Spirituality, and Religion

In ST, there are times when the use of limited and judicious self-disclosure can be very effective. It is one source of modeling. If done well, it will increase respect and trust. It is potentially helpful to see a therapist in his or her humanity.

> Ollie was struggling with stress and generalized anxiety. His therapist, Jamie, said, "I think I understand some of what you feel. I've struggled over the years with anxiety and I found that a regular practice of mindfulness discipline helped a lot. Would you be willing to try something similar?"

Self-disclosure reveals that everybody struggles to some extent, because we are human. This is reassuring. We journey through life starting from different points but often dealing with similar issues. The therapist does not need to be perfect but can provide a model of the Healthy Adult in dealing with stress. This might include taking some deep breaths to get out of a current schema activation, standing up to get a new perspective, or taking a few minutes of time out if overwhelmed.

Therapy Tip: Self-disclosure helps the couple to avoid feeling inferior or damaged. It creates a collaborative, warm, and understanding working relationship.

We look for healing metaphors to assist the recovery process. Think about how you might identify models who are relevant to the couple from their cultural, family, and religious history. Using metaphors can be vivid and effective because there is a potentially deeper impact. A metaphor can activate associations of related neural networks. Potentially, even years later, this is what a person may remember from the time in therapy.

Individuals may have "heroes" in their family history, or people in their life who they have looked up to or been influenced by. These can be made models of Healthy Adult. Showing a sensitivity and appreciation for these people, their religious family history, and relationships is often both empathic and highly encouraging. It can also provide a balance for a person who believes that much of what they learned from their dysfunctional family was all bad.

Reflect: Who are your family heroes? To what extent is Healthy Adult modeled by them? How do you draw on such healthy role models in your therapy?

To Do: Think about a couple you are seeing who have a strong religious faith. Who are the central role models held up by their religious beliefs? How can you more effectively use their example?

> Betty has a traditional Roman Catholic faith. She used the example of St. Claire, identifying her patience and hope in God, to strengthen her resolve to move past a bitter disappointment in her marriage.

7.5 Balancing the Level of Activation

While conducting the course of therapy, the therapist finds a balance between self-actualization (Millon, 1990) and self-reflection (see Figure 4). Think about adopting different therapeutic stances. The couple could be sitting or standing up, each talking directly to their partner, talking to you about the partner, or talking about himself or herself in the first person or in the third person. First person "drives the elevator down" and increases emotions, while second person "lifts it up" and helps distancing from the emotions.

The goal is not to be completely detached or shut off from the emotions, but to be aware of them without getting "drowned in the emotional flood." Teasdale (2002) called "desactualization" being mindfully aware about our thoughts and feelings ("being" mode) but abstaining from taking action ("doing" mode). Establishing an internal observer is essential to getting out of schema activations and shifting gear into Healthy Adult. Standing up and looking down on the scene in the chairs below also aids emotional distancing.

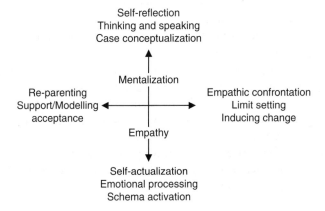

Figure 4 Balancing the therapy relationship. Source: Based on Roediger, Behary, and Zarbock (2013).

In addition to monitoring the level of emotional activation, the therapist also has to both actively soothe the couple and drive the therapeutic processes of change. If at some point you are apprehensive of losing the couple, it may be helpful to ask, "I have the feeling of losing you. I'm wondering what you might need now? Have I moved too quickly? What do you think is the next step?" Open questions invite the couple to engage in the process. Paradoxically, slowing down may result in the fastest progress.

Asking the couple to practice between the sessions is essential for progress, so there might be a need for empathic confrontation: "I fully understand your difficulties to meet for a *jour fixe* to train your communication skills. Nevertheless, progress needs training to lay new tracks in the brain. Do you have any ideas about what could help you to take the first step?" If the couple does not start training, reducing the session frequency can be a first step, proving that the therapist will not "carry the couple up the mountain."

7.6   Dealing with Volatile Couples

If a couple is highly reactive in their clashing, here are some suggestions.

Destructive conflict has to be interrupted (use the "pause button"). Say "Stop" repetitively with a firm voice. Eventually, hold your chart between them to interrupt eye contact between the fighting couple (another reason why it is helpful to sit rather close to them). If that does not work, you may have to separate the couple. Ask one to go and sit in the waiting room, but commit to soon exchanging them. Remember what we do with struggling children!

If you can work with the couple together, identify and label what you see happening in the relationship. The focus is on the here and now. This channels the conversation and keeps the focus on the concrete interaction. Detecting the mode cycles is far more important than discussing the content. It is sometimes hard to convey this message to the couple, but it is an important step in healing the old wounds.

To Do: Try to validate the reactive stance (coping mode) if you know something about its origin in childhood. Ask what they really feel deep inside or what the child mode actually needs.

Think about creating a metacognitive position for the couple, "above" the ongoing process. You can induce mentalization or mutual understanding with questions like:

- How did you feel doing that?
- What did you feel in your body?

- What thoughts were running through your head?
- What was your intention in that moment?
- What actually happened?
- What do you really need?
- What do you think your partner felt while you did that?
- How did you expect them to react?
- How would you have felt standing in their shoes?
- How would you have probably reacted yourself?

> Charlie was given to explosive reaction and instant blame of Violet. She would sulk and then nag about some insignificant infraction in their relationship. They were seeing a schema therapist who insisted that they slow the process down and carefully look at their process of interaction. They were able to identify triggers and reactions. What did each step look like for the partner? What did it feel like from within? This discussion helped to weaken the emotional polarizing of the couple.

If you can identify the couple's interlocking coping modes, you can tell them that it is not their fault. It is non-blaming to remind them that it is a legacy from the past, but creates what is "their cycle" in the here and now. You might use Seneca's metaphor of emotions being like wild horses: our role is to pull on the bit and keep a tight grasp on the reins. Later, we will consider how to separate out the different modes, place them on separate chairs and reconnect with the Healthy Adult.

Reflect: Watch the movie *Who's Afraid of Virginia Woolf* (1966). What would you do with Martha and George? How would you introduce enough control to limit their destructive interactions?

7.7 Working with Passive Individuals

There are common "roadblocks" to therapy. Sometimes an individual or a couple will remain emotionally detached and unmotivated. An individual may refuse to do an exercise or homework assignments. Generally, resistance in therapy reveals that a client, or even the couple, has not formed a working alliance. This behavior should be recognized and empathically addressed.

> Kathy began to miss couple sessions. She had a busy job but it was soon clear that she was not making the relationship a priority. She was halfhearted in sessions and commonly looked bored. This was undermining the work. The couple therapist asked to see Kathy for an individual session to address his concerns.

Sometimes you will suggest an exercise and a client will refuse to be involved. At that point, it may be helpful to disclose some frustration and perhaps disappointment, but without accusation:

> "I'm frustrated because I think it would be a good idea just to try this exercise out instead of talking about it. We gain insight through experience. I understand that it's a bit frightening for you to do things you've never done before and show your vulnerable side. I felt the same when I did an exercise like that for the first time. What can I do to reduce your fears or create some trust so we can try it?"

The questions are driven by a serious interest to fully understand their inner motives. It may be helpful to explore reasons using the mode model. Also remind the couple that ST is effective because it is highly experiential.

Here are some of the most common reasons why people resist:

• There is a lack of understanding about what is being asked. Remain patient and ask for feedback about what they understand you want them to do.

• The person remains in an avoidant coping mode because of a fear response. We may have to move from the front stage (protector) to the backstage and ask the child mode what is needed to feel more assertive and empowered. The therapist might ask, "What exactly are you afraid of? What's the worst thing that might happen? Did you ever have a bad experience trying something similar?" Usually, this inquiry reveals interfering parental voices that can be disempowered as described in the next step. Afterwards, the therapist soothes and assists the revealed child mode: "What could I do to help you feel less frightened?" Do not forget to use a childlike language while talking to a child mode.

• The punitive or over-demanding parent modes are activated. The individual is afraid to fail. It is easy to think that doing nothing is safer than making a mistake. The "thoughts in the head" of the backstage have to be detected, placed on a parent mode chair and challenged— "impeached" if possible. Sometimes these modes are too strong and persistent and, after acknowledgment of their presence, are best ignored.

• There is an Undisciplined Child or Obstinate Child mode that is "voting" to abstain from the exercise. Such modes have to be detected and then empathically confronted: "I understand that it takes a stretch to get this experiment started. Let me make a suggestion: instead of arguing beforehand, let's give it a try and discuss later. I'll accept your doubts if you're unhappy with the result. What's the first little step that you can imagine taking?" The idea is to lower the bar to the point that a person cannot get under it! This strategy also works with the depressed.

- There is secondary gain in remaining passive. If, for example, a client was able to leave the house, then returning to work is expected. The partner might be more absent if they are recovering from panic attacks. Being less submissive means taking more responsibility. These motives have to be dismantled carefully, the cost–benefit ratio has to be clarified, and acceptable alternatives must be developed. If there is no serious gain in sight, the couple will stick to their old coping behavior.

Orlie resisted chair-work with his therapist. Rather than change seats, the therapist simply asked him to address the mode that was represented by the chair. As this became more natural, Orlie was prepared to sit in a chair to represent the mode he had previously spoken to. This is an example of making small steps in the right direction.

When in doubt, it is better to go with the person instead of following a strict agenda. Miller and Rollnick (2002), in *Motivational Interviewing*, said: "The patient is always right." It is better to "roll with resistance" instead of arguing with your client, so leave them with a choice. People like having choices. It is not a matter of right or wrong. We try to evoke an experiential attitude. They have to try it out, draw their conclusions and then take the next step. Overcoming emotional or experiential avoidance (Hayes et al., 1999) is also an important goal in ST.

7.8 Enhancing Communication Skills

There are countless communication manuals for couples, but ST has its own perspective on communication skills. We want the couple to be in touch with their needs and goals. This will help progress, certainly more than mechanically following a training skills manual, because they both understand why change is necessary. It is helpful for the couple to become familiar with communication skills even before they start talking directly to each other. The therapist will often have to intervene as soon as the couple falls back into old habits. The gravitational pull of the attractors into the old repetitive clashing style is usually strong. Naturally, the therapist will model communication skills.

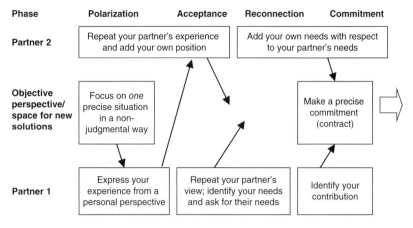

Figure 5   Movements of a conflict-solving communication

Simeone-DiFrancesco and Simeone (2016a,b) have conceptualized skill-ful communication as "Connect-Talk." The goal of the communication skill is connection (see Figure 5). The therapist encourages the couple to achieve the following:

1. *Focus.* Focus on the same interaction, not on feelings or assumptions.
2. *First to talk.* One individual expresses a point of view and associated emotions on the chosen issue and nothing else. The partner empathically "echo-listens" what was heard. This is basically saying back, in one's own words, what was heard, without any defensive reaction, aggression, negative analysis, turning it into a weapon, or adding contempt (c.f. the "Four Horsemen of the Apocalypse," Gottman, 1999).
3. *Reverse roles.* The roles are then reversed, with the partner expressing a view and the initial "talker" echo-listening. This often involves extensive clarification to understand what the other means by their words. Making the effort to clarify before echo-listening demonstrates a caring investment in really wanting to attain understanding. And it creates a certain sense of being heard and understood, creating a feeling of reconnection. This role is often what the therapist demonstrates and models intensively. It is at this juncture that the clarifications will also involve an emotion-focus, often bringing startling new awareness of the other's inner realities.
4. *Wishes.* Then the first makes a wish. The partner repeats the wish and adds their own one.

5. *A suggestion.* One partner makes a concrete suggestion for a solution. The other partner echoes this and makes a suggestion as well.
6. *Agreement.* Both come to an agreement (and echo-listen to each other to see whether both have fully understood). The agreement includes a precise description of the desired behavior. The outcome will be followed up in the next meeting.

The movements shown in Figure 5 are the tango. Susan Johnson (2004) used the metaphor of the dance of the couple. In our example, one takes a step and offers something. The first person, leading in the dance as it were, then steps back and invites the partner to join. Again, a similar movement for asking and responding, each time stepping back or up to agreement. Echoing increases the bond of understanding and provides security for the submissive or avoiding partner to be heard. Encourage the couple to adapt their pace to suit each other or very little will be achieved.

Therapy Tip: Automatic thoughts come up fast—the new brain circuits are fragile and perhaps slow to change.

In the beginning, the therapist attends closely and interrupts if one of the partners falls outside the guidelines. If necessary, you can suggest and model a skill, such as empathically listening without a contemptuous comment. Later in therapy, the couple will "dance" more naturally with their Connect-Talk between sessions and report their successes in later sessions.

7.9 What Schema Therapy brings to the Communication Process

ST-C gives the couple a language to communicate vulnerability (schemas) and inner states (modes) and to analyze their interpersonal interactions (contained in what we later refer to as mode maps). Emotional connection is the key to getting in touch with the Vulnerable Child mode. Once you have moved out of problem solving, when one of the couple says something deeply revealing you can place it in the "empty space" between them. It is of value and should be respected. You will need to limit negative judgments from the partner. Nobody is permitted to "throw dirt in the water." The pool between the clients has to be kept clean.

After something has been placed in the empty space, you can invite the partner to contribute something as well. The best invitation is a clarifying question. Clarifications can open up the space. Equally, though, such questions can put someone on the spot. The exploration has to be on a mutually acceptable topic. It is not about you, as the therapist, going with your own curiosity or analyzing hunches.

Identifying an unmet need can lead to mutual understanding and vulnerability. At other times, making a wish is less demanding. A wish is not an essential need but might reflect an underlying need. Expressing a wish *as* a wish provides the partner with greater choice and respects their autonomy. People like to choose (this is why there are so many shampoos in the supermarket). Asking for a wish is the right kind of "submission." When done appropriately, it will invite help and emotional bonding.

Therapy Tip: Remember that what works with children also works with adults. We can easily feel like a child inside, even when physically grown-up.

It is best to have a very clear agreement. Sometimes it will make sense to write down what was mutually understood. The agreement is binding, and should be precise and leave no space for "interpretations." If an agreement is violated, that can become an issue to start a new communication dance.

Vikki and Bart agreed: "We'll meet every Wednesday at 8 pm to talk about current issues." Initially they thought of "We'll continue our talk next week," but their therapist insisted on being precise. Bart found that there were occasions in the next month that he had to postpone because of work commitments. He then offered an alternative time that was acceptable to Vikki. Once, the date for the dance was not kept, and this was discussed in the following session.

Reflect: Keeping agreements provides building blocks for trust in the couple relationship.

A good dance-floor is necessary for the communication dance. This is not street dancing—you need a safe space for practice. Initially, perhaps communication will happen in therapy sessions, but encourage the couple in treatment to make a regular time (*un jour fixe*, in French) of an adequate length (between a half-hour and one hour, no longer), and with agreed "escape clauses" when talking bogs down or becomes unproductive. Meeting twice the week for half an hour is more productive than once for a full hour. Rhythm helps! Make a *jour fixe* a regular part of your life.

Therapy Tip: All distractions have to be kept out (children, phones of all kinds, doorbells). No alcohol, of course! No snacks. Create a warm but serious atmosphere. Ritualize it a bit by lighting up a candle. During the talk, the dance steps should be followed. Try for a soft start-up.

When the couple have mastered some of the basic ST skills (recognizing modes, knowing how to chart their mode maps and mode cycle clash-cards), they will be progressing to the Healthy Adult mode.

Note: Progress may be agonizingly slow—very much like a game of Snakes and Ladders, with setbacks—but will eventually occur because the couple keeps rolling the dice.

Summary

It is natural in therapy to notice what a couple say. However, it is the form of interaction that is most important. In this chapter, we have made some suggestions about providing a safe place, especially with volatile couples, therapeutic attention, tonal regulation and using self-disclosure. We have made suggestions for helping couples with the dance of communication.

8

Mode Mapping and Mode Cycle Clash-cards

Some very useful tools have been developed for our approach to ST-C. They include mode maps and mode cycle flash-cards (Roediger 2012a and adaptations such as Roediger and Simeone-DiFrancesco's mode cycle clash-cards). These tools conceptualize individual and couple dynamics. We can track a couple's interaction in a session, and the couple gradually learns to understand their out-of-session interactions. This chapter is devoted to more fully understanding these tools.

8.1 Introducing the Dimensional and Dynamic Mode Model

The modes are regarded as "parts of the self" with emotions, thoughts, bodily sensations, and behavior. There has been an attempt to define specific sub-types of the major mode categories in order to link their presence in the schema mode inventory with DSM-4/5 personality disorders (e.g., the Perfectionistic Overcontroller mode with the obsessive-compulsive personality disorder, the Self-aggrandizer with the narcissistic personality disorder or the Attention Seeking mode with the histrionic personality disorder). Presently, only some of the 14 modes from our listing in Chapter 6 are specific to one or two disorders (e.g., the Bully and Attack mode for the paranoid and the borderline), while most modes are used in a range of personalities (Lobbestael et al., 2008). To avoid an implicit influence of theories, the model remains descriptive and proceeds

Schema Therapy with Couples: A Practitioner's Guide to Healing Relationships, First Edition.
Chiara Simeone-DiFrancesco, Eckhard Roediger, and Bruce A. Stevens.
© 2015 John Wiley & Sons, Ltd. Published 2015 by John Wiley & Sons, Ltd.
Companion website: www.wiley.com/go/difrancesco/schematherapywithcouples

Table 3   Comparing the two mode models

Traditional "Dutch" model	Model used in this book
Categorizing	Dimensional
Descriptive	Interactional/dynamic
Idiosyncratic construction	Normative framework
Bottom-up	Top-down
"Psychological"	"Medical"
Research orientation	Clinical orientation
Dyadic interaction between Healthy Adult and one mode	Getting an overview over an internal map of modes
Stand-alone model	More closely connected with the cognitive behavioral therapy model and 3rd wave therapies

"bottom up" from describing to labeling the modes.[9] This may be helpful for differentiating and grouping participants in research studies and for designing specific interventions to create high levels of adherence.

The model we present in this book (to distinguish it, we call it the *dimensional mode model*) is slightly modified from that used in the Netherlands and brings the mode model a step closer to psychodynamic, transactional analysis or emotion-focused therapy models. We want to assist therapists in getting an overview of the dynamics of client presentation and conducting therapy in an efficient, goal-oriented way. Couples come seeking help and we try to help them by using our knowledge and presenting them with an understandable model. This is a more medical "top down" approach that still works in emergency situations. Table 3 highlights the major differences.

There are two major sources of human consciousness. Looking from a developmental and physiological perspective, the underlying biological processes in the body result in primary emotional activation. On a parallel track, we internalize appraisals of our environment into our view on the world, which creates our internal belief system. We can portray two levels (front and backstage) by distinguishing visible behavior (coping modes on the front stage) from the internal motivational level (backstage).

The two major motivational systems (backstage) are basic emotions or child modes deriving from subcortical activations streaming up from the

[9] Bottom-up is a grounded approach, from observable facts to more abstract concepts. Top-down is, of course, the reverse.

limbic system and the internalized core beliefs and display rules or parent modes, possibly stored in the mirror neurons of our cortex since childhood. According to current neurobiological models (Siegel, 1999), these impulses are merged in a convergence zone, in the orbital frontal cortex, which Botvinick et al. (2001) called the "conflict monitor" (i.e., in the anterior cingular cortex). There, the visible coping behavior is executed. Small changes in the balance of the activated motivational systems can result in mode flipping (e.g., from an externalizing to a self-mutilating behavior in the borderline). The dynamic model reflects these changes in a complex way and helps people better understand their "bizarre" behavior and solve it better by separating and acknowledging any motives.

In this way, we can move from the descriptive level to the emotional and cognitive origins of behavior. Tracking back to the roots of our behavior is like analyzing a color. All colors (coping modes) comprise three primary colors (blue, red, and yellow). Basic emotions such as fear or grief belong to the Vulnerable Child (blue). Disgust or anger belong to the Angry Child (red). The internalized beliefs, for the purposes of this illustration, are yellow. Coping modes are primarily regarded as executive behavior accompanied by social emotions resulting from a composition of trans-formed basic emotions (between the poles of blue and red) and simulta-neously activated core beliefs (yellow). In order to present and distinguish how these modes are truly different, we regard them as a mixture of emotions, cognitions, and behavior but split them up into essentially dif-ferent groupings: a) behavioral (coping modes), b) primarily emotional (child modes), and c) cognitive (parent modes).

This is, of course, somewhat artificial, because even in a child mode we express our feelings with words (cognitions). But, essentially, we try to per-ceive and express our core emotions that are not tainted by beliefs. Experiencing our innocent child can be likened to showing our true colors. This is the part that we try to get in touch with and care for in a "secondary childhood" in therapy. Additionally, parent voices have an aura of negative affect. But they convey toxic beliefs that are uncritically entrenched in our appraisal system and have the potential to still make us suffer. It is an impor-tant goal of ST to dismantle these toxic beliefs and reduce their power by impeaching them. Therefore, we have to bypass the coping modes that clients bring into therapy to reach the backstage as soon as possible. While the beliefs in a coping mode sound rational to some degree, the entrenched core belief is more toxic, so you will see the real difficulties as soon as you access the backstage. The mode map will provide this direction.

It is the backstage dynamic that this model is designed to present. It is dimensional rather than categorical. This allows the representation of all

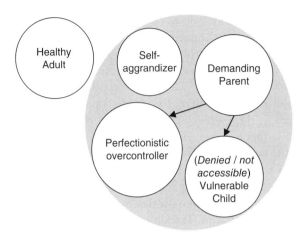

Figure 6   Descriptive mode map. Source: Modified from Arntz and Jacob (2013)

possible emotional, cognitive, and behavioral aspects through the modes. Despite its complexity, it keeps the model clear and manageable—once you understand the underlying ideas. You can place all basic emotions on the spectrum between Vulnerable (blue) and Angry Child (red). Internal voices are either inside or outside directed and the resulting behavior is somewhere between internalizing-submissive, passive or active avoidant, or externalizing-dominant. There are no more modes needed. Like a lens, this reduces the complexity of our experiencing and places it neatly on the stage we work on.

The relevant modes are found in both of the models, but are ordered independently in the case conceptualization form, as shown by two figures. The major difference is that the *Descriptive* map (Figure 6) does not include any dynamic influences or interactions between the modes, while the multiple arrows of the *Dimensional* mode map (Figure 7) describe complex intrapersonal interactions. This provides a broad overview of the inner world of the couple, including inherent conflicts. Clarity is provided for the problem-solving function of prior coping modes, moderating internalized parent-voices and involved child need motives. This can assist chair-work (explained in Section 9.8), when the chairs become the outer landscape for the internal mode map. Finding such concrete ways of expressing internal dynamics is a strength of ST.

Being able to shift from the narrowed perspective in a schema activation to a broader Healthy Adult perspective in therapy assists the move from a hypothesis to a solution. This gives clients a comprehensive internal working model, not only of the self but of others (i.e., the partner). This

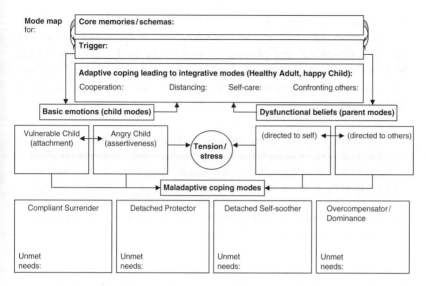

Figure 7 Dimensional mode map. Source: Based on Roediger (2011)

helps with the *why* and the *how* to move into more balanced and adaptive behavior. The mode map can be useful for all of us, continually providing orientation and guidance to more flexible and balanced ways of acting. It has also been used in therapy supervision (Roediger & Laireiter, 2013).

8.2 Mode Maps

Mode maps provide a comprehensive case conceptualization in ST. The map is based on the mode model shown in Figure 1 in Chapter 1. We describe its use in detail in this chapter. The map helps to limit the complexity of the mode model that arises from an increasing number of sub-modes, as mentioned in Section 6.3. It contains the four major classifications of modes: child modes, parent modes, coping modes, and the Healthy Adult mode. There are other mode models, but this model goes beyond categorizing the modes to include interactional relationships between the mode groups. It differentiates the four groups at two (or at least three) levels: the coping modes as behavior that can be seen (on the front stage), while the child and parent modes are hidden on a motivational level (backstage). The Healthy Adult mode floats above both of them.

The child modes indicate emotional core needs that are not adequately met. These emerge as basic emotions from the depth of the brain's limbic system, where our emotional regulation systems are located. People will usually experience child mode activation with intense and often overwhelming emotional and physical arousal in the body. In everyday life, child modes do not present unless we are regarded as "childish," although there are some "playgrounds" for the Happy Child mode, such as games and having sex.

> A supervisee working in the forensic field reported a client killing his spouse with 40 stab-wounds from a large kitchen knife. Suddenly, the client stopped and called the police. A few minutes later he continued stabbing her, seemingly without any control. This attack can be viewed as the rare direct expression of an Enraged and Impulsive Child without any reasoning involved, interrupted by a short flip into Healthy Adult or Demanding Parent and then reverting to the child mode.

We feel the child modes in our bodies. Sometimes it is difficult to put such sensations or emotions into words. Being in a Vulnerable or Angry Child mode indicates that core needs have not been met. More positively, this can invite the partner to meet the needs.

It may be helpful to think about basic emotions. Ekman (1993) named six:

- *anger* and *disgust* (belonging to the Angry Child mode and indicating that the need for self-assertiveness is threatened)
- *fear* and *sadness* (belonging to the Vulnerable Child and indicating a painful activation of the attachment system)
- *happiness* (belonging to the Happy Child, which is encouraged to grow in therapy)
- *surprise* (which is neutral in our context).

The first four emotions named are relevant to making a connection with the Angry and Vulnerable Child states. The question, "What do you feel in your body, in your chest or stomach?" usually helps people to access their basic emotions. Consider offering an individual having difficulties identifying their basic emotions the multiple choice of the four relevant basic emotions and ask which of them might be a best "fit." Almost all are able to do this and feel the model "from the inside."

Note: We are not talking of primary emotions, which is the term used in emotion-focused therapy. In that model, basic emotions can be primary or secondary, depending on chronology or onset. In our model, the time sequence is irrelevant. What matters is the distinction between secondary (or socially modified by internalized parent modes) and basic (spontaneous expression of child needs) emotions. We want to guide clients back to their full spectrum of innate motives expressed by basic emotions. The dominant coping mode is usually driven by one pole of the emotional spectrum that we call the Active Child mode. Shifting from the cycle to the solution requires including the formerly blocked child mode as an essential ingredient for an emotionally better balanced Healthy Adult solution.

In addition, it is important to appreciate that the two child modes are not categories but a spectrum of emotional activation, and we constantly move back and forth. If you take the "soother" out of a baby's mouth, he or she will probably react in Angry Infant mode. After some minutes of helpless crying, the sound may change to moaning, indicating sadness, and finally might turn into an expression of fear. There is no "jump" between the two modes, but more a smooth shift. Sometimes both systems (the assertiveness and attachment systems) are activated at the same time and we might feel a mixture of anger and sadness (or a quick flipping between them). The categories in a mode inventory cannot fully represent such varieties of emotional movements. Hence this model is not only interactive but dimensional. Research may need categorizing models for data purposes, but our clinical understanding is more nuanced. A dimensional model is helpful because you can place each existing mode somewhere in the given dimensions while keeping the model simple.

On the motivational (backstage) level, we also find the internalized appraisals from significant others (parents or carers). This is a legacy from childhood. The messages are probably stored in mirror neurons in the brain's parietal cortex and are experienced as "voices in the head." This commentary continually assesses current situations and child mode activations. People find this easy to identify, and even recall the origins (whose voice it may be), so these are called "explicit motives." Often these appraisals are in contradiction with the child's needs (implicit motives). The child tries to reduce the resulting emotional tension or dissonance between its needs and the acquired rules of the parent voice or later introjected parent modes. This results in the development of coping modes. The current coping mode is probably the "best" solution found so far. It might appear maladaptive from a Healthy Adult perspective, but at the very least it has worked for years and it was adaptive in childhood. The therapist should acknowledge this positive contribution before moving on to develop more adaptive solutions.

Brad was an auditor for a large accountancy firm. He was a perfectionist at work and this was highly rewarded. But at home his demands resulted in a very unhappy de facto partner. Kerry complained, "He's so controlling of me, and now he wants children. Does he want a whole 'tribe' of us to control!?!"

We used the simplified mode map to see that Brad had a coping mode of Surrender. We called him the Perfectionist. This was justified by his self-directed Demanding Parent mode with rigid rules about what is "right," with which he coped by surrendering to it, and to the concept of himself as inadequate without such perfectionism. He needed to be perfect to avoid making mistakes and getting accused. In his work life, this coping was functional unless it resulted in burn-out.

In the couple's family life, the Demanding Parent mode was directed to Kerry in an overcompensatory way. Brad turned into an Angry Child mode when she did not fulfill his standards. What was hidden, and protected, was his Vulnerable Child. So there were two goals of therapy. When dealing with Kerry, he should bring the Vulnerable Child onto the front stage, softening his approach to her. At work, the opposite was true. He was too much influenced by his Anxious Child mode and needed to strengthen his self-assertiveness side, connected with his Angry Child pole.

Usually, people do not enter therapy because of a coping behavior. It is considered part of personality and experienced as "ego-syntonic." Nevertheless, coping modes can clash in the couple relationship, which can result in therapy. Brad, in the case above, was happy with his way of interacting with people in his work life. He was convinced that he was justified and normal. This is one reason why each of a couple typically believes, at the beginning of therapy, that they are normal and their partner has to change. Developing a mode map is an important tool to take the couple on the journey from the front-stage coping to the back-stage motives.

In ST, the goal is to strengthen the Healthy Adult mode. This is a way for an individual to be aware of both motivational drivers and to make adjustments. The negative automatic thoughts of the parent modes have to be reappraised, and the needs of the child modes have to be acknowledged and fulfilled in their full spectrum when possible. If the child's needs are met, the Vulnerable Child becomes an open and sensitive child again, willing to socialize with others. The Angry Child, when their needs are met, calms down and becomes an empowered child ready for exploration with realistic assertiveness. It is the "job" of the Healthy Adult to reappraise the old beliefs and care for the child and then develop functional coping behavior for a successful performance in life.

Therapy Tip: If you were to treat Brad, you would probably see Angry Child before Vulnerable Child.

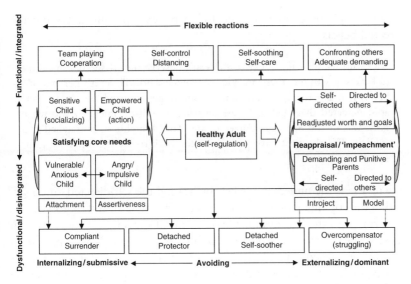

Figure 8 The extended dimensional mode model. Source: Based on Roediger (2011)

Figure 8 shows the extended dimensional mode model.

The orbital frontal cortex in the brain seems to play an important role in developing coping modes derived from motivational activations. The anterior cingular cortex, especially, has emotional and cognitive representations and has been regarded as the "conflict monitor" (Botvinick et al., 2001) where the coin tumbles to one or the other side: Go or No-Go? We assume that the more differentiated reactions are organized in the prefrontal cortex. They are able to overrule the spontaneous decisions made in the orbital frontal cortex, so we locate the Healthy Adult function in the prefrontal cortex.

People come into therapy identified with their belief systems. These are ego-syntonic: "I have to fulfill the wishes of my partner or she'll leave me" or "I have to be perfect or my boss will fire me." A helpful question to make the belief more ego-dystonic is: "Where you born with these beliefs?" Obviously not! So social influence is at work. Beliefs can be other-directed too: "A man who cries isn't a real man!"

This rigidity indicates a coping mode. Such beliefs are mixed with some kind of secondary or social emotions. In social contexts, the original basic emotions (such as fear, anger, or disgust) are merged with beliefs, leading to the social emotions of hopelessness, guilt, or shame (Leary 2000). You can see the coping mode of Self-aggrandizer when the social emotion is grandiosity or contempt. The following example illustrates outside-directed beliefs.

Nick said to himself, "Ricky just doesn't deserve me. If she doesn't want to have sex with me, there are a lot of women who will. So it's her fault if I betray her. The therapist said I have a right to get my needs met!" His therapist detected these beliefs by asking what his self-commentary was while Nick was in the Self-aggrandizer mode. The thoughts were detailed and explicit. The therapist gave permission for Nick to say them in an uncensored way.

Try to access the underlying beliefs by hearing the self-directed "message" within the coping mode voice and then translating it from the ego-syntonic "I-form" into the ego-dystonic "you-form." In this way, "I have to fulfill these wishes" becomes "You have to fulfill these wishes," or "I have to be perfect" is turned into "You have to be perfect." The outside-directed beliefs, such as "A real man doesn't cry," remain unchanged because they are already directed to another person. These ego-syntonic sentences reveal their origin because they sound like the voice of significant others.

Nick recognized the voice of his mother, who raised him thinking he was special and that other children were unworthy to play with him. He began to see how his mother programmed him from childhood.

In this shift of first to second person, *intra*personal conflict becomes an *inter*personal conflict that is available for clinical work.

Vonnie and Ron came for counseling. She was on the verge of leaving him: "I just have to get away." Ron was puzzled and could not understand why the "sudden" change in her attitude: "We've been married for 25 years. Why now?"

What was soon obvious to the couple therapist was the way Ron put extraordinary demands on his wife ("He wants the house perfect at all times of the day!"). The therapist re-expressed this as "Ron, I want you to hear this demand coming from me. *You* have to be perfect in everything you do! *You* are not allowed to be human. No human frailty will be tolerated."

This shocked Ron and he was able to see the unreasonable demands he placed on Vonnie: "I've been like a Nazi in the home. No wonder she's so fed up. Please give me a chance to change."

In explaining this to couples, it is helpful to start with the simple model. It is not unlike various psychodynamic models that pervade popular understanding. Indeed, this is a strength of ST, since the theoretical models are quite simple. But for understanding a couple´s interpersonal dynamic, including their cycles of conflict, we need the comprehensive model in Figure 8 and the mode map in Figure 7 as the basis for the mode cycle clash-card bringing together the essentials of the mode maps of both partners.

Think about the shift as one of perspective. The mode map works like the zoom lens of a camera. It gives a closer look, with the four basic mode groups in greater focus. The child modes are described in the continuum between Vulnerable and Angry Child modes. The Vulnerable Child is striving for attachment and safe belonging. The Angry Child strives to become assertive and tries to get control and fight for needs to be met.

The parent modes are also described in terms of polarity. These modes were generated by an internalization of the values, appraisals, and demands of parents, carers, and authority figures. Naturally, these messages were internalized. This probably has links to the concept of mirror neurons in neurobiological research. Those neurons allow us to feel like other people feel and detect the intentions of others. We build up internalized representations. This is the neuronal basis of empathy and "theory of mind" (Fonagy et al., 2004). Significant others are internalized in a dual way:

a. We build up a representation that continues to speak as they did. This is the self-directed voice of Demanding or Punitive Parent modes.
b. We also internalized these significant people as a model of how to treat others. This is why parents often treat their children just as they were treated as children. Only the actors change, not the patterns! This explains how victims became offenders, unconsciously "trained" by the parental model.

The model has an additional box for the parent modes turned outwards. The blaming words may be the same, but the direction can be internal or external—to self or others.

In the bottom level, we split up the coping modes into four boxes, describing a continuum between a submissive and internalizing behavior on the left and an externalizing and dominant (overcompensating) behavior on the right. In the middle are the more passive (Detached Protector) and more active (Detached Self-soother) avoidant coping modes. These boxes just represent the most important coping modes, but with some training you can place any behavior somewhere in this spectrum.

Therapy Tip: Practice with your family members or colleagues to become familiar in detecting the relevant mode (i.e., separating coping modes from the underlying child and parent mode activations). Try to get to the interpersonal meaning of a behavior and include your own feelings activated in the interaction (the child mode within yourself). Consider your schema activation as the therapist. This helps you identify subtle manipulative messages of coping modes that might appear "innocent" at first glance. Or the other way round: become aware of a protective anger.

> Tracey, a young borderline patient, came to a session swearing, "This stupid therapy doesn't help me at all. Let's stop!" Her therapist initially thought it might be an overcompensating mode, such as Bully and Attack, but she did not feel threatened. So the counter-transference reaction led her to identify Angry Protector, which was keeping the therapy away from her Vulnerable Child.

This mode can be placed somewhere between the Self-soother and the Overcompensator. Another person might come in stating, "You're wasting your time with me. I'm a hopeless case. Better spend your time treating more promising people!" This might look submissive. But does this person try to connect with you? No—they are keeping their distance. So this is another self-defeating protector that could be placed between the Detached Protector and the Compliant Surrender box.

A third example: a person might seem completely calm (as many antisocial personalities will present) but feel threatening while saying, "I know where you park your car!" Although there is no anger, you perceive it as Overcompensator because the person tries to control you.

A final example: somebody might be very active or perfectionist and because of that appear overcompensatory, but as long as they are driven by the will to please you this is surrender or at least submission. Sometimes behavior can incorporate aspects of two coping modes. Obsessive hand-washing to "wash away" guilt feelings is evidence of Detached Self-soother mode, but requiring others not to touch anything in a room becomes overcompensatory. Making gifts may appear surrendering, but getting angry when they are not acknowledged reveals a manipulative (and by that, overcompensatory) foundation. Take time to explore the layers driving the behavior.

Therapy Tip: When uncertain, be like Colombo, the TV detective. Play ignorant and ask seemingly foolish questions until the person reveals their real needs or implicit beliefs of the motivational level backstage. Then insert the behavior in the box that fits best (but remember that it may be somewhere in between or have to be located in two boxes.

This model is also dimensional, with an interactive perspective. Every coping behavior is "fueled" by underlying emotions and "directed" by parental mode appraisals. In this way, an anxious Vulnerable Child when combined with a self-directed parental mode will lead to surrender. An Angry Child and an outward-directed parental mode lead to overcompensation. If an Angry Child's tendency to fight is blocked by a Punitive Parent, this might result in avoidant coping, such as Detached Protector or Detached Self-soother (i.e., self-mutilating behavior). Following the arrows will reveal the dynamics.

The more complex mode map will also show how Healthy Adult can function. This mode cannot "invent" new coping tendencies, because they are well established. But Healthy Adult can modify the reaction, adapt it to the situation and the needs of others, and include a long-term perspective. And Healthy Adult can change in a more flexible manner from one coping mode to another, instead of "mode flipping." They are able to make the best out of a given situation. The large box on the top level of the figure shows how the exaggerated coping modes in the bottom level can be modified by the Healthy Adult.

Therapy Tip: The basic goal of working with child modes is to encourage people to care better for their own emotional needs. With time and progress, such needs will be better expressed. Note also that some coping modes can be very rewarding and can be entrenched by secondary gain, especially overcompensating, stimulating, or attention-seeking ones (Arntz & Jacob, 2013).

Coping modes are like defense mechanisms. Help an individual to identify the coping mode and recognize it in daily life. It may be easier for an individual to accept the negative effects of a mode after the therapist has acknowledged some positive aspects (Arntz & Jacob, 2013).

8.3   Using Mode Cycle Clash-cards

Roediger developed the mode cycle clash-card for working with couples. With Simeone-DiFrancesco, he has adapted it to understand a mode cycle and to guide the couple in finding a better solution (see Figure 9).

Start with the triggering situation. Try to detect activated schemas and core memories if they are accessible. Then follow the downward arrows to the second line and add the parent voices. Then move to the center part of the second line and record the resulting visible coping mode for each

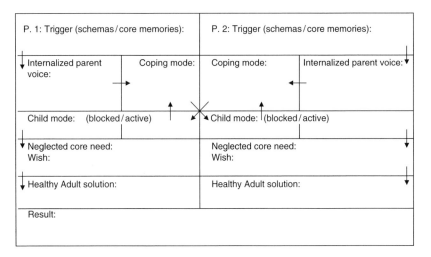

Figure 9 Mode cycle clash-card. Source: ©Roediger and Simeone-DiFrancesco (2013)

person. The next step is to assess the dominant affect (child mode activation) behind this coping mode and then help each partner to unblock the more hidden child mode that is connected to unmet needs. Then find a Healthy Adult strategy. The arrows indicate how the cycle is perpetuated by the mutually evoked emotions of the coping behaviors.

> For example, Amanda had an Angry Child who could not show needs because a Punitive Parent prohibited such expression. She then resorted to self-mutilating behavior (Detached Self-soother). Her treatment involved disarming the Punitive Parent and allowing the Angry Child to express its anger.

The therapist can use clash-cards to educate the couple about their core needs and how those needs can best be met. The way to escape the cycle is to detect the blocked or neglected emotions and relate them to unmet core needs. The following question is always central in ST: "What does this child mode really need? What is being asked for?" After inserting the blocked child mode, follow the arrow downwards and fill in the core need and the related wish. In the line of the Healthy Adult response, note realistic means to fulfill these needs and wishes and state the effects in the bottom line.

The mode cycle clash-card provides goals for the developing work with the couple. The card is especially helpful for couples in understanding triggers and the dynamics of conflict. In this way, they become more empathic to one another. Eventually, the card can be used as part of the partner-to-partner re-parenting process. It can also be used with couples who have intense clashes (described in Section 2.5) by redirecting their anger and introducing a joint point of reference.

The mode mapping model is dimensional, without being categorizing, and allows the therapist to identify behavior on the given dimensions in a specific way. Couples usually use several mode cycles (e.g., starting with an Overcompensator–Overcompensator loop). Then the more vulnerable partner shifts into an avoidant coping mode, leading to a Detached–Overcompensator cycle. Sometimes the roles change and the other partner moves into a Detached Protector mode and you are stuck with a Detached–Detached state. After a while, the formerly detaching partner becomes accusing, cycling back to the original coping mode clash formulation of the cycle's start. The drama between George and Martha in the 1966 movie *Who's Afraid of Virginia Woolf* illustrates this. So you might need several clash-cards to reveal the mutual deficits in understanding and coping style dynamics. Usually, two or three clash-cards cover the relevant mode cycle a couple presents. The clash-card leads to a better understanding of underlying motivations. It is practical and clinically useful, with a natural focus on what is happening and what is needed.

Therapy Tip: ST allows you to separate behavior from schema activations or mode states. The treatment goal is to change behavior, not the basic emotions or automatic thoughts or core beliefs. However, traumatic memories of abusive parents may be deeply entrenched in the brain. When the memories of abuse continue to nag, a more helpful goal may be to label them as "ghosts from the past," to accept the past imprinting, to cope by distancing and letting them go, perhaps through thought diffusion (in acceptance and commitment therapy), and to focus on healthy action.

> Georgie is a survivor of childhood trauma. She began to confront her parental mode messages. Her therapist tried a mindfulness approach: "Just hear the messages as monkey chatter." But Georgie responded, "I won't feel better if I just ignore the negative parental messages. I do better when I debate them with evidence to the contrary."
>
> Her therapist changed tack: "Yes, this is good. I'll join you in debating the messages. 'Pushing back' is new for you and it should work because there's a lot of evidence to counter those messages. I want to help you accumulate all the evidence. One day you might get tired of the debate, being in a court room, and maybe you'll feel strong enough to say 'I don't even need to answer you. I don't need to listen to you. I already know you're talking sh**!'"

Think about using the mode map when guiding therapeutic intervention. *Exercise:* Use a mode cycle clash-card to think about the following case:

Edmund was dragged into couple therapy by his de facto partner, Suzanne. He was a lawyer who had engaged in multiple affairs over the past five years. He had been an over-functioning child in a neglectful home environment. The therapist identified the following modes as relevant: Detached Self-soother, Impulsive Child, Detached Protector, Punitive Parent, and Self-aggrandizer.

How could you use Edmund's competence at work to strengthen his Healthy Adult?

Reflect: Watch *Who's Afraid of Virginia Woolf.* Have a stack of clash-cards and try to analyze the mode sequences.

8.4   Extended Case Example

The mode cycle clash-card can help us understand Tom and Betty. The therapist noted the information in a clash-card on a flip chart.

Tom's perspective. Tom had to stay longer at the office because of some urgent work. He knew he had committed to an appointment with his wife Betty at 8 pm. He watched the time on the clock pass. The project turned out to be much more demanding than he expected. His anxiety grew. Soon it was already after 8 pm. He knew from past experience that if he rang her she would become angry and call him names, so he tried to finish as soon as possible. He arrived home an hour later. The prediction proved correct. After he arrived, Betty started yelling, cursing him, and hitting him in frustration. He escaped to his study and locked the door. Betty continued shouting and hammering at the door. Tom became worried what neighbors might think. He turned on some music, waiting for the storm to pass.

Betty's perspective: Betty had cancelled an appointment with her best friend, Joan, in order to have enough time to prepare the dinner with Tom. Betty was aware of the effect of Tom's work on their marriage, but she enjoyed time with him and she wanted the night to be special. Then Tom did not come home. She had everything timed for 8 pm. For a moment she worried about what might have happened. She tried to phone him, but he was not answering. She texted him but got no reply. She imagined him having fun with his new colleagues, and her anger grew. She started to drink the wine bought for dinner alone, and by 9 pm she was slightly intoxicated. When Tom finally showed up, she reacted in a rage. When he withdrew to his study, she felt worthless. After some desperate minutes, she went to their bedroom, crying herself to sleep.

Here is the clash-card (Figure 10):
First we focus on the triggers for both partners and reveal the underlying schemas and childhood memories we already know from the mode maps of each partner. The therapist might assist with some additional information from prior work. Next, we identify the "voices in the head" (deriving from the parent modes) fueling the emotions. Then we label the coping modes and take a look at the child modes behind them. This allows some self-focus and enables a joint perspective on the problem. Both can agree, to some degree, that they are victims of past experiences and the schemas deriving from them! This helps the couple move out of a blame position. The historical perspective helps them calm down. They begin to understand that they are fighting "ghosts from the past." This identifies a pattern in which both are stuck, which is not simply the result of victimizing behavior by the partner.

This background understanding opens the way to a better solution. The first step is to rediscover the neglected child mode. For Betty, this was the Vulnerable Child mode. As soon as she got in touch with her Vulnerable Child, she could feel her neglected core needs and was able to ask Tom for what she needed. Tom had to get in touch with an Empowered Child to overcome his fears and tell Betty what he needed.

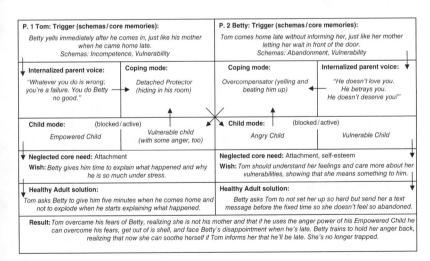

Figure 10 Mode cycle clash-card of Tom and Betty. Source: ©Roediger and Simeone-DiFrancesco (2013)

When the avoiding partner deprives the other of what is needed, it is like wanting to lean on somebody and he or she moves aside: you drop! Most overcompensating individuals hope for someone in a relationship who is strong enough to resist, confront, and tame their anger. The deepest need is for someone they can trust and rely on. So, too, for Betty. She doesn't really hate Tom—she needs him!

The therapist assisted the couple to learn to go through this process step by step until they were able to express their needs and wishes in modest and solution-oriented ways. It helped to be able to shift into Healthy Adult informed behavior to mutually fulfill mutual needs. In the beginning, the therapist had to interrupt strongly when the couple re-engaged in clashing. Think about ways you can slow down the pace by interrupting automatic reactions and giving time to build up new neuronal pathways leading to better solutions. Finally, with the clash-card the couple have to document the result. In the next session, you can work with them to find solutions that might work with another clash.

Once you have demonstrated the use of the mode cycle clash-card, the couple can be encouraged to fill it out for themselves. Homework can be set to follow up on an incident of conflict by filling out their own clash-card. They can both wait to discuss it in the next session. It may also be worthwhile for the couple, when both are more calm, to try to compare their clash-cards between sessions. So, step by step, the couple learn new skills and gains insight into the process of working out problems. Sooner or later they will be able to go through these steps without the aid of a therapist and then later even without the clash-card. In this way the couple experience a positive "problem-solving" schema.

Here is some further advice on using the mode cycle clash-card:

1. *Psycho-education.* You may need to provide psycho-education about identifying and understanding the modes. Think about giving the couple a handout a week before the session when you plan to begin using the maps or cards. Give a variety of examples to explain the modes.

2. *From schemas to modes.* It can be confusing for both therapists and couples already exposed to the early maladaptive schema coping model. There is an overlap of concepts. For example, trying to be perfect from Unrelenting Standards can be put in the Compliant Surrender box because it becomes a strategy to maintain affiliation in the couple relationship. Unrelenting Standards towards others, though, is placed in the overcompensating box because it becomes demanding and aggressive through attempts to control the other.

3. *Overcompensation.* Generally, fighting indicates overcompensation. Grandiose behavior associated with narcissism can also be included here.
4. *Avoidance.* All types of avoiding go in the Detached Protector boxes. A distinction can be made from those who avoid in an active way, so consider Detached Self-soother. Detached Self-soothers may come across as very active.
5. *Parental messages.* Consider what is done with parental messages. If they are believed, that may indicate Compliant Surrender. If the messages are also acted out, it is surrender. If the person believes the messages but detaches, this indicates that the person is in Detached Protector mode. If the person assumes a "one-up" position in relationship to the partner, then the mode state is overcompensating. Interpersonal behavior will reveal underlying beliefs. This is relevant to understanding both causes and interactional sequences.
6. *Basic emotions.* Be careful that the basic emotions do not trickle down into the other boxes. They belong in child mode boxes. Happy Child is an exception because it is protected by a caring Healthy Adult. Try to get in touch with both poles of the emotional spectrum. Go after the blank boxes.
7. *Developmental perspective.* It may be helpful to estimate the age of the child mode when you fill in the box (especially if you sense that the age is very young; see infant modes).
8. *Needs and wants.* You might think about Simeone-DiFrancesco's differentiation of needs and wants. The first are universal and the second tend to be specific.
9. *Healthy Adult.* Understand the role of Healthy Adult in integration. Use Roediger's simple model, which specifies four core needs of the adult:
   * attachment
   * assertiveness
   * self-esteem
   * happiness.

Compared to the needs Young describes, the need for limit setting is missing here. Adults should usually have internalized limits, so there is no general need for further external limit setting (although traffic offences, say, might suggest something else).

Once you identify a need, consider what behaviors from Healthy Adult might be helpful. This may need some guidance from you, at least initially, as some people have no idea what Happy Adult might look like. Make suggestions and see how it feels for the person.

Caution: Sometimes a personality-disordered client will nominate a goal that that is clearly not healthy. The goal will be narcissistic, avoidant, or whatever. Then you have to go back to the drawing board and work more with the motivational modes backstage (i.e., the parent modes) to detect the subtle influence of not yet discovered and reappraised beliefs. You might wait to fill in this box. Finally, you might also try another strategy and suggest tentatively, "Let's try that out and see how it works, then you can re-evaluate it. This is what Healthy Adult does: it's flexible, learns from experience and is open to re-evaluating."

People who strictly avoid behavioral experiments may be in Detached Protector mode, which has to be empathically confronted.

> Alex was a foreman in a building company. He was very demanding on his workers, often exploding in Bully and Attack or berating in Punitive Parent. A labor inspector found that his behavior had been bullying. He was required by company policy to attend counseling. His therapist suggested that he list ways he could listen more to the concerns of his workers, but he came back with a lack of insight: "I know what's needed. Why should I waste time listening to complaints?"
>
> It was a struggle, but his therapist eventually encouraged Alex to try some behavioral experiments with delaying his immediate response, counting to 3, and then asking, "What do you think is important?" The idea was to encourage him to pretend he was in Healthy Adult and see if it felt different from his usual Self-aggrandizer or Bully and Attack.

Reflect: Can you try out the idea of encouraging a client to pretend to be in Healthy Adult mode?

8.5 Advantages of Mode Maps

The dimensional and dynamic mode model is relevant. Roediger outlined the following:

1. *Neurobiology.* The linking of child modes to emotional and physiological activations is closer to neurobiological models.
2. *Parent modes.* Parent modes are understood in terms of toxic messages or a negative "voice in the head." This makes it easier to use a range of techniques, such as disputing the voice (Beck, 1963, using a cognitive behavioral therapy model) and acceptance and commitment therapy's thought diffusion or mindfulness. There is also chair-work in ST.

3. *Distancing.* However, it is likely that distancing from internal modes is more effective than fighting them. They are "hardwired" and will reoccur. People might get disappointed when they cannot manage to "fight" them successfully.

4. *What is revealed.* The map can reveal deficits and excesses in the coping modes. Following the arrows back behind an empty coping mode field leads directly to the blocked basic emotions and forbidden cognitions. This will guide your therapeutic interventions.

5. *The metacognitive treatment goal.* The goal is to change behavior and social emotions, not the basic emotions or automatic thoughts. Those have to be accepted, reappraised, and sometimes let go. At times, use Healthy Adult as a "wise mind." If you can get Healthy Adult to act, the results may be beneficial.

6. *Overall view.* The mode map gives the couple an overall view of the full spectrum of basic emotions, balanced appraisals, and coping behavior. So it is not the therapist but the mode map that confronts the individual, and this assists the couple to shift to observer perspective. This "joint referencing perspective" (Siegel, 1999) is also helpful in clashes between client and therapist during the sessions.

7. *Child needs.* It helps to answer the question, "What does the child really need?"

The following is an example of using acceptance strategies to deal with a mode, showing how a metacognitive approach looks in ST:

> Frances had difficulties with her Demanding Parent mode. The internalized voices (mostly from her mother) included, "Your house must be spotless. You're not trying hard enough at work. You don't deserve a promotion. You must be a perfect mother ..."
>
> She tried to dispute these voices but reported, "I feel bogged down in the fight with them. And I lack energy to overcome them." She found it better to take an acceptance stance, mindfully observe, and not judge (either the voices or herself): "The demanding messages are there, but I accept them as if I were watching cars go past me on the road. I visualize myself in a roadside coffee shop, enjoying a cappuccino and watching the traffic. Then it doesn't seem to matter and I don't have to obey the dictates of my parental mode."

This technique from acceptance and commitment therapy (Hayes et al., 1999) is called "thought diffusion." It separates thoughts from emotions.

Exercise: Here are some ideas to help to visualize modes in homework. Draw a representation of common modes (Simpson, 2012, p. 158). Use a large piece of paper and represent the interaction of couple modes visually. Look through a stack of popular magazines. Find and cut out pictures that represent the most common modes. Label them as a couple and make a relationship poster.

8.6   Tim and Carol: Another Extended Example

Mode mapping is integral to case conceptualization and treatment in ST-C. Often the clash is on the level of behaviors—not intrinsic personality attributes or needs. This can lead to a dominant cycle or multiple cycles in the couple relationship. Indeed, mode maps provide mutual understanding as well as suggesting helpful ways forward. The following extended case had an individual and a couple therapist involved.

> Tim, a coal miner in his early 60s, had a history of being abusive to Carol, his wife. Alarmingly, this included repeated experiences of domestic violence. Carol was dependent in the relationship, saying, "I love him. I know I have to forgive him." Tim had been seeing an individual schema therapist for about two years. However, driven by his own self-soothing needs, he persisted in frequent, often daily, unwanted sexualized touching of Carol. This proved to be retraumatizing for her, which stopped any possibility of growth in trust. Tim periodically felt self-disgust and remorse, but his behaviors continued.
>
> It became clear in marital therapy that Tim had a history of being subjected to anger as a child. The marital therapist suspected that Tim was emotionally and physically abused, based on his sister's recitation to Tim's wife of the family history, although this was hard for him or the individual therapist to really see due to his minimization. Individual therapy helped Tim to control overt violence, but there was still a legacy of dysfunctional behaviors.
>
> The individual therapist validated that Tim was emotionally deprived and made progress with limited re-parenting, but the sexualized behaviors continued. One day, when Tim's wife described how his family was treating him, the marital therapist noticed a huge disconnect between his usual presentation in a "happy" state and the emotional reality of his life. This allowed an important connection. She saw that Tim was in fact a victim of severe control and abuse, and used this in her conceptualization. Tim was avoiding this reality. This legacy of abuse, past and present, would contribute to him feeling bad about himself and desperate for soothing. He was driven to pursue this illusory comfort in a sexualized way. Tim recognized that, at some level, all this was self-defeating. Like many men, Tim used sex as a pathway to feel intimacy. Women usually need intimacy to feel sexual desire.

This perception of the marital therapist created a key conceptualization shift, from a man who had trouble with emotional deprivation, limits, and impulsivity, to a man who actually went into a Compliant Surrender mode out of extreme anxiety over impending rejection and hurt, and from there into a Detached Protector mode of "acceptance" and then to an artificial and detached self-soothing focus on only the positive aspects of his life. This acceptance was of no benefit, since it was essentially a denial of reality. It paralyzed his Healthy Adult mode from taking any protective action towards his inner Vulnerable Child. In relating to his family and mother-in-law he was continually being revictimized, although with little cognitive awareness of this reality. The Healthy Adult was too weak to provide self-soothing or be appropriately self-protective (see Figure 11 for Tim's mode map).

Mode-mapping his coping behaviors in the bottom two left boxes of Compliant Surrender and Detached Protector Modes, it suddenly became clear to Tim why he kept acting out. He saw the cycle of moving into a third coping mode of determined Self-soothing by his wife and Overcompensation/control to get what he "wanted" with desperate

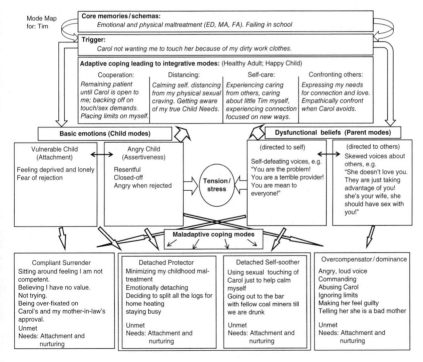

Figure 11 Tim's mode map

intensity. It was as if a person, dying of thirst, thought there was a drop of water on his tongue, only to discover again and again that the water was only a mirage.

In two years of therapy, without the mode map, Tim had no clarity about what was driving his behaviors. In minutes, the mode map crystallized it for him. It also enabled him to see the triggers, identify the child mode, identify the voice in his head with the parental blaming/controlling voice, and see how he fell into a predictable pattern in the lower boxes on the map—coping mechanisms that encompassed behavioral patterns.

This opened up an entirely new and more positive self-appraisal. No longer was he acting out of being defective, weak, or bad. Now he could recognize the reality of his abuse—so he had to accept it and refocus. The option of Healthy Adult was now a possibility. His Healthy Adult validated how miserable he really felt, and was ready to protect him and show him respect. Eventually, he could begin to re-parent himself, which in turn drained off the "driven-ness" in his overcompensation behaviors towards his wife (irritability, anger, raised voice, controlling behavior, and intimidation) and his Detached Self-soothing use of sexualized behaviors. The happy ending is that Tim took this new information to his individual schema therapist, who worked cooperatively in her own caring way with the couple therapist in the new case conceptualization. At last he could feel the care that was there for him.

The mode cycle clash-card enabled a clarification and shift in the conceptualization. It facilitated a different therapeutic approach. Notice the differences between the two case conceptualizations. The previous was:

Tim was emotionally deprived and got triggered in lonely feelings, going into Lonely Child (Vulnerable Child) mode. He acted impulsively (without any clear understanding of why), and he needed better empathy for what his wife was feeling about his off-putting behavior. This deviant self-soothing behavior needed to be *better controlled*. By limited re-parenting, the individual therapist could help him with acceptance of the situation with the wife, who was also wounded and needed to regain trust and confidence in him. So the conceptualization here is, in brief: Lonely Child turns into Angry Child acting out impulsively. Re-parent to comfort and increase emotional empathy and sensitivity. Result: Tim is calmed down for a while and acts briefly with more restraint and stops groping his wife for a short period. He quickly relapses.

By contrast, with the conceptualization yielded by using the mode cycle clash-card (see Figure 12, based on Tim's individual mode map in the background), the intervention becomes quite different.

Mode Cycle Clashcard
©Roediger and Simeone-DiFrancesco, 2013

Tim: Trigger (Schemas/Core memories): Argument with my sister, Karen, criticizing my wife's cake and complaining we had bad manners. *Schemas: Mistrust/Abuse, Emot. Depriv., Subjugation*		**Carol:** Trigger (Schemas/Core memories): *Sexualized or unwanted touching by Tim, memories of intimidations by brother and being raped by Tim. Schemas: Mistrust/Abuse, Emot. Deprivation, Subjugation*	
Internalized Parent Voice: *You should be nice and apologize for both of you! You're a disgusting dirty coal miner, and not a good husband or father. You're the problem. You will stay alone. You are not worth being respected!*	Coping mode: *Subjugation towards Karen and later forcing Carol to touch him* (Overcompensation)	Coping mode: *First going along (Subjugation), later withdrawing (Detached protector)*	Internalized Parent Voice: *Be nice, but never trust him. He doesn't respect you. All he wants is sex like all males. Watch out and get away from him! Don't tick him off!*
Child Mode (blocked/active):		Child Mode (active/blocked):	
Vulnerable and lonely Child	*Angry and needy Child*	*Vulnerable and anxious Child*	*Angry Child*
Neglected core need: *Attachment and nurturing* Wish: *Being soothed by body contact.*		Neglected core need: *Control and Self-esteem* Wish: *Tim respects her and keeps the limits*	
Healthy Adult solution: *Instead of assaulting Carol physically I will try to be aware of my true needs and express them verbally. I will try to be patient until Carol wants physical contact too.*		Healthy Adult solution: *Instead of withdrawing automatically I will try to get in touch with my underlying anger and use my power to set clear verbal limits towards Tim; Knowing I am safe today I will try to be more open and care a bit for his Vulnerable Child.*	
Result: *It does not always work but I feel less driven by my greediness knowing where it comes from. It takes a lot af courage to address my needs towards Carol.*		Result: *I feel much safer now knowing I am allowed to set clear limits. Being less anxious allows me to open up towards Tim. Beside that I find him more attractive (sexually too!).*	

Figure 12   Tim and Carol's mode cycle clash-card. Source: ©Roediger and Simeone-DiFrancesco (2013)

Tim had no awareness of his trigger. Collateral information from his wife helped. Tim realized that he was "disrespected and abused" in his family of origin, and his wife's distancing only served to solidify the voice in his head. This parent mode would usually conclude that he was unworthy and just a dirty coal miner.

Through the use of limited re-parenting, the couple therapist was able to be a strong and empathically confronting "parent" who "cut the crap" and helped him see the reality of what was actually happening in his life. This felt liberating to Tim. The internalized Parent Mode directed at him had been protecting Tim from feeling the abuse, especially the emotional aspects, that he had been dismissing and minimizing all his life.

Then the therapist developed the mode map with him to chart what happened when this abuse occurs. Why did he dismiss it? Here the mode map shows its robustness in creating a much more accurate conceptualization of what is really at the heart of this repeating pattern for Tim. In the child mode box, Vulnerable Child was quickly identified as being extremely anxious. Parent mode threatened disconnection and blame should he speak up or not comply. Tim automatically pulled in all past memories of what happened in the family system when he or others dared challenge his sister. It always turned around on him, with his parents joining in as well. Tim moved down to the bottom left box of behaviors/coping mechanisms and, surrendering, did what was demanded of him and accepted the ridicule, the foul language, the horrible blaming, and the lack of recognition. When triggers occurred, he quickly went from this internalization and Surrender to a "happy" Detached Protector mode and used his perceived "yoga" resources to accept the situation. He then got even more stuck, and when the intensity of the lonely miserable feelings welled up too high, he then compulsively acted out in overcompensatory outbursts.

We call this kind of mode flipping an "anger/guilt see-saw" because people having it show exactly this typical (and predictable) movement: driven by the Vulnerable Child and Punitive Parent voices, they surrender so much that sooner or later the child mode activation moves over to the Angry Child pole, giving way to outside-directed Punitive Parent voices such as "I have done so much for others; now it's up to them to give something back!" facilitating an overcompensation outburst. Soon after this acting out, the Punitive Parent voices turn inside again, blaming the individual and activating fear, and the person flips back to an exaggerated submissive coping again, and so forth.

How do you escape this? Try to open the door to be in touch with the energy of Angry Child to avoid excessive submission. In this way, strive for more balanced and assertive behavior.

Revealing the "guilt/anger see-saw" (you can label it both ways, unless it is a cycle) called for an entirely different modeling of Healthy Adult.

> The therapist helped Tim focus on his upset feelings, and validated rather than dismissed the hurt and anger striving to protect him. She helped Tim see and feel the internal turmoil, and explain just how "yucky" it felt. She then helped him see how the internalized parent voices pushed him down into the submissive coping boxes on the internalizing, left pole, coupled with the past memory activation and the inability of a child mode to handle such a situation without a Healthy Adult. The defenseless child was then given the therapist's help through limited re-parenting by protecting and objecting to such abuse, and not standing for it any longer. Tim was educated about the Healthy Adult, which can help to keep Vulnerable Child out of situations of abuse, and instead advocate for self-respect.
>
> The therapist showed Tim how he needed to soothe himself in a healthy way, without being detached, by giving himself what he actually needed, including protection, validation, and respect. This helped Tim to channel the anger feelings in a more constructive way instead of defeating them first

and acting out later in an externalizing way, followed by guilt feelings again on the see-saw. Tim began to see how the avoidant coping mode, which functioned as Detached Protector, would then move into Overcompensator Control mode towards his wife, and then into Detached Self-soother by his addictive acting out. The sexual groping and aggressive push for contact was an unhealthy temporary "solution" that only made his emotional deprivation worse and did not remove the source of the pain.

Tim also experienced, from the therapy with his wife, validation of the abuse she saw from his family of origin, which was a type of re-parenting. She also began to affirm, empathize, and urge him to protect himself. Carol found in Tim's sister a great confidante to help her in the more difficult times, so she felt more protected as well. She pledged that she would continue to support him in the face of the abusive members of his family. This shone a light into the pit of his darkness. She also told Tim that she loved him but would not tolerate his coping behavior, which did nothing for either of them.

Carol drew close to him as she said this and touched his hand. He melted. He saw that this was not because he was so defective. He just kept failing in his efforts because he had no healthy coping mechanisms to offset the intensity that feeling abused was creating in himself, and to offset the parent voice in his head. The wife actually allied with Tim, opposing and blocking the effect of the parent voice. She was taught by the therapist how she needed to target what this voice was saying to him.

In this case, the therapeutic intervention was different. The mode cycle clash-card facilitated the change in conceptualization and led to interventions that affected all four: the couple and the two therapists. The mode map enlightened the therapeutic process and suggested an effective way to work.

8.7   Progress Mapped Out

ST-C has the capacity to target unmet needs and past wounds. This may be unique to our approach to couple therapy because it provides both a conceptual framework and powerful techniques for change. We go further than simply identifying a cycle, dealing with bad behavior and changing destructive negative communications and interactions. In ST, the target relates to specific memories behind the cycles. The art is in unlocking this information at an experiential level and being able to transmit that to a partner whom you have positioned to become receptive. Most couples are sincere in trying to obtain help, so eventually providing this target in such a clear fashion becomes the key to restoring their relationship. All this takes considerable preparation and work, but once experienced by the couple, who have made progress, it is wonderful to see them begin to give to each other again. This reconnects them with what established their relationship in the beginning.

The therapist can help an individual to re-parent him- or herself and experience what it is to have a safe relationship that meets needs. ST-C is all about "co-parenting": co-parenting of the person's inner child mode by the therapist and the partner's Healthy Adult; co-parenting of spouse to spouse, partner to partner, in both directions, reshaping one's inner experiences. After some progress, individuals will begin to feel what it is like to have an unmet need finally met. The therapist assists at a number of points in this process by limited re-parenting with an individual, helping the person to re-parent themselves. Later, the couple mutually re-parent each other and experience what it is to have a safe relationship. This rediscovering of the "emotional fire" between the partners is often a deeper experience than the couple had before. They can find an emotional connection that creates a limited dependency with another human for meeting needs, yet at the same time is completely respectful and builds individuation and resilience. It also builds the capacity to transfer this experience of nurturing their own inner self into connecting with their partner. ST-C goes beyond cognitive therapy because it addresses the emotional basis of the relationship.

This emotion-based learning experience with the therapist becomes a bridge to a healthy connection with the partner, as well as a positive relationship commitment with one's inner self to meet one's own needs. Actually walking a person through this "road map to fulfill an unmet need" eventually puts them on the right track to desire and to obtain a true healing of their relationship with a partner with whom they have already invested time, and even endured rejection, emotional hurt, and pain. Who would want to waste that? All of the past—hurt, misunderstanding, and even abuse—can be transformed into gain, as two now-bonding partners struggle to conquer and transcend past negativities.

On the other hand, what would result if unmet needs were set aside or foolishly endured? To merely escape and not deal with one's own past dynamics ensures that either the painful pattern of unmet needs will break one's current relationship and follow, still unfulfilled, to the next, or sadly remain as the status quo with the current partner.

Therapy Tip: It is often helpful in a session to have the couple stand up with the therapist to give their view in a third-person perspective while looking down on the chairs below. This introduces a different perspective and may encourage a joint perspective on the problem. Standing makes it much easier to distance from the activated schemas and shift emotionally into a solution-focus by getting in touch with the core needs, rather than being lost in former "battles."

Advanced Therapy Tip: Think about the modes as "vibrating" with the influence of childhood experiences and messages, archaic coping styles, and present emotional reactions. What you see in a session is the present tense of a lot of past tense. Indeed, you can infer backwards, somewhat like a psychoanalyst interpreting transference. Modes are a window to the past when you acknowledge the schema background behind them.

8.8   A Road Map

Using these ST resources, the therapist can devise a personally customized "road map," offer it to the couple, and with their informed consent proceed to treatment. The therapist determines how to navigate to achieve goals with the couple. Simeone-DiFrancesco (2012) has recommended the use of a battery of inventories. These help to identify schemas and modes that can be linked to the couple's history. Presenting symptoms can be incorporated into a traditional treatment plan and informed consent to treatment. However, under the treatment goals the clinician can specify a case conceptualization for each partner with a mode or a schema they would like to highlight for the person. In this way, the individual is involved with the treatment planning phase, and the plan also serves as a point of psycho-education about schemas and modes.

THERAPIST: "Sally, we want here to weaken the Demanding Parent mode speaking in your head. This is an echo from how your mother treated you. You see how you scored this here on the SMI 1.1? Do you agree with this being one of your treatment goals? Also, we may want have the goal of being able to empathize with Nick's Vulnerable Child mode. This is why he gets locked-up and unable to respond to you the way you need. If we can understand him and feel with him, perhaps we can help him become stronger and be more there for you. How do you feel about that goal?"

Therapy Tip: This can be put in writing for the couple. You might also offer a copy of the treatment plan. This is not only good ethically, but it engages the couple and keeps them on track with a road map that they agree to travel on together.

Summary

In this chapter we have introduced some important tools, including the dimensional and dynamic mode model, mode maps, and mode cycle clashcards. These have been illustrated with the extended cases of Tom and Betty, and Tim and Carol. We again emphasized the importance of a comprehensive schema case conceptualization and gave some guidance on how progress might be mapped out.

ST-C provides an opportunity for a dynamic clinical understanding that includes developmental origins, past trauma, and emotional focus, but with the clarity of cognitive therapy. This is further explored and developed with interventions in Chapter 9.

9

Interventions in Couple Treatment

Progress in ST usually proceeds from cognitive, to experiential, and finally to more behavioral interventions (Farrell & Shaw, 2012). In this chapter, we look at a range of interventions commonly practiced in ST, including imagery work with limited re-parenting, mode chair-work, couple re-parenting through the use of language, and behavioral pattern breaking.

The couple will usually arrive for a session emotionally activated. This is an opportunity for an emotional focus. Young (2012) recommended that therapists look for a prototypical conflict in the couple relationship. Usually, this is an example of a *repeating* conflict. A recent incident in the couple relationship will often become the focus of a session. Initially, allow the argument to continue for some minutes (until you detect the mode cycle), because this will indicate their way of mismanaging conflict and display coping modes. ST tends to begin with more of an emphasis on feelings and empathy than on problem solving (Kellogg & Young, 2006). Eventually, problem solving is based on case conceptualization using mode maps and mode cycle clash-cards, followed by emotional reconnection.

9.1 The Role of Empathy

The role of empathy is important. Another contribution of ST-C is that it clearly *defines and separates the behavior from the person* (i.e., the child modes and their needs) by asserting that acceptance has priority over agreement. Acceptance leading to agreement must travel over a bridge of mutual empathy. The empathic understanding of the therapist leads

Schema Therapy with Couples: A Practitioner's Guide to Healing Relationships, First Edition.
Chiara Simeone-DiFrancesco, Eckhard Roediger, and Bruce A. Stevens.
© 2015 John Wiley & Sons, Ltd. Published 2015 by John Wiley & Sons, Ltd.
Companion website: www.wiley.com/go/difrancesco/schematherapywithcouples

the way. This experience of being understood helps the couple to give it to each other.

> An ST-trained social worker confronted Ricky's binge-drinking behavior. He linked it to emotional deprivation in his client's childhood. Ricky was able to avoid taking it personally and said, "Yes, I get that. I go into Detached Self-soother mode instead of taking the needs of my Vulnerable Child seriously. Just seeing this means that I have shifted into Healthy Adult." His therapist was able to validate this insight and not worry as much about a therapeutic break in their working alliance.

The therapist was able to confront unhealthy behaviors while at the same time being empathically understanding through linking current coping modes with childhood origins.

In ST-C, the therapist and the couple stand side by side, looking on the mode map, identifying the current behavior as a coping mode, and looking at the parent voices and child mode activations "backstage." It helps to look from a joint reference perspective (Siegel 1999). This experience nudges the couple out of a defensive stalemate. The limited re-parenting attitude encourages each to give their partner opportunities to grow. It is easier to find a healthier self in the relationship once each recognizes that caring does not mean agreeing with or accepting the offensive behavior itself.

9.2   Imagery Work

Imagery work in therapy is like driving a Porsche. It is powerful, and can surprise and even overwhelm an inexperienced therapist. However, the power is in the potential impact for change. Affect is quickly engaged. Roadblocks are bypassed. And it is a way of gaining access and potentially changing childhood memories that profoundly affect adult relationships. The main goal is to help an individual establish new emotional patterns (Arntz & Jacob, 2013).

Reflect: Think about how you address emotional learning in therapy rather than simply trying to change patterns of thinking.

Imagery work is now more common in shorter-term therapies, such as cognitive behavioral therapy (Hackman et al., 2011). It has been found to be highly effective in the treatment of trauma with imaginal exposure (Creamer et al., 2007). Imagery work is also important in ST and can be easily adapted for couple work.

Therapy Tip: Start with a very basic visualization, such as a safe place or an unemotional childhood memory, and practice it with a number of the people you see. In this way, you will soon build up your confidence.

Advanced Therapy Tip: If a client finds it hard to create a safe place image (but is emotionally stable), then work to strengthen positive feelings at the end of imagery work or rescripting. In this way, rescripting can become a substitute for initial safe-place imagery (Arntz & Jacob, 2013). If a client tends to be flooded by emotions (like some borderline personality-disordered or traumatized individuals), you should work on their ability to stabilize and soothe themselves in individual sessions first. Farrell et al. (2012) suggested using the image of a safe bubble because this proved to work well in group ST with borderline patients.

9.3   Starting Imagery Rescripting

The past is not past in ST. Through imagery work, significant events are made present in therapy. This can be done in a variety of ways:

1. *Memory* therapist: "Vikki, we want to heal some of those past hurts you spoke about. Is it okay that we proceed in a way that you first image being safe, and then we leave that nice spot and deal with the pain? We'll come back to the safe spot later, I assure you. [Therapist continues with client agreement.] In the first session, when I was asking you about your family history, you said that you were rejected by your peer group when you were 11 years old. Do you remember that?" Vikki: "Just like it was yesterday." Therapist: "Can you see it visually?"
2. *Affect bridge* therapist: "Vikki, I see that you're upset. Can you identify what you're feeling now?" Vikki: "I feel sad and alone." Therapist: "As you feel those feelings, sadness and being alone, can you recall a time as a child when you felt the same way? Let yourself float back in time to your childhood. What picture comes up?" [see Weertman, 2012, p. 104].
3. *Somatic bridge* therapist: "Where are you feeling that tension now? Yes, I mean in your body?" Vikki: "I feel really tight across my chest." Therapist: "Can you member a time, perhaps long ago, when you felt the same way? Let yourself float back in time. What picture comes up?"

To Do: Before doing imagery work it is helpful to have visualized a safe place with your client. You should also establish a safe person (which could be you, the therapist) whom they have experienced as protective and nurturing. This person can be introduced to the memory to meet the needs of the Vulnerable Child who is often evoked in this work.

These techniques help to elicit an image from childhood. You can enhance this by saying something like, "If you were holding a video camera, what would have been recorded? Describe the scene in as much detail as you can recall. Include all your senses. Start with a picture. Then let the picture start moving like a film."

It is important to check Subjective Units of Distress Scale (SUDS) levels and try to keep the person being treated in a therapeutic window of about 40–80/100. In imagery work, their SUDS score is raised by asking them to keep their eyes closed and describe what they see in the present tense. ("I'm standing in the living room. My father is in a rage, throwing things around. He's shouting at my mother.") If the SUDS level goes too high, first stop the "video" by pushing the "pause button":

THERAPIST   "Everything is on hold right now. You have the remote control in your hand. Nothing happens unless you push the start button again. You have full control. What does the child feel? What would be helpful? Can you picture yourself entering the scene as the adult person you are now?"

Note that the situation becomes safer if the therapist enters the scene together with the client, so that therapist and client watch the scene standing side by side. This creates the opportunity for the therapist to immediately intervene if the client is not able to adequately rescript the scene.

THERAPIST: "What do you feel now, as an adult, coming in and watching the scene? [Eventually the anger gets stronger if the therapist describes the scene in some clear words.] What do you feel now—in your body? [The client needs to feel the anger power before they will be able to impeach the opponents in the picture.] What do you want to say or do now, using your anger power?"

After impeaching the offenders, ask for the feelings for the child. They should be a kind of compassion. Out of that feeling: "What do you want to say or do now to care for the child? How does the child react? What else does the child need?" And finally: "How do you feel now at the end of this exercise. How about your body feelings? Can you feel the difference?"

If the SUDS levels do not go down, instruct the person to open their eyes and talk in the past tense. If it is too overwhelming, let them tell you exactly what they had for breakfast. Or give up visual work and return to grounding: "What three things do you see now in my office? What three things can you feel? What three sounds can you hear? What can you smell?" These are grounding techniques. In the next step you can combine that with walking around with them a bit in your office. Remember: changing sensory input induces attractor changes.

> Danny remembered a scene when she tried to tell her mother that her uncle (her mother's younger brother) had been inappropriately touching her. This was dismissed, "Oh, it's just Uncle Terry being affectionate." Danny was devastated and felt that she was completely unprotected in childhood. Initially in therapy she rated her SUDS score at 50/100. She went back to the memory through her safe place and was surprised that her score quickly went to over 80/100, so her therapist had her abandon the image and return to her safe place.
>
> Danny identified Ms. Smith, her primary school teacher, as her support person. This time when she returned to her memory, her therapist had her visualize Ms. Smith entering the scene and intervening on her behalf.
>
> Ms. Smith said to her mother, "What Danny is saying is important. She's only 10 years old and it takes a lot of courage to tell you this. You need to believe her and act to protect her when Uncle Terry is visiting your family. Unless you do this, you are failing your responsibility as a parent!" The therapist then did rescripting to lead to a better outcome.

Arntz & van Genderen (2010) have provided an outline for imagery work. They described stages after usually starting with safe place imagery: a) seeing an original childhood event as a child and entering into the emotions; b) rescripting the event by protecting the child and meeting the child's needs, initially by the therapist entering the scene; and c) if there is enough Healthy Adult in the person, entering the imagery as an adult and carrying out rescripting themselves. It is very important to make the rescripting experience a success. This is why Arntz and van Genderen (2010) suggested the therapist doing the rescripting first. In Arntz and Weertman (1999, pp. 725–726) there is a good example of a therapist intervening to process the childhood memory in a more adaptive way. Now the process will be explained in more detail.

There has been some misunderstanding about what the term *re-parenting* means in ST. The basic assumption is that people who have experienced deficits in parenting "must experience positive parenting before they can learn to do this for themselves ... the goal of ST is autonomy, so this early focus on the therapist doing the re-parenting is ultimately replaced by a developed and strengthened Healthy Adult mode where an individual performs these functions" (Farrell & Shaw, 2012, p. 17). Many people with personality problems have never had the experience of being adequately cared for. The therapist initially models a functioning parent until the person has learned to "take over." You might consider setting up a "task force" between you as therapist and your client's Healthy Adult so you can decide who does the rescripting in the given situation. In a sense, this becomes "co-parenting," as you and the Healthy Adult mode of the person re-parent the child mode until the Healthy Adult is able to function autonomously.

Always think about what is needed in imagery work. It is usually helpful to have the client and therapist enter the scene standing side by side. The therapist intervenes first and then asks the client how they feel watching the therapist. What outcome do they want? Sometimes it is necessary to spend time "standing" at the edge of the scene and watching it from a third-person perspective to give the client enough time to become aware of their basic emotion (such as constructive anger). If the client basically agrees to the therapist's intervention, the "baton" is handed over to the client with the therapist assisting. The client is asked to repeat the sequence in their own words, speaking directly to the significant other. During the rescripting procedure (either by the client or by the therapist), you can monitor thoughts related to doubt or guilt within the client (such as, "Don't be so hard. It's your father. He's been maltreated as a child himself. He only wanted your best," etc.). Then you can label them Punitive Parent voices. It is hard, if not impossible, to work with these voices with the imagery rescripting technique, so try to put the voices aside. You can also work on the voices using chair-work in one of the next sessions.

Therapy Tip: Watch your client's level of conviction about their belief in the "truth" of the Punitive or Demanding Parent voices. You might rupture your therapeutic alliance if you rescript against their convictions.

9.4   Impeachment

It is helpful to work with the constructive anger of your client. This is a potential energy for change. However, sometimes a person may get stuck in an anxious, submissive child mode. There are ways to address this. It can be helpful to ask them to enter the scene as a Healthy Adult.

Therapy Tip: Do not let the client try to rescript the image unless they perceive that their anger is empowering their Healthy Adult in the imagery, since the confrontation of the abusive person may fail. If the client feels too inferior (e.g., a woman standing up against her father), in a first step you can "blow her up" to 10 feet tall, enabling her to look down onto the father (as he did onto the child in the first part of the imagery).

If the client remains in submissive coping mode, leave them in the child's perspective, watching you doing the rescripting. This makes sense in very traumatized or low-functioning clients.

Think about how you can use the Angry Child within your client. This is promising if the client shows outbursts of anger on other occasions, proving that this power is accessible within them. It makes sense to unblock this anger and give the client an experience of how their anger can be used a constructive way.

Following a "third-wave" approach, we do not dispute the contradictory Punitive Parent voices blocking the anger. There are two major ways to proceed: extension and substitution.

In *extension*, the therapist asks the client to step into somebody else's shoes and watch the scene from a different perspective:

> Tom was often hit by his father. However, even the memory of this did not bring up anger for him, so his therapist used the extension technique by bringing into imagery Tom's best friend, Peter. The therapist said, "Hello, Peter. Thank you for coming in to help us. When you see your friend Tom in this imagery being treated badly, how do you feel?" Tom was able to finally get in touch with anger through the reaction of his friend in the imagery.

However, some clients are so withdrawn that they might not have a best friend. In such instances, this technique can be extended to figures from fairytales or movies.

In *substitution*, you replace the child in the imagery with a known child, such as one of the client's offspring, and ask the client, "If you see your son, Brian, treated so badly in the image, what do you feel?" This will almost always bring out a vicarious anger. This activates the brain's "hard-wiring" of protection and empathy for offspring. If a client has no children, you might use a related child or a child of friends.

Unless constructive anger (Greenberg, 2002) is unblocked, the client will not be able to escape the "dungeon of submission." This is why we spend time on this crucial procedure to reinforce the client using adaptive anger for self-assertiveness under the control of the Healthy Adult.

The client should not be responsible for caring for significant others in imagery. Many clients were "parentified children" (see Chapter 4 for details). In the rescripting, we prefer to leave them to the care of professionals (e.g., psychiatric care for a depressed mother, inpatient treatment for a drug addict parent, or a jail for an abusive person). You might affirm the reality that the abusive situation will not return and that the child is safe now. The role of the Healthy Adult is not to care for the others, but for the child!

Therapy Tip: Do not forget to rate SUDS. Do not worry if the SUDS score is elevated if it was high at the beginning of the intervention. A significant reduction is a satisfying result. Generally, SUDS scores will not drop further until you take care of the child.

Another Tip: If a perpetrator appears to be very overwhelming, include police or military figures into the imagery to guarantee the superiority of the "client–therapist task force." Caution: watch the use of guns, because this can be frightening to some clients.

9.5   Caring for the Child

In a session, when you get space from parental modes, you can ask the client how they feel. This will lead to child modes. If you detect doubts, then see whether they are traces of parental modes (especially Punitive Parent). It is a good sign, after rescripting, if the experience of change goes deep (changing body feelings). This might be described as feeling "right and strong" about the rescripted image. Smucker and Dancu (2005) recommend that impeaching parental voices be done in front of the child mode(s). Often, Vulnerable Child has to witness such a process of disempowering the parental modes to gain trust in the Healthy Adult (and, once more, the therapist).

Therapy Tip: Remember that many clients are identified with the internalized images of significant others. The reappraisal part of the imagery work weakens this identification and supports trusting one's own Healthy Adult instead of ongoing submission to internalized parents.

Advanced Therapy Tip: If the Vulnerable Child is very anxious and weak, you can make their perspective safe by placing them behind a thick wall of glass for them to watch the scene.

To Do: Identify some healthy parent messages for the following case examples:

> You are doing imagery work with Mary. One of her formative experiences occurred when she was 12 years old. She saw her parents argue. When intoxicated, her father hit her mother and then stormed out of the house, never to return. She was raised by her mother as a single parent.

What healthy parent messages would Mary need to hear? Think about her needs for understanding, being protected, not blaming herself, and identifying what she needed as a 12-year-old.

Robert was molested by his Uncle John for a number of years. When he was 9 years old, he found the courage to tell his mother, who did not believe him and told him, "It's just your uncle being friendly." What messages would Robert need to hear as a 9-year-old?

It is important to explore the effect of such visual work. The image might change, becoming more distant, the emotional distress might be reduced (with a lower SUDS score), or both. Graham Taylor (ISST Couples Special Interest Group) has emphasized the desired outcome of holding a more adaptive view of the situation and the self after such work.

Charlie did imagery on an incident of bullying in the school yard. He felt very helpless, and his therapist encouraged him to visually shrink the bullies and age them to be decrepit old men. Charlie felt more empowered through this visualization. He also came to a more realistic view of his past: "I can't really change what happened. But I can change my relationship to the incident and how I see myself. I no longer feel 'under it'."

Memory is remarkably plastic. It is surprising, but imagery rescripting a past event can actually weaken a formerly overwhelming memory. But the essence of imagery rescripting is not changing history. We try to change the meaning, not the memory. This phase is really about the needs of the child in the situation.

An important goal is to reappraise the situation from a Healthy Adult perspective and then care for the child. The new message is: "They never had the right to treat me (as a child) this way. They just had the power to do so. But this wasn't right at any time!" This fundamental shift in the meaning of the old scene unblocks resources. It is possible to write a new story rather than argue about the past.

It is less important to encourage clients to talk about old experiences. We would rather support them in fighting for their needs today.

Therapy Tip: Think about continuing the imagery work by doing a role play with current partners, especially if relational skills need to be learned or practiced.

Visualization has been adapted to working with couples (Atkinson, 2012). Essentially:

1. *Identify.* Identify the intrusive mode that is causing problems in the couple relationship.
2. *Use the partner.* Ask the watching partner be a supportive spectator while you work with an associated childhood memory and re-parent the working partner.

3. *Partner visualizing.* Encourage the partner to visualize the scene as vividly as possible, be empathic, and communicate understanding.
4. *Soothing.* Ask the watching partner to soothe the working partner as if the working partner were their child.
5. *Discrimination.* Finally ask how the working partner experiences the soothing partner.

Having the partner involved in this way leads to a deeper engagement than simply registering any new information cognitively. The real value comes when the partner can *picture* it and does the re-parenting. This visualizing of child experience has great impact. This helps the experiences to have staying power. When couples share negative experiences from childhood, it builds a sense of connection and empathy.

Therapy Tip: Sometimes it is helpful for the couple to bring in childhood photographs to help "picture" experiences (Behary, ISST Couples Special Interest Group, 2012).

9.6   Making Imagery Work Safe for Individuals and Couples

Safety is important for imagery work. We advise as follows:

1. *Permission.* Always ask. Is it okay to have the partner there while imagery work is done? Do they feel safe enough, or is something needed to feel safer? Find out what will increase the sense of safety. You are a model for dealing with emotional needs!
2. *Support of partner.* It can help to mention that the partner will not to be in the room in a detached way, but to grow in their own feelings of caring and understanding and to work with the therapist to assist the healing process. Later, roles will be reversed.
3. *Role of partner.* Clarify whether the person would like their partner to hold their hand, or just sit alongside, or be somewhere else (including not being present).
4. *Eyes.* The partner is generally asked to close their eyes as well, so the person does not feel stared at. Some therapists initially close their eyes, too, but it may be important to closely monitor the person doing imagery work.
5. *Enter image.* Ask permission of the person before you enter the image.

6. *Be sensitive.* Note any possibility that the person you are working with might feel that their partner is treating them "one down," as if they were stupid, childish, or in some way disrespected. Stop this immediately! You may sense this developing. Try to offset it from the beginning by acknowledging the mutual strengths of the adult self: "This child mode is just one part of you, the part where the hurt is, so please be assured that a focus on a child mode doesn't mean that the adult is less capable." You can also tell the couple that it will be the turn of the other partner next.

7. *Participation.* The technique usually involves asking the person to *help you to help them.* Say something like, "Help me understand how you feel. Describe to me. Help me see what it is you need. What expression is on the face of Little You right now? Can you do this? Can you help me with this?" This is a very gentle way to enter the details of the scene and guides you, as therapist, into whatever the client needs. The safest path is to be person-centered. Trust the person to guide you where they need to go. You will often be surprised! Take your cues from the individual.

8. *Partner active.* After you model empathically, feeling what the child in the image is feeling, involve the partner in helping you feel this as vividly as possible. This will help the person feel more understood and supported. What can the partner add to the picture of the child? Or what would they wish to say to reassure the child or offset the child's hurt, confusion, and disappointment? If you sense that this would be useful, encourage the partner to say it.

9. *Involving partner.* If the partner needs to learn more emotional resonance, you may have the child get more detailed with the partner in sharing their feelings and asking the partner for help. You can ask the partner, "If this were you, or if this were your little child, how would you feel?" Then you can ask the individual whether this feels similar.

10. *Closure.* In ending the imagery it is important to allow the person to gather up all their feelings, contain them, and also switch to a safe place (if not already there). Later, most people like to process the experience on a cognitive level for a few minutes. Some appreciate the therapist making sense of what they learned from it, including underlining some of the connections between the past and the present. Ending with an affirmation about how much courage it took to face the memory is helpful.

11. *Check out.* You will want to check out the experience of the person doing imagery work. Also learn what happened for the partner.

Invite the partner to share this. Is there anything that was confusing for either one of them? Was it difficult for them to do this in front of the partner? What would make it easier next time?

12. *Feelings at end.* If possible, try to ensure that the person leaves the session feeling safe and that their partner understands.

Sometimes an individual will be lower functioning than you might have suspected. Maybe they held it together and did not let on. Sometimes an individual begins to disassociate. If they begin to regress, you may need to stop the process and contain them using some grounding exercises, as mentioned above. Do not be discouraged from using imagery. It just means you need to take it more slowly. Re-emphasize the safe place. Use it as a base for imagery and re-parenting work.

Therapy Tip: It is a good idea to have a signal with the person in treatment, such as raising the hand, when exposure becomes too intense. Then the visualization can be regulated down or stopped.

Exercise: Try this brief couple visualization with a couple. Both identify "one thing I would have liked to hear from my mother or father." Reduce this to a single sentence, then guide each in turn, with the partner's support, to visualize being a child and seeing the parent say what needed to be heard. Encourage the couple, in turn, to hear the words in the parent's voice. This will help to check out whether both can do visual work without complications and be mutually supportive.

Also teach the couple to use the pictures to bridge to empathy and understanding.

Bryant and Hetti noticed that certain issues erupted with great emotional intensity. Their therapist taught them to first notice when triggered, to pause, float above and notice with "detached observation." Hetti noted that her trigger often led to flashes of rage, but Bryant observed that "I feel myself collapsing inside. I want to hide from her anger. Then I feel that everything's hopeless." The therapist used these memory bridges for re-parenting work, and "seeing" this in sessions developed a deep common understanding.

Once the Vulnerable Child's needs are met in a session, the person will have a different "corrective" experience. This will provide an antidote to dysfunctional schemas and disruptive mode states.

There are some couple risks in this vulnerable space. The partner's Demanding Parent or Punitive Parent may get in the way. This may be expressed in relation to a jarring partner response. You may need to strongly intervene: "Wait, where did that come from? Which part is talking that way? [Detect and label the parent mode.] What happened to you as a child?" [Build a bridge to the schema onset.] This might not be a "pure" voice from the parent, but more of a composite voice, which may include what the child felt in response to hearing the parental message. A therapeutic confrontation may be more acceptable when it is explained in this way and linked with childhood origins. At the first opportunity, the therapist will return to the partner's experience of needs not being met.

Therapy Tip: When working with traumatic memories, ST is not the same as exposure work, although sometimes this will happen naturally. In ST, it is not necessary to relive the whole trauma; for example, it may be sufficient to go only to that point where the individual feels threatened. The goal is to move towards resolution through re-parenting. It is important that the client feels safe at the end of the exercise. Make sure that they fully feel the positive emotion associated with change: this will anchor progress (Arntz & Jacob, 2013).

Note that ST goes beyond replaying emotional cycles and gives a clear focus on treatment targets. When the targets are hit, there is a pay-off for the couple in connection and more stable attachment (see Chapter 11 on needs versus wants). In this way, ST assists the couple to reattach. This is illustrated in the following clinical example.

9.7   Case Study: Michael and Amanda

> Michael (age 48) was a very senior consultant to large corporations. He was used to earning more in a month than many people earn in a year. He was "a bit of a bully," irritable, easily slighted, and quite grandiose. Needless to say, he had narcissistic traits, but managed to function highly in his employment. He met Amanda (age 22) when she was "on the job" as a sex worker. This began a very turbulent and explosive relationship. She was very demanding and had high dependency needs. Both were easily angered. Therapy was like an emotional roller-coaster ride.
>
> In one session, Michael was complaining about Amanda constantly ringing him and texting. He said, "Don't you realize I have a very demanding job. I don't have time to answer your calls, or respond to 20 texts a day!"

The therapist remembered from his assessment that Amanda's father had left the family when she was 12 years old. This scene was used for limited re-parenting in which she visualized when her father fought with her mother, pushing her over and then angrily slamming the door when he left. He did not say goodbye and had no contact with his daughter over the next 10 years.

The therapist entered the scene and confronted the father: "You've frightened your daughter. She needs to be told that all this isn't her fault. Maybe you're leaving your wife, but you're walking out on your responsibilities as a parent and neglecting your daughter when she needs you."

The therapist also asked Amanda what she needed. She wanted a hug from an older sister, which she was able to visualize. As a result, Amanda began to feel some comfort in this terrible incident.

Michael watched "through a window at her childhood house," patiently holding Amanda's hand through the visualization. Periodically, the therapist asked him, "How does Amanda look now?"[10] Later, Michael was better able to understand why she put such demands on him: "I guess she's only experienced men leaving her. She's so anxious at home during the day, she feels she needs some kind of reassurance from me—that I'll be there for her."

In the next session, Amanda said that Michael was often "too big for his boots." The therapist remembered a time when Michael said that he brought home a report card. His father said, "Yes, you got five As but also a B. What went wrong in that subject?" This scene was visualized and Amanda saw how he believed, from his father, that nothing he ever achieved was good enough. She could understand the demands he made on himself (and also on her!).

We can think about addressing the mode clashes in this clinical example. Amanda was caught in Vulnerable Child feeling abandoned, quickly becoming Angry Child if Michael did not return her calls. At times, she might enter the overcompensating Bully and Attack mode. Michael also had a Vulnerable Child, but he overcompensated with Self-aggrandizer and had a powerful Demanding Parent mode. He could resort to Bully and Attack as well. ST allows the therapist to directly engage, distinguish,

---

[10]   Ida Shaw suggested this way of involving others in a visualization exercise. Try to balance such interventions.

label and externalize the modes, and then begin to make interventions to deal with the impact of each mode on the relationship.

There was continued progress in therapy. After working on her mode map, Amanda was better able to tolerate and understand her anxious feelings. She could mostly ignore them when they crept up during the day: "I think about my work, accept the anxiety, and realize that it's a kind of noise in my day." Michael was also able to "target" her need for reassurance in a reasonably negotiated way without feeling resentful. It helped him to keep in mind the visual picture-image of Little Amanda.

Michael also did some individual mode mapping on his over-compensation mode and the pain he felt with his father when nothing he did was ever good enough. When Amanda would complain (overcompensation) and feel abandoned (Vulnerable Child), this would activate his feelings of helplessness (Vulnerable Child) and memories of his father's criticism (schema and memory activation). He learned to intercept this parent mode in his head and recognize that, although the voice from his father "felt" the same with Amanda, he was often able to please her (unlike his father). He would pull out a note of hers that he kept in his wallet and a picture of her when she was 12 years old. Then he would remember that this was her abandonment "baggage" from childhood (development of empathic resonance through photos). Then he could relax, knowing that they, as a couple, could get over it (blocking or ignoring Punitive Parent mode). He was free to be in touch with his emotions, assertive, and realistically affirming of Amanda (Healthy Adult mode).

Amanda and Michael decided on a ritual for morning partings, which felt very special (c.f. Gottman's technique of creating shared rituals, 2009). She was able to recall this memory during the day (developing a sustained sense of connection/attachment) whenever she felt anxious (Healthy Adult Amanda taking care of her Vulnerable Child and re-parenting herself), so there were far fewer complaints (Healthy Adult reducing ineffective Overcompensator mode). Michael was in a much better mood when he came home (Happy Child as needs get met), and he in turn was able to be more enthusiastic (Playful Child) with Amanda in greeting her. He was able to let go of the failure feelings (ignoring Punitive Parent voice) and just focus on her, and at times he would ask her for reassurance (Healthy Adult asking help to fulfill a need), so there was a mutual meeting of needs.

Over time, not only did this become a habit, in the best sense of the word, but they both changed in healthy ways (result of personal re-parenting of self and mutual re-parenting of each other). Amanda gradually became more secure, and Michael became softer and more empathically sensitive (the fruit of mutual re-parenting). This had the additional benefit of being less triggering for her. It was a big step for Michael to learn how to ask Amanda for reassurance (assertive Healthy Adult taking care of his Vulnerable Child) when he was feeling he wasn't measuring up, or to even bring up the subject. The therapist walked this journey with them (Healthy Adult on the part of therapist). She began to see his vulnerability (Young's technique to help the therapist attach more to a narcissist and to retain empathy when the person becomes difficult). Amanda also felt more secure (core need finally being satisfied), and her lapses into Bully and Attack mode (overcompensation) became less frequent.

Her gratitude towards Michael (a component of Healthy Adult love, which includes reciprocity) made him feel more respected and less controlled (fewer clashing coping mechanisms) and he was able to use some of his humor again (Playful Child mode emerges as needs get met), as in the days when they first met. Amanda was able to "call" Michael out on his unrelenting standards on himself (becoming an equal, a partner, able to also re-parent him, and a helpmate) when he was becoming over-pressured (partners learning to soothe each other, a new coping mechanism), and help him get to his more vulnerable self (wise-mind technique to soften her and engender her empathy).

Although Michael didn't really like this aspect of therapy (in ST, we go out of our comfort zones), he gradually got used to it (acceptance of body feeling) and stopped resisting it. He eventually began to like talking about some of his softer feelings (Healthy Adult mode is self-reinforcing), but only with Amanda (only she got to this level with him and proved to be a safe person), although naturally some of the old personality patterns, nevertheless, remained.

Reflect: This case also gives a good example of an ST-C case formulation.

9.8   Mode Dialogs on Multiple Chairs

ST uses chair-work (Kellogg, 2012). This technique has been used in other therapeutic approaches, such as gestalt therapy, but ST uses it in a very specific way. Chairs represent the modes concretely: the modes are placed in different chairs. In this way, chair-work allows a representation of "psychic entities" to display inner dynamics, especially when encouraging a conversation between the modes or chairs.

We suggest using the modes from the mode map and placing the chairs always in the same way. Working in this consistent way creates an internal mental map for the clients, in which the chairs in the room align with the printed mode map you have given to them. From our vantage point, it is neither necessary nor helpful to differentiate into too many chairs and label them in an idiosyncratic way. It is fine to use personalized names, but the modes should match with the modes on the map. This makes it much easier to achieve an overview.

Therapy Tip: This is a good way to work with parental modes. It leads naturally to a more realistic reappraisal of their "voices." Alternating perspectives through changing chairs makes change easier. This process works more deeply than just following cognitive procedures.

Consider the following example:

Barry felt guilty after an affair. He had talked it through with Caroline, his wife, who had forgiven him—but he could not forgive himself. This became a problem when he became more depressed and withdrew emotionally from his wife. The therapist recognized the blaming voice was from Demanding Parent and used a chair to represent the voice. He then asked Barry to sit in the chair and speak with that voice.

In this case, Barry felt guilty, and judgmental thoughts appeared as a blaming "voices in the head." Initially, the voices may have seemed ego-syntonic, or an accepted part of the self, but when the therapist labeled them Demanding Parent mode voices and put the mode in a chair, this introduced a sense of distance. The parent mode chair could be addressed or "heard from." The mode, represented by a chair, began to speak clearly to Barry after transforming the ego-syntonic message into a "You" sentence: "You're guilty. You didn't do the right thing!" The therapist encouraged Barry to enter Healthy Adult mode and evaluate such messages.

An additional chair was then used to represent a child mode. When Barry sat in Vulnerable Child chair, he was asked, "How do you feel hearing this voice? What do you need now?" Each time Barry switched back into surrendering or identifying himself with the parental voice, the therapist interrupted and labeled this mode flip by pointing to the chair the person was sitting in at the beginning of the chair-work: "This isn't a child mode speaking—it's still surrender. Were you born with that guilt or desperation? Obviously not! So how do you feel deep inside you, being called a complete failure or loser?"

We suggest using the chairs in a way consistent with the mode map to build up an internal (or mental) map. After separating coping modes, parent modes, and child modes into three chairs, the individual and therapist can stand up together, looking down on the chairs side by side. This "floating above" position is quite similar to the way therapist and client enter the image in an imagery rescripting session. Following the same script in imagery and chair-work helps clients understand the inner movements of the modes and how they come about. People usually like standing beside the therapist because it makes them feel that there is a working alliance.

You might ask how the client feels, watching Punitive Parent beating up Vulnerable Child through such negative messages. This may release anger resources to take a stand for the child. You can validate this anger and place an additional fourth chair to represent Angry Child close to the Vulnerable Child chair, so both poles of the child's emotional spectrum of the mode map are now represented on separate chairs. This fosters a distinct mental representation of both poles. Then encourage the client to use their assertiveness feelings to fight for the child's needs and rights.

Remember: It is always the Healthy Adult acting for the child, never the child itself! The emotions within the Healthy Adult (e.g., constructive anger) derive from the child. The adult is connected with the emotions of the child modes, which fuel and empower, but the action comes from the adult mode. The adult integrates the emotions, enabling them to act in a balanced way.

The voice of Punitive Parent is very destructive. It is vital for the therapist to support the person in challenging it: "What do you want to say to the Punitive Parent?" After everything has been said, it may be helpful to throw the Punitive Parent chair out of the office into the corridor. Check out the feelings of the client after the chair has been removed. There is often considerable relief at this symbolic banishment of parental voices, but it is equally common for doubts or guilt feelings to return through the "back door." It may be helpful for the client to hear your assertion that they are old enough to decide what is right or wrong and no longer need anyone telling them what needs to be done! It is better to work on these "pull-back messages" in session, instead of leaving the client alone with them after the end of session.

Therapy Tip: The client can hear from the banished Punitive Parent chair. This can help to establish whether the impeachment of the Punitive Parent was effective. Usually, Punitive Parent will not accept being treated that way and will predict that the client will not get along well without them.

Another Tip: Do not argue with the Punitive Parent voice. Encourage your client as a homework exercise to try banishing Punitive Parent for one week. Think about this as an experiment. Then consider the result. Did it work? And then problem solve.

Towards the end of the session, the client can be placed on the Healthy Adult chair, between parent and child mode chairs, instead of the initial coping mode chair and, we hope, feeling more comfortable with the new situation. From that chair, they care for the child chairs: the Angry Child is calmed and has to obey the guidance of the Healthy Adult; the Vulnerable Child has to feel safe and trust the Healthy Adult. Once more, it is helpful using two separate child mode chairs to address them in this specific way. Sometimes you have to move back and forth until the needs of both child mode chairs have become clear and have been fulfilled by the Healthy Adult.

Remember: Do not hesitate to assist if the client shows difficulties acting as a Healthy Adult. What is important is that they feel good during the exercise and it comes to a successful end.

Therapy Tip: You might consider using acceptance and commitment therapy's thought-diffusion techniques. But note that chair-work is helpful in distancing from the Punitive Parent because it is externalized and the person can come to understand that this is "not part of me." It is not easy to tone down the negative voices, but we can repeat the procedure of letting them go again and again. The Chinese metaphor can be encouraging: "You can't keep the birds of sorrow from flying above your head, but you can keep them from building their nest in your hair" (c.f., Parfy, 2012).

Being the mode in a chair helps the individual "completely get into the mode's perspective" (Arntz & Jacob, 2013, p. 125). This results in an emotional deepening of the work of therapy. If you are working with Bully and Attack mode, you can assign the mode to an empty chair and forcefully address that mode. Clients should not be placed in a Bully and Attack chair during the session, because we do not want to reinforce that mode! The client can also be encouraged to "speak back" to the mode. This might be contrasted with them in Vulnerable Child mode. It is useful to keep the focus on the negative emotions related to dysfunctional parent or child modes after the person is able to bypass the coping mode and relate to the emotional triggers (Arntz & Jacob, 2013).

Reflect: John Gasiewski (ISST Special Interest Group, 2012) saw a therapeutic role in assisting an individual to change Punitive Parent messages into more empathically attuned versions of parental introjects (via limited re-parenting) that allow adaptive coping modes to gain hold. How might you use your creativity to honor the positive aspects of a client's belief system and make it more useful to the development of Healthy Adult?

Remember: It is up to the client to choose their own personal values. Even if this includes some of the values that the Demanding Parent mode stands for, that does not mean that the parent modes are "right." The values may be right, but not the way the parent modes forced them on the child. An adult has grown out of the need for parents!

> Helen would often come to sessions in the numbness of Detached Protector mode. The therapist said to her, "I know that this feels safest. But I'd like you to shift into another seat. You are now the Detached Protector speaking to me." She said, as Detached Protector, "I keep Helen safe. I know that she can't cope with strong emotions. She's easily overwhelmed. I'm doing my best to protect her." But Helen, after hearing this exchange, went to her normal chair and said, "I do understand that Detached Protector is protecting me, but then I don't feel anything. And since I'm like a zombie, does anyone ever get to know the real me?"

Another approach is to highlight the choices Helen made to go into Detached Protector:

> The therapist said to her, "I want you to go back to a time today when you felt something intensely." She said, "Yes, when I was driving here, I was cut off in my car by another driver. I was so angry I felt like driving my car into his BMW!" Therapist: "What happened then?" Helen: "I felt guilty and I didn't want to come today so stirred up. So I shut down." Therapist: "So that was the point of choice. You went into Detached Protector?"
>
> The therapist then continued with somatic awareness for Helen to iden-tify a place of tension in her body. This led to more awareness of emotion, leading to Vulnerable Child and progress in the session.

Chair-work is especially helpful with the dysfunctional parent modes. It is important to understand that, with the more personality-disordered, the voice of a Defectiveness-Shame schema ("I am flawed") can come through Demanding Parent messages. But even more damaging is Punitive Parent, which can contribute to self-injury and ultimately to suicide. We need to oppose such "life and death" ramifications of modes with great vigor.

Kellogg and Young (2006) thought that chair dialogs can be used to affirm and nurture the abandoned child and to fight or impeach the Punitive Parent.[11] These are core therapeutic interventions in ST. This allows the person to conceptualize the critical voice as separate from the core self. It is best to label the mode as a coping mechanism, clarify through chair-work, and then "float above it" in a calm way, or literally stand above the child or infant mode.

Standing up induces a different pattern of self-experiencing and thus helps people to step out of their previous mode attractor, change into a more healthy state again, and cope with the old modes using the resources they developed while growing up. In intense schema activation states, people are so drawn into their current modes that they feel "trapped" and cannot get out to shift to a Healthy Adult perspective. Moving physically can help to shift into a different mood state—in therapy and between the sessions. This is one reason why we ask clashing couples to move to different rooms or to stand above the modes placed in chairs. Moving to another place helps to activate different neuronal patterns.

Therapy Tip: Chair-work will normally intensify feelings. Do not ask a person to sit in a chair representing either Punitive Parent or Bully and Attack. Instead, have an empty chair represent those modes while the client remains in either Healthy Adult or Vulnerable Child, or stands above the chairs next to you, as Healthy Adult, to address the mode. Safety is always an important consideration (Arntz & Jacob, 2013). Simeone-DiFrancesco notes that at times she and her clients stand for so long in the session that they place Punitive Parent barstool chairs behind them as props to lean against, and at other times spin around the stool to impeach it and turn it away from the child!

Another Tip: The more punitive a parent mode is, the greater the need to work against it (at first to impeach, then to block and neutralize) by catching its influence in therapy through both re-parenting and chair-work. Also, note that patients with a strong Punitive Parent will tend to interpret even neutral comments from a Punitive Parent perspective.

Chairs can be used to represent anything you want to work with in therapy. You can put a coping mode in a chair for investigating (as described in Chapter 6), or a chair might represent longing for an affair (Chapter 10). When working on clarifying emotions, it may be helpful to have two chairs

---

[11]   This fighting aspect has been modified in the current application of ST. Although it may take on this characteristic initially with the client, it moves rather quickly to impeaching its power and accepting its presence as chronic, but to be ignored. This can help to eliminate a sense of frustrated powerlessness over its persistence.

represent the two poles of the emotional spectrum of the child modes, as introduced above. So, even if the client feels just angry, there is still a Vulnerable Child in another chair watching the scene from his or her vantage point. Offering additional chairs helps people remember that there are other factors beyond their currently overwhelming emotional activation.

Therapy Tip: A Vulnerable Child mode can represent attachment needs. This can be made concrete through a chair and facilitated by moving it closer to the Healthy Adult chair, meeting attachment needs.

Originally, chair-work was used in individual sessions, but in ST-C it might be helpful doing it in the presence of one partner to enhance their understanding of the other partner's inner world. In a second step, the non-working partner can be included in reappraising and looking for adult solutions, and co-parent together with the therapist. Mutually applied to both partners, the mode chair level becomes a neutral "stage" that both partners and the therapist are looking down upon in a joint reference perspective while standing side by side above the chairs. This helps to create a working alliance in the session.

Emotions are closely connected with body sensations (Damasio, 1999). Physical activities are able to block negative emotions (Ekman, 1993).

Reflect: Put a firm smile on your face in a purely mechanical way and then try to feel sad. It just does not work!

The body is like the body of a violin that gives resonance to the sound of the strings. It is a two-way street. We can guide our attention and thoughts and, in that way, influence our emotions from the top down. But we can also induce body changes that influence our feelings bottom up. ST uses both channels.

There is another reason why standing up together with the couple can be very helpful. While sitting in front of a client, face to face, you are in a dyadic setting. This setting might be connected with memories of being accused by parents or a work instructor, examined by teachers, or ashamed in a peer group in front of others. Standing side by side and "watching the game" on the chairs below induces a very different relationship between you and the person. You both look in the same direction and the "enemy" is the scene in front of you. This is a triadic setting, like chattering with somebody about a third person, kids talking about their parents or a teacher, or—later in life—students trying to solve a difficult problem together. Tom Anderson (1990) called this a "reflecting team" perspective: you talk with an individual about him- or herself as if they were a different person. So, while being connected with them on the Healthy Adult level, you can talk about conflicts or ruptures on the mode level on the chairs. These perspective changes in the "therapy lab" induce perspective changes outside the sessions because they involve not only mental processes but body movements, too. All this goes deeper.

Standing or walking in the therapy room weakens rigid neural activation patterns. You can use this more fluid state to induce additional perspectives, for example from a best friend. Ask for the name of the best friend and address them directly: "Welcome, Sue. I'm happy that you try to help us out. Why is Mary reacting like that? Do you know this from other situations, too? What do you think she really needs?" It is fascinating how this movement works! Usually, the person will activate inner images of the friend and then make an effort to seriously step into the friend's shoes. Besides real people (some borderline people lack good friends), you can introduce a "friendly observer," a personal "hero," or a well-known wise person, like Gandalf from *The Lord of the Rings*. This technique allows us to use resources that people usually have but that are blocked by intensive emotional states. Physically distancing helps emotional distancing and gives access to the full knowledge of the Healthy Adult state.

It is possible to stand up simultaneously with both partners, but separate them by standing in the middle and keeping them on both sides of you, as we do with struggling kids. And be aware: always work on the same level with both! Do not stand up while one of them remains seated, or vice versa. Being on separate levels induces unintended strong emotional responses.

Therapy Tip: Sometimes, with a room full of chairs and one partner needing to be in a child mode chair, you may need to get used to going on bended knee near them as the re-parenting and caring parent. Make sure you check whether it is okay to approach this close, and also ask the partner whether they would be willing to do this with you. (Simeone-DiFrancesco has seen amazing results with this.)

9.9 Dealing with Anger

Anger can spread like fire. This has been called the "kindling effect" (Solomon & Tatkin, 2011). As therapists, we commonly have to deal with anger in the couple relationship. The following steps have been suggested by Kellogg and Young (2006):

a. *Ventilate.* Express anger fully. Clarify what is at the core of it, so long as it is not abusive or destructive, especially to the partner in a session. Working with multiple chairs can separate reactions.

b. *Empathize.* The therapist responds empathically to the wound that was activated with an acknowledgment of the pain that was caused.

c. *Reality testing.* For the "reality check," it is helpful to stand up together and physically take a new stance, too. By not being punitive or defensive, the therapist acknowledges what is seen accurately, which is followed by looking at what aspects have been schema-driven and are distortions of the situation.

d. *Rehearsal of appropriate assertiveness.* After anger has abated, both therapist and couple explore how needs could have been expressed in an assertive rather than an overcompensating aggressive manner.

You can even use chairs to represent a negative reaction to the therapist. For example, the "stupid therapist" can be placed in an empty chair in front of an angry individual, while the "cooperative healthy therapist" sits in a chair close to the working person to maintain the therapeutic alliance while expressing the anger towards the "stupid therapist" chair. Then the individual is encouraged to say what they need to say, and the therapist may even add fuel to the fire: "Is this really all you have to say to this stupid therapist? Tell him how much he hurt and disappointed you. He can stand that. Let it all out. It won't destroy him; I'm still on your side!" Later, it might be helpful to clarify what might be called "old anger" deriving from childhood injuries left buried for years, but emerging now, triggered by the therapist's or the partner's behavior. This may help the watching partner to realize that it is not personal, that they are the trigger for an old feeling.

While standing up side by side, both can speak in the third person about "the client" and "the therapist." This can introduce more emotional distance. You can ask questions like: "What do you think the therapist might feel if an individual accuses him this way?" or "How do you expect the therapist to react to being treated this way?" This helps to strengthen the person's capacity for mentalization (Fonagy et al., 2004), which is a skill of the Healthy Adult. Questions such as, "It seems as if the person acted out more out of the Angry Child mode, but what does the Vulnerable Child need?" broaden the scope on the full spectrum of child needs. Asking, "Have you had similar experiences in other situations, too?" helps to connect current conflict with a pattern of schema activation outside therapy. All this work can be done with one partner in the presence of the other.

9.10 Working with Impulsive and Undisciplined Child modes

Impulsive and Undisciplined Child modes appear to have different childhood origins from the anger-related modes. The anger modes often come from a childhood experience of being punished for expressing needs or feelings.

People with strong impulsive modes, on the other hand, often report being spoiled in childhood and not being taught to take responsibility, but sometimes being overburdened by responsibility (of, say, caring for an unwell parent). The person may be attracted to hedonism, indulging in promiscuous sex, bingeing on alcohol, buying or stealing things, and so on. The Undisciplined Child mode avoids normal responsibilities, especially tedious tasks, and may seem demanding in a very childish way.

The response of the therapist is to be a good parent, affirming legitimate needs but reality-testing the expression and empathically setting limits on destructive behavior (Arntz & Jacob, 2013).

Therapy Tip: Watch out for the Obstinate Child mode. Generally, this is the result of an activation of the person's assertiveness system through striving for autonomy, not being respected in adolescence, or being stressed by overwhelming social demands. Encourage the person to look at the pattern in a realistic way, and ultimately to decide against it in order to receive help (Arntz & Jacob, 2013). Consider the possibility of this mode if you are stuck with a person who is seems willing to change but is not actually changing.

Cultural and family prejudices have been identified by Simeone-DiFrancesco and Simeone (2016a,b) as quite a significant trigger:

> *Example*: The way we celebrate birthdays and holidays, or handle it when someone is ill, tends to be part of a family tradition. Many a negative image of a partner is formed by unexpressed expectations. While unexpressed, they cannot be negotiated. Just try to convince a spouse who expects to go to his mother's for Christmas that you do not think this is the best way to spend the day and have a higher priority in bonding with your children at home.

Reflect: These mode dialogs require specificity and flexibility in the forming partnership of the couple. If such issues are not addressed, there is not much left but role-relating through parent modes. Using the dialog tools to articulate these traditions and expectations is a starting point. Then a tool, such as the needs vs. wants tool (Chapter 11), gives the therapist a way to address these seemingly rigid and gridlocked issues.

9.11   Rewind the Video

Simeone-DiFrancesco and Simeone (2016a,b) share a technique they call "rewinding the video":

> Dora, a sensitive wife, recalled in therapy, "My husband, Dan, and I tell of when we were first married. He walked in one day, looking forward to

seeing me. But something had activated my schema, and I acted morose and withdrawn. He got really mad and gave me a big lecture about this. He said that we had promised each other, as part of our marriage vows, that enthusiasm would be part of our relationship, no matter what. He didn't want to let this expectation go, even though he was perfectly willing to entertain what had triggered me.

"He asked, at the very least, that I could greet him nicely, because we were still friends and not enemies. No matter what had happened between when he last saw me and now, it didn't just turn us into enemies. He was, of course, right and this was about the end of my trying to get away with this 'bad behavior'."

Dora's awareness did not mean that she was instantaneously healed of her schemas or forever changed from wanting to withdraw. In fact, it took some mode mapping to help her get there more consistently. But as the couple learned about modes and schemas, her head told her there must be a better way (the clashes became more ego-dystonic), so she had better "hang in there," calm down, and figure it out.

To help the couple start over, Dora and Dan were taught to use the "re-wind the video" technique. The couple noticed that greeting time, after a day being apart, was highly apt to spark an issue pretty quickly, and it was amazing how from being excited and happy to see each other, it could deteriorate in minutes to both feeling miserable and unhappy. The re-wind the video technique works to handle this. The one who came into the room goes back outside. That person returns to replay the scene: calling out and finding the partner in the agreed-upon ritual of the greeting. Smiles, a kiss, a tickle or two, a nice word about missing the other, a nice long hug. The couple then goes into "This is what I meant to say," and they re-say and re-do in more Healthy Adult mode; the other responds in a new edited version, having learned what the unhealthy, inattentive, or reactionary response did only moments before. All this may seem silly, but it works to change the interaction. It also functions to "yank upward" the downward spiraling depressed feelings precisely because it is so "corny." Sometimes, though, it takes a few re-plays! (Simeone-DiFrancesco & Simeone, 2016a,b).

9.12   Behavioral Pattern Breaking and Homework Assignments

Young et al. (2003) understood behavioral pattern breaking as behaving in a way to counter an underlying schema and help to develop a new Healthy Adult mode. This is often the last and longest phase of treatment. After modes begin to change, guide the clients in applying what has been learned to their interactions outside the session. This involves a shift to healthy coping strategies, rather than the former automatic schema-driven responses (Farrell & Shaw, 2011, p. 94). Then, after some success, have them reward themselves for doing the new behavior. Clearly, this will have a beneficial impact on the quality of the couple's relationship.

Therapy Tip: People who have strong coping modes typically express their needs in exaggerated, distorted, aggressive, or over-dominant ways (Arntz & Jacob, 2013).

The therapist can also draw on traditional behavioral techniques, such as relaxation training, assertiveness training, anger management, self-control strategies (self-monitoring, goal setting, self-reinforcement), and graduated exposure to feared situations (Kellogg & Young, 2006). Target the behaviors that are having the most negative impact in the couple's relationship.

> Lee-Ann noticed that she was less reactive with Brett. Her Punitive schema tended to lose some of its edge in her irritability and occasional explosions. She had practiced assertiveness and was better able to negotiate a reasonable level of getting some of her needs met. Brett had strong Social Isolation and Failure schemas, but with less perceived "hostility" from Lee-Ann he began to risk beginning conversations, and at times they found they could discuss sensitive topics in some depth. Lee-Ann said, "He has come out of his shell. I feel like he's meeting me halfway—and it's great!"

The main behavioral pattern breaking interventions are emergency plans, mode management plans, evidence logs, and role play practice (Farrell and Shaw, 2012, p. 34). All of these can be applied to ST-C. Another ST technique to overcome rigid thinking is letter writing. This can be used to express feelings towards people who have caused injury. Once written, the letters are read in therapy but not sent! You can also use cognitive restructuring. Black-and-white thinking about the actions of a partner is not especially helpful. Instead, "use approaches that can serve to develop a more moderate, complex, nuanced, and reality-based interpretation of the behavior of others" (Kellogg & Young, 2006, p. 451).

Think about encouraging the couple to use the mode cycle clash-card and do imagery work between the sessions, but with a shift in focus to behavior change. The couple is first trained in solving everyday conflicts during sessions by using the following sequence:

1. *Stop*—recognize and stop schema clashes immediately.
2. *Distance* physically from each other (go to separate rooms) for an agreed-upon time.

3. *Analyze* the conflict individually by both filling out mode cycle clash-cards, readjust to Healthy Adult and reveal the unmet core needs.
4. *Reconnect* with the partner by comparing clash-cards. Step into the partner's shoes to share their perspective.
5. *Mutually* contribute suggestions about how to solve the conflict and meet core needs in a functional way.

The therapist coaches the couple through this process and assists with problem solving as required. Later, the couple try to apply the principles in daily life. Homework might include writing out alternative responses to core schemas through the use of a diary or flash-cards to be read when schemas are activated. Encourage the couple to practice new behaviors and get feedback. This can build mode management strategies, establishing boundaries, and assertively asking for needs to be met.

This might be combined with behavioral experiments for the couple (used in cognitive behavioral therapy; see Bennett-Levy et al., 2004). There are plenty of opportunities for behavioral experiments in couple therapy (for example, to try to increase affectionate exchanges, but also rate anticipated SUDS and negative–positive outcome predictions). This will give a baseline for comparison.

Therapy Tip: Think about ways you can use the therapy relationship as a setting for the couple to better express their needs. Aim for a "good enough" meeting of needs.

Another Tip: The Angry and Enraged Child modes are connected with hot, negative emotions. To be effective, you need to work with an emotional focus, either with re-parenting or chair-work. The Impulsive and Undisciplined Child modes seem more "spoiled," and the therapist needs to provide empathic confrontation and limit setting.

9.13 The Role of Mindfulness

When we think about behavior change, we imply that people are able to choose between alternative behaviors, but making choices does not happen in a vacuum. The context will often include activated schemas. You can think about schemas as laying down the tracks for neural activation in the brain. Schemas function like attractors, leading the activation in the pre-existing pathways. To be able to get out of these "life-traps," as Young called them, we have to find a state of mind that allows us to distance from the pull of the emotional activation. This counterforce can include mindfulness.

In mindfulness, we focus on the here-and-now content of our consciousness. The next step is to recognize the content but to immediately let it go and refocus in an undirected state of awareness. This allows a measure of detachment. This kind of awareness is like a putting a spotlight on something, which may include current thoughts. Most disorders (such as generalized anxiety disorder, depression, obsessive compulsive disorder, hypochondria, or anorexia) are related to automatic thoughts or endless ruminating.

Mindfulness clears the mind of such intrusive thoughts triggered by schemas. Some training in mindfulness techniques helps those in treatment distance from preoccupying emotions (e.g., child modes) or thoughts (often parent modes). It is the role of the Healthy Adult to "raise the head above the water."

The function of the Healthy Adult can be likened to the three steps of shifting gears (Schore, 2003): shift out, choose a gear, shift in (see Figure 13). Shifting out means mindful disidentification (Teasdale et al., 2002) from the spontaneous activation. Choosing a better gear means reappraising the content, including core needs and long-term goals and values, from a more distanced perspective, such as a "wise mind" (Linehan, 1993), or through "a best friend's eyes." We can shift in by using self-instruction techniques (Meichenbaum & Goodman, 1971) to weaken intrusive thoughts, calm down or soothe child modes and lead attention and action in the desired direction.

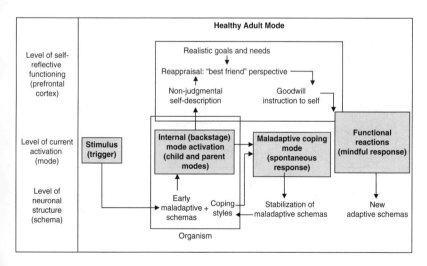

Figure 13 The movement of the Healthy Adult. Source: Based on Roediger (2012b)

The first two steps of this mental movement are an essential part of most so-called "third wave" therapies (Hayes, 2004), which are having more and more impact on the development of cognitive behavior therapy. Some, such as dialectical behavioral therapy, mindfulness-based stress reduction or mindfulness-based cognitive therapy, include Buddhist philosophy, and perhaps *Lectio Divina* prayer modeling of Healthy Adult figures in the New Testament. Where the more Buddhist-influenced techniques abstain from taking an active influence on the mental state, other approaches, like ST, try to guide consciousness in a desired direction (Roediger, 2012b).

The goal of changing thoughts, emotions, or behavior is intrinsic in behavior therapy, but the road of change might become rocky. When people have a more severe or chronic disorder, the recovery process may be hindered by a lack of motivation or biological or social limitations. Then disappointment may be inevitable for both client and therapist.

There is satisfaction when a goal is attained. Consistency theory (Grawe, 2004) may help to explain this process. The degree of personal satisfaction depends on the level of inconsistency in our mind (what has been called "cognitive dissonance"). If the state we are in differs from the desired state, inconsistency is high and there is a feeling of emotional tension (see Figure 14).

This is a useful lever in the change process. If we reach the desired state by changing the situation, we reach consistency for the price of a certain effort. This is the traditional Western approach to consistency: getting what we want. Buddhists do the opposite: they practice acceptance and

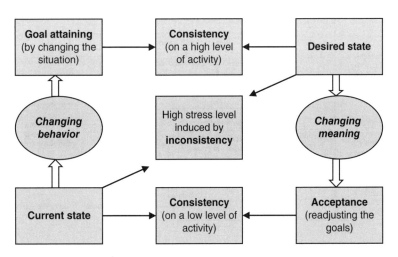

Figure 14   Two ways to consistency. Source: Based on Roediger (2011)

abstain from desires and by that path also reach consistency—with mental efforts only and no need for any other resources.

ST tries to mix both approaches. In the beginning of therapy, we usually try to change behavior. When we realize the limitations of an individual or a couple, we support accepting non-essential differences that do not dehumanize and have proven hard to change. The TV show *The Odd Couple* provides an example of non-essential qualities that are just the way we habitually tend to be. For example, one person is neat and tidy and the other person is never organized. Such a couple may both move more to the middle, with the neat person learning to relax and getting out of a parent mode, and the "slob" learning to be more responsible and not create additional work for the partner, or else getting a maid! However, the whole idea of this type of acceptance is to not be in Demanding Parent or Undisciplined Child mode. An acceptance of some shortcomings and attempting to "match sides" may well prove to be a more promising strategy. To be in Healthy Adult mode is to maximize the contributions of each and allow for limitations.

> *Example:* Husband to wife: "You value the house being tidy. I like it, too, but I don't see half the details you perceive, so why don't you focus on the house, and I'll do the specific things you ask me to do. And then I'll focus on doing the accounting, which you hate. Deal?"

In a couple relationship, differences often express our roles in the relationship and hitherto unexpressed expectations. Expectations that are not discussed can lead to one person dominating the other and become destructive of mutual respect.

9.14 A Couple Schema Plan

At the end of this chapter on intervention, we want to tie this together with a case vignette developing the brief outline of an ST-C therapy strategy. It is, of course, open-ended and as a work in progress it can be changed at any point.

> Umbretto and Maria were helped by their therapist to work out an individualized treatment plan. They had been married for more than 20 years and had struggled with the empty nest when their two children left to go to university.
>
> Umbretto's main schema modes were Self-aggrandizer ("I feel puffed up"), Demanding Parent ("Nothing I'm doing is ever good enough"), Detached Self-soother ("I get over-involved in my accountancy work"), and Angry Child ("It just feels like I want to burst and have a tantrum").

Maria identified Compliant Surrender ("I feel desperate to do anything to please Umbretto"), Vulnerable Child ("I feel lonely and lost"), Punitive Parent ("There's a harsh tone in the voice"), and Enraged Child ("It's like I hate everyone and want to lash out").

They worked out how each mode looked from the outside, and then the childhood needs for Umbretto: "I need to be looked at and to say that I'm OK how I am" (Self-aggrandizer); "Remind me that Demanding Parent asks too much of me on a regular basis" (Demanding Parent); "Say my work isn't everything and give me a hug" (Detached Self-soother); "Listen for five minutes and let me run down. Set some limits if I get aggressive" (Angry Child). He added, "I think my Vulnerable Child is actually the motive behind all these modes that try to protect me." Maria agreed to try to see his Vulnerable Child behind the modes that were most common.

Maria identified her needs: "Remind me to stand up for myself and say what I need in a clear way" (Compliant Surrender); "Just give me a hug and don't let go for five minutes. That will soothe me" (Vulnerable Child); "Speak sharply to that voice and tell me not to tolerate it at all. Throw it out of my head!" (Punitive Parent); "Give me some time to vent, but limit set and then hug me" (Enraged Child).

The "escape strategy" was for the one who reached 6/10 on SUDS first to initiate separation, promising to come back in 30 minutes, and for both to do the mode cycle clash-card on the incident. Then it was the responsibility of the first to separate to come back to the issue and check whether both had SUDS scores under 6, so that the issue could be talked through. Both were to try to get into Healthy Adult to facilitate this. They agreed that they would later write in their relationship journal what had been learned or gained from that encounter and at a later time share for mutual understanding.

Therapy Tip: Empathic confrontation is an important skill. With this technique the therapist incorporates enough of the person's biographical background to give the reason for dysfunction and explains the dysfunction as a coping strategy that now fails to meet adult needs. It is the focus on finding a way to meet needs that helps the confrontation work.

THERAPIST: "Vlad, I know you've struggled with your grandiosity. It made sense when your mother treated you as very special, more special than your brothers and sisters. But it led to a lot of relationship problems, initially with your siblings but later with work colleagues and your wife. But, while you may feel special, usually in a fleeting way, the real need for connection and understanding from others goes unmet. That's not a good 'relationship deal'!"

The presence of the partner adds a valuable resource in a session. There are a lot of potentially comforting behaviors that can be drawn on. Reassuring touch is generally fine. The partner can also suggest ideas for rescripting or can visually be part of a rescripting scene. Naturally, all this is subject to therapeutic timing and judgment, but the partner is an important resource.

9.15   Conclusion

There is no neutrality in working with couples. The only effective therapist position is to give full support for both in a relationship, but alternating the support as needed. With lower functioning couples you will need to keep an eye on the partner when you work with an individual in couple therapy. They may need frequent indications that you are continuing to notice them and support them in the session. Eye contact helps, as do the following:

- *ST tools*, such as cognitive case conceptualizations of the schemas, coping mechanisms, and modes (with a mode map)
- *mode clashes*, which can be conceptualized with the mode cycle clash-card
- *imagery work* to enhance emotional activation
- *chair dialogs* to work through inner conflicts and access the full spectrum of modes
- *the therapy relationship*, which we use in examples of schema activation and adult problem solving
- *homework assignments*, including working with mode cycle clash-cards.

These specific techniques might be combined with various techniques that therapists are familiar with. We want to emphasize the importance of applying these techniques within the schema case conceptualization framework. Eclecticism on a technical level works, but can lead to confusion on a conceptual or theoretical level.

Summary

In summary, the general pattern of individual growth involves the following: *help* the child modes develop and find safety through emotional processing of traumatic childhood experiences, acknowledging the original childhood needs and corrective experiences; *eliminate* punitive and demanding parental modes as much as possible and replace them with healthy attitudes to needs and emotions, healthy standards, and moral principles; and *let* the Healthy Adult side develop, with the result that the dysfunctional coping modes become less necessary (Arntz, 2012b).

This has been illustrated with a variety of interventions in this chapter. They include important interventions using imagery, chair-work, and behavior pattern breaking. A number of specific topics were addressed, such as empathy, anger, and Undisciplined and Impulsive Child modes. This chapter ended with the development of a schema plan for treating a couple. In Chapter 10 our focus is on common roadblocks in couple therapy.

10

Common Problems in Couple Therapy, Including Affairs, Forgiveness, and Violence

The therapeutic course rarely runs smoothly with couples. There are many potential roadblocks. A number are examined in this chapter.

10.1 Affairs

Affairs are often part of the breakdown of relationships. Sadly, it seems that few people have much psychological insight into what happened or are wiser after the event. ST can help us to understand and possibly find some resources to deal with this common challenge in couple counseling.

The statistics indicate that over half of marriages break down. One interesting trend is that younger wives are now more unfaithful than their husbands; two-thirds of women and half of men who were having affairs did so in the first five years of marriage (Lawson, 1988). Until a couple of decades ago, men were more likely to have an affair, but now the genders are about equal. However, if a man is unfaithful he is more likely to have more partners.

Many factors contribute to the current crisis in romantic relationships: higher expectations of emotional fulfillment, a general lack of communication skills, changes in what is acceptable in society, and a greater proportion of married women in employment, making them financially more independent.

Andy and Margo came for therapy. They were an attractive young couple who seemed to have everything going for them. The husband was a high

Schema Therapy with Couples: A Practitioner's Guide to Healing Relationships, First Edition.
Chiara Simeone-DiFrancesco, Eckhard Roediger, and Bruce A. Stevens.
© 2015 John Wiley & Sons, Ltd. Published 2015 by John Wiley & Sons, Ltd.
Companion website: www.wiley.com/go/difrancesco/schematherapywithcouples

school teacher. He had an infatuation with Kirsty, another teacher in his school. Kirsty had recently separated from her husband and Andy was "being supportive." Margo was in a state of near panic, and she felt acutely the threat posed by Kirsty to their marriage.

Almost all people enter a romantic relationship, whether marriage or living together, with a conscious intention of remaining sexually faithful, so an affair is inevitably a falling from an initial ideal, whether a religious or a personal value. It is usually secretive, guilt-inducing in the person involved and anywhere from infuriating to shattering for the partner who finds out. Although most of our discussion of this topic focuses on the affair in relation to a marriage, the dynamics are similar for an engagement, de facto partnership, or longer-term committed relationship. In those cases, there may be less of a public dimension than with vows made in a marriage service, but often there are children involved and the legal situation can easily become entangled.

10.1.1   A Symptom

While affairs may be erotic and intensely sexual, there is a sense in which they have little to do with sex. The real dynamics are unexplored conflict, anger, fear, and emptiness. Such is the pain of an unhappy relationship that an affair tries to keep at bay. It is the symptom of a deeper malaise.

> Will and Marg have been married eight years. There has not been much sparkle in their relationship for a few years. Will became attracted to a colleague, and what began as a few drinks after work ended up with sexual involvement. Will is now less troubled by Marg's emotional coldness, and the affair has drained away some of the tension from the marriage. This is a false calm before the emotional storm when Marg finds out about the relationship.

An affair almost always represents an externalization of an unhealthy process in the original relationship. In this way, an affair may help to keep the real issues, such as unresolved conflict over differing wants, "safely" underground.

An affair is often in a fairyland of unreality. The relationship begins with excitement, compelling attraction, and the thrill of "forbidden fruit." But it is a protected relationship:

> It does not have the everyday worries and chores of marriage or the pressures of living intimately with another person over time. It is a hidden relationship, shared only with one or two confidants who are chosen for their

ability to be supportive and to keep the secret. The secrecy provides a shell against outside pressures. (Brown, 1991, p. 24)

The marriage still impinges on the affair. The spouse still comes first in finances, family crises and celebrations, and in public, so the unfaithful partner is torn between competing demands, especially as the lover becomes more impatient.

If we are to understand the dynamics of an affair, the larger picture of the family is important. This includes the children, the respective families of origin, and behavior patterns of near relatives, and what is considered permissible in the wider ethnic group. The family of origin, for example, can leave an adult with "unfinished business." There may be patterns of avoidance, seduction, secrecy, and betrayal. The precedent for turning away from relationship difficulties and escaping into an affair may be set over the generations. It becomes so much easier as the pattern repeats. It is a two-way street: an affair is the result of various dynamics in the family and, of course, it will in turn influence other dynamics whether or not it is discovered.

The family is a primary place of belonging. It is where we long for attention and the need to be needed. This is the place where we hope that the person we love will love us back in the same way. An affair threatens the glue that holds everything together, and therefore the very basis of belonging. It arouses and fuels the fear of abandonment. It is no wonder that emotions run hot!

10.1.2 The Nature of the Affair

The couple will tend to respond in very different ways:

For the spouse, the betrayal seems unbearable. Yet for the unfaithful partner the affair is an aphrodisiac. The aura of romance and intrigue is compelling, especially when reality feels barren or boring. Affairs promise so much: an opportunity to pursue dreams that have been dormant, to come alive again, to find someone who truly understands. Their hidden promise is pain. (Brown, 1991, p. 2)

The destructive aspect of unfaithfulness was spelled out in Proverbs long ago: "For a prostitute's fee is only a loaf of bread, but the wife of another stalks a man's very life. Can fire be carried in the bosom without burning one's clothes?" (6:26–27).

Involvement in the affair can be sexual, emotional, or both. Women are more likely to be emotionally involved. The combination of sexual and emotional elements represents more of a threat to the marriage than either alone. Some generalizations might be made about gender in marital dissatisfaction: women tend to see sex as flowing from intimacy, whereas men see it as a path to intimacy. Therefore, it is natural that women's dissatisfaction will most often come from emotional issues, while males will complain about of lack of sex. While such distinctions seem to be breaking down, clinical experience suggests that when the woman has an affair it is usually more ominous for the future of the relationship.

Gottman described the "distance and isolation cascade," which is characterized by flooding (of emotions), seeing problems as severe, believing that it is best to work out problems alone, leading parallel lives, and loneliness (Gottman, 1999, p. 72). It is hardly surprising that as a person descends this cascade they will be more open to having an affair. However, while it is an option, an affair is never a solution.

Depression may be a factor, and this should be carefully assessed. Mid-life issues can add another dimension of potential complications. So often, the conclusion is reached after yet another unresolved fight ("This is not where I belong!"). There are also a number of ways that schema vulnerability, hidden behind coping modes, can contribute to an affair. But first we will build on Brown's (1991) model of five different kinds of affairs (Table 4).

10.1.3 The Conflict Avoidance Affair

In the conflict avoidance affair, there is a shout: "I'll make you pay attention to me!" Sometimes a couple will have a "nice" relationship, like a pond with hardly a surface ripple. Every difference of viewpoint is

Table 4 The six types of affairs

Type of affair	Characteristics
Conflict avoidance affair	"Peace at any price" leads to problems through the avoidance of relationship issues.
Intimacy avoidance affair	Hurt and difficulties with emotional intimacy lead to seeking it elsewhere.
Sexual addiction affair	The affair is part of a pattern of repeated infidelity.
Empty nest affair	Children have left. This is an affair to meet the emptiness of home life after raising children.
Out-the-door affair	The decision to leave has been made. This is the transition.
Homosexual affair	Perhaps sexual orientation issues have long been denied, but are now acknowledged.

avoided, and eventually this "peace" becomes suffocating. Usually, the more dissatisfied spouse gets into the affair and then manages to get quickly discovered. This takes the covers off problems in the relationship. It is a relief to have things out in the open.

> Rob confessed the next day to Marlene: "I have no idea what happened. I have no particular feelings for Sally. We were both at the conference, and after dinner drinks led to ... well, you know. I feel so guilty—and I promise never to see her again. Can you just forgive me? I want to make things right." Marlene was certainly prepared to forgive Rob, but she realized that something was wrong in their marriage.
>
> The therapist saw them a week later. Rob and Marlene had only a vague sense of dissatisfaction in their relationship. It was puzzling: why the affair? But they soon began to realize that underneath the avoiding of "hot" issues, even just "warm" ones, there was deep dissatisfaction. After the violation of the relationship, Marlene found it easier to be angry. Rob was obsessed with his guilt, but gradually he, too, was able to express resentment, especially about Marlene's frequent unwillingness for sex.

The threat to the marriage is more in the avoidance of conflict than in the affair. There is hope for the relationship if the couple are willing to face underlying issues. Ending the marriage or quickly forgiving are both cop-outs.

10.1.4   *Intimacy Avoidance Affairs*

All affairs reveal problems in intimacy, but in the intimacy avoidance affair it is the core issue. The outside relationship is a shield against hurt and disappointment with a barely conscious message: "I don't want to need you so much, so I'll get some of my needs met elsewhere." It is easier to argue than to be vulnerable and risk intimacy.

Intimacy avoiders appear to be very skilled at fighting (though not resolving conflict). Whether it is hot or icy, conflict is endless. Exchanges are filled with criticism, sarcasm, and blame. The mutual hostility may provide a justification for turning to someone else. The affair then becomes a weapon in the fight, and the partner may counter with another affair.

The way the couple stay in contact is through conflict, but paradoxically the anger gives the safety of distance as well. It is easy to justify the affair when there may be quite abusive conflict. Expressions of guilt are rare even after the discovery of the affair. Under the surface, there is a great deal of pain and fear. It is a dance in which both want the assurance of the other's love.

Val called early in the morning asking for an emergency session: "Can I see you first? I've just found out that my husband has been seeing prostitutes when he's overseas." There was high tension in their relationship. It was hard to get the story straight, but eventually it came out that Paul had caught a venereal disease when he was last in the Philippines.

The relationship was entangled and surprisingly strong for all the mutual blame. Neither raised the issue of leaving and both quickly engaged in the counseling process. They talked about experiences growing up. In Val's home, the parents were continually in an uproar. In contrast, Paul's parents never spoke to each other: there was a constant tension between two people who appeared to be strangers. Gradually, Paul and Val realized that they had no experience of healthy communication in family life. After about 10 sessions they had made such progress that they wanted to see whether they could make it on their own. They had managed to get behind the wall of conflict and found a new reward in getting to know each other.

If the issues of vulnerability and dependency are not addressed, affairs can become a way of life. The "open" marriage is a variation of this theme of intimacy avoidance.

Therapy Tip: You will need to be accepting of different values and life-style choices, but in ST it is important to look at dynamics from the perspective of modes. Is this evidence of a coping mode? Sometimes it might be helpful to say something like:

> "Some couples who have come being very adamant about an 'open' marriage have discovered that they have actually never been able to be emotionally intimate with anybody. We often see it when a partner goes along with the other's desire for a variety of sexual experiences because they are dependent in the relationship and use Compliant Surrender as a coping mechanism."

In therapy, the surrendered partner may become empowered to share their inner reluctance. Look for the buried hurt and anger. There may be a similar dynamic with couples who use pornography together. The consenting partner may feel that the initiating partner has more of an attachment to the pictures than to them, and a significant increase in a sense of failure and defectiveness haunts the relationship. Sometimes, the partner who wants to use pornography has deep-seated feelings of pressure and failure in his or her sexuality and sees the pornography as a model to be achieved or as a help in performance. Potentially mode-driven alternatives here harm the attachment bond. Ask what kind of bond this is. In both conflict avoidance and intimacy avoidance affairs, there is a deep bond in couples for which the search for attachment and acceptance is high on the needs list.

10.1.5   Sexual Addiction Affairs

The "womanizer" or "temptress" is a special case. This kind of person avoids dealing with personal needs by making conquests, perhaps with the expressed hope of finding "true love." Such individuals usually come from a deprived past, sometimes involving abuse or neglect, and experience themselves as empty—nothing fills them up in a lasting way. The conquests compensate for feelings of isolation, shame, and low self-esteem. The sexual addiction affair is addictive behavior, being compulsive and seemingly out of control. It usually continues despite the cost. This can also be a pattern with people who have a personality disorder or, at least, strong personality traits. Sometimes you might notice an adolescent quality, expressed in bragging about conquests. Risk may be something of a narcotic "hit."

Perhaps the only hope of change is through providing a measure of re-parenting through extended psychotherapy. It may also help that the partner uses the leverage of abandonment in the event of the continuation of this bad behavior. ST is well suited to this challenge.

In this type of affair, the lover is usually of little significance, although they may have attractive surface qualities, such as good looks or power of position. It is safe to predict that there will be many lovers over time and that there will never be enough. Such affairs tend to happen throughout the marriage. Often there is a defiance, a sort of "Catch me if you can."

Nicholas came to therapy after his new wife, Bess, threatened to leave him. She found out that he made a pass at one of her close friends. He was in his late twenties, tall, with an athletic build. He was very engaging and quite charming.

In the next three months, Nicholas proved to be very motivated. His mother was an alcoholic who had never married, and he came to realize that his emptiness was related to a lack of nurture when he was a child. He felt empty and tried to fill that intense need with the excitement of a hidden sexual relationship. Bess was very helpful in the process in holding him accountable and keeping lines of communication open.

It is helpful to understand the principle of "change talk" (from motivational interviewing), which encourages the therapist to position himself or herself in such a way that clients are encouraged to talk about change (Miller & Rollnick, 2002). Matthew Kelly calls it "becoming the best version of yourself" (Kelly, 2004). This is the principle of mode work in which we ally with the person to help change to a healthier coping mode or Healthy Adult. This is illustrated in the following:

THERAPIST   "So, as I understand it, you like the excitement of the chase and the novelty of different partners. But you've found some heavy costs as well. What do you see as the main disadvantages?"

NICHOLAS   "I think it's the Alfie syndrome. I always end up alone and full of regrets."

THERAPIST   "And?"

NICHOLAS   "I end up losing my self-respect, and I want to build something lasting in terms of a relationship ..."

Therapy Tip: Think about sexual "addiction"[12] in terms of the Detached Self-soother mode.

In ST-C, pornography can be taken out of the "blame arena" of the parent modes and more realistically explored as a Detached Self-soothing coping mechanism. This leads to dialog between the modes that prompted the need for self-soothing. Does the parent mode need to be blocked? Is there a seriously deprived infant mode that does not know how to self-regulate negative emotions and other unpleasant body feelings? Do the child modes need more re-parenting from the therapist, from the spouse, or from both? What is stopping the client's Healthy Adult mode from seeking a more adaptive coping mechanism?

Denny realized he had a sexual "addiction," primarily to pornography but also to occasionally engaging sex workers on business trips. He identified this as an escape. He would feel very overwhelmed, and when he fell below his sales targets he would hear his parent mode accuse him of being a failure.

There is a danger of superficially dealing with pornography as an addiction and intervening with motivational interviewing. We think it is preferable to work with the modes. Healing will not be lasting until a person changes the unhealthy coping mechanisms and resolves unmet needs. This will have a reinforcing effect in the couple's sexual relationship. It improves and becomes more mutually satisfying. Interpersonal connection is a challenge, but the rewards are great.

---

[12] There is emerging scientific evidence that "sexual addiction" as such might not truly exist. Brain studies using electroencephalography show some indications that this conceptualization may be misleading (see Steele et al. 2013). It remains to be seen whether these scientific analyses may be supporting the mode conceptualizations of such behaviors described as "addictive".

The schema therapist is uniquely positioned in understanding of how the modes operate, and helping people in a non-blaming way to fill the positive lack in the "need" area. As Rafaeli et al. described in their book on ST (2010), limited re-parenting seeks to satisfy a person's need within professional boundaries, rather than fear that they will become dependent.

Just as this takes "considerable emotional investment" (Rafaeli et al., 2011, p. 155), it is considerable emotional investment that ultimately brings healing in a relationship. Why do we bring this up here? Because sexual disorders, addictions, and seeming incompatibilities are based in the emotional connection or disconnection of the couple. If only the symptom is treated, the couple may be temporarily "satisfied" but may miss out on the richness of connecting, when the needs of the both are fulfilled.

Therapy Tip: Change-talk, a technique from motivational interviewing (Miller & Rollnik, 2002), is useful in dealing with addictions and can provide a good initial therapeutic stance.

The goal is a more intimate connection for the couple. Lacking that, the relationship becomes messy:

> Love consists of a commitment which limits one's freedom—it is a giving of the self, and to give oneself means just that: to limit one's freedom on behalf of another. Limitation of one's freedom might seem to be something negative and unpleasant, but love makes it a positive, joyful and creative thing. Freedom exists for the sake of love. (Wojtyla, 1993, p. 135)

Intimacy is the goal. The couple can experience it without the baggage of their "schema-walls" interfering and their maladaptive coping modes creating "escape hatches." Psychiatrist Richard Fitzgibbons clarified the sex-to-person connection:

> This connection between sex and the person is manifest in the special awareness of the "I" by which every sexual giving always requires a giving of the whole person. Betrothed love absolutely needs the other forms of love, especially goodwill and friendship. Without these "allies," self-sacrificing persons might find a void within themselves. They would then become helpless in the face of internal and external problems. (Fitzgibbons, 2005–2011)

10.1.6   Empty Nest Affairs

The empty nest affair signals a marriage that has been held together by a belief in family rather than a strong emotional bond. A family man, married 20 years, now admits that he has never really loved his wife. Or he says that he had doubts since the beginning but went ahead anyway. On the surface, it appears that he tried to "make a go of it" by doing his duty. But there are an equal number of wives who have filled the same role for a decade or two and now look elsewhere for intimacy.

While the children are still at home, the focus is on them. When it becomes obvious that the marriage is empty, the person is tempted to seek fulfillment elsewhere. It is the relationship rather than the individual that is empty. Communication may be limited to purely practical matters.

The affair tends to be a serious matter and may last for years. The partner in the affair then becomes idealized, while the spouse is devalued. Participants tend to be more discreet and do not invite discovery. However, when the affair is revealed it can be deeply wounding to the spouse, especially if they remain committed to the marriage.

> James saw me only at the demand of his wife, Fiona. He explained to me, "I really have no energy to work on the marriage. It's pointless. Fiona has finally found out about my relationship with Michelle, and I suppose that clarifies things for me. I want to move to Sydney so I can be with her. Our son, Mike, has nearly finished his law degree and he can come to see me on the odd weekend."

There is usually some reluctance to enter counseling. But if there is any willingness, try to clarify what is at stake. It may be helpful to see the couple as individuals for a while, with marital counseling following later. Sadly, a typical motive for seeking counseling is to leave the abandoned spouse in the care of the psychologist.

10.1.7   Out-the-Door Affairs

The erring spouse is seriously thinking about ending the marriage, so this affair is an attempt to answer such questions as: "Can I make it on my own?" "Am I still attractive?" "Can I be happy in another relationship?" and, most important, "Can I get you to kick me out?" The purpose has two aspects. There is usually a quest for self-validation, but less consciously there may also be a desire to avoid taking responsibility for ending the marriage. The affair is a distraction from the difficulties and the pain of ending the marriage.

The lover is usually portrayed as "understanding," and the relationship may have been built on a close friendship. They are someone to talk with about marital dissatisfactions and hopes for the future. The affair confirms that the marriage is unsatisfactory, and this justifies the impending separation. The unfaithful spouse will usually ensure that they are found out, and sometimes they are disappointed that even then the spouse will not end the marriage. The task of counseling is difficult because the unfaithful spouse may only be coming to self-justify: "I did everything that I could." Usually, the spouse being left is more willing to face issues such as the loss of the marriage and adjustment to a different life. There may be some need to improve communication, which will help them in facing their parenting responsibilities.

> Trudi had married Clarence, a successful medical specialist about 15 years older than her. They had two children in their marriage. She was initially very reluctant to tell her husband about her affair with Frank. In therapy, she made that decision.
>
> Trudi said to her therapist, "Yes I will leave, but it's more to leave Clarence. I'm not really in love with Frank. I may see how it goes with him for a little while, but I really want to get on with my life."

Generally, the prognosis for the marriage gets worse as the assessment moves from conflict avoidance to an out-the-door affair. It is helpful when both can accept responsibility for creating the unhappy nature of the marriage, and a schema therapist can help to define the underlying nature of the problems in the relationship. Rebuilding takes time, whether it is focused on the marriage or on the future after separation. Sometimes forgiveness is possible, and it has a healing effect (Gordon & Baucom, 1988).

10.1.8   The Homosexual Affair

The homosexual affair is another category to add to Brown's five types of affairs. It is an affair with a gay lover after being in a heterosexual relationship. There are some similarities with the out-the-door affair, because the prognosis is usually poor for the marriage. But it also has elements of the empty nest affair, in which there may be a deep attachment to the lover.

There are differences, including in the apparent change in orientation. Some people are aware of attraction to their own sex in their teens but hold back for reasons of personal, family, or social disapproval. The social stigma may lead to trying to make a traditional marriage work. Moral values or religious beliefs may also add to the determination to make a success of the marriage. This resolve can later break down.

Bennie experimented with some homosexual encounters when he was a teenager. He tried to dismiss it as "sexual exploration," until he found the urge to visit gay bars irresistible. He had a troubled marriage, and when his wife found out about his homosexual activity she left him and refused to speak to him except through her lawyer. He was confused and somewhat ashamed of his desires: "I can't understand it. I still only want to have a steady relationship with a woman, but I go for casual sex through a gay bar."

In some cases there is a more recent attraction, and this can be confusing.

Mark rang in a state of panic. He had found out that his wife, Gabrielle, had a female lover. On the phone he poured out, "Damn it! We have four children, all teenagers. How the hell could this have happened?" He sent Gabrielle for the first session. Mark was hoping that therapy would change her back.

Gabrielle: "I met Angie at church. We both help with a coffee house ministry. It involves outreach to the unemployed. We began with being good friends."

But Gabrielle had no interest in reconciling with Mark: "The thought of Mark touching me disgusts me. I can no longer sleep in the same room, and I think it's hopeless staying together for our children. This sounds like I've made up my mind to leave, doesn't it?"

The rejection of the partner is possibly the hardest to bear in this kind of affair. As Mark later said, "It's not just me personally. I could understand it if she went with another man, but a woman? She's so turned off that she's rejecting my gender as well. How could I fail her like that?"

10.1.9   Schema Therapy with Affairs

Often the vulnerability for having an affair can be traced to schemas. Consider how each of the schemas might contribute.

Some schemas indicate a strong sense of need, and if a person becomes desperate this might lead to trying to seek comfort elsewhere. Abandonment, Emotional Deprivation, and Approval Seeking reveal deep unmet needs. Angie said that she needed more than Barry could give, "And I found it with Hank at work."

An affair with schemas such as Entitlement and Insufficient Self-control will be very different. Nick said with self-justifying anger, "I believe that I am due recreational sex! What's the big deal?"

Some schemas indicate a lack in the sense of self: Defectiveness-Shame, Social Isolation, Dependence Incompetence, Vulnerability to Harm or Illness, Enmeshment, Failure, and Emotional Inhibition. Amie was very dependent in her relationship to Brad. She lacked any sense of autonomy. She was getting more frustrated at his lack of availability for her to "lean on" but found a work colleague who began to show an interest in her.

An affair might be seen as a distraction or an attempt to "break out." Nick felt inferior to others because he did not feel athletic enough. He tried bodybuilding but it never worked. But at the gym he found the interest of Mike quite intoxicating.

Or there may be vulnerability because of attitudes: Mistrust-Abuse, Negativity Pessimism, Failure. Vella felt a constant failure, especially in her marriage. She did not live up to the expectations of her husband, or his mother, but she felt more accepted by Dennis, who lived nearby.

Sometimes anger leading to an affair may be influenced by Punitiveness. Charlie said, "I'll show her. The bitch! She'll feel bad when she finds I'm screwing around."

Look for the schema dynamics:

> Mary was a personal assistant to a demanding boss. She never complained when he was sexually harassing her. But what began with suggestive comments ended up as sexual advances, which she could not refuse due to a life pattern of subjugation.

So understanding the affair in terms of schema vulnerability is important. There may also be complementary dynamics from the spouse. ST-C heals these vulnerabilities by re-parenting. It helps change the underlying personality coping mechanisms. Other marital and couples therapies bring about empathy and some measure of understanding, but do not generalize to the entire stance and towards the very personal cycle that the couple is perennially trapped in.

> Nick's wife Brenda tended to accept Nick's self-serving justifications. She was heavily into Self-sacrifice with Emotional Inhibition schemas.

ST can work with such patterns through some of the techniques already outlined. Limited re-parenting is especially important with entrenched schemas that contribute to affairs. Angie had to deal with memories of abuse that resulted in emotional neediness, Mary with her violent father, who insisted on subjugation, and Brenda needed to trust her feelings and to change her passivity into appropriate assertiveness.

10.1.10 Mode Work with Affairs

It is also valuable to think about the mode, or state of mind, in which an affair is attractive. While a schema-based conceptualization looks on the underlying personality traits, a mode perspective focuses on the here-and-now reaction of the person and leaves the history aside. In complicated cases, such as those involving the personality-disordered, this helps manage the reactive elements within the couple relationship.

Think about the following cases using this list of modes: Vulnerable Child, Angry Child, Enraged Child, Impulsive Child, Undisciplined Child, Happy Child, Compliant Surrender, Detached Protector, Detached Self-soother, Self-aggrandizer, Bully and Attack, Punitive Parent, Demanding Parent, and Healthy Adult.

> Natalie talked about the affair: "I just needed the comfort of being with him." (Detached Self-soother)
>
> Val said defiantly, "I just wanted to get back. Stick it to her and rub her face in it—the worthless bitch she is!" (Bully and Attack)
>
> Desmond said with a sad tone, "I felt totally alone. I needed comfort. My wife was no longer talking to me." (Vulnerable Child)
>
> Nerrida spat out, "I hate Ben. I was glad that his brother was interested in me. I know it hurt Ben that I screwed his younger brother, but I deserved to get some attention!" (Angry Child)

An affair might "feel right" when the person is in a child or coping mode. If you can understand the mode, then it becomes possible to introduce some circuit breakers to bring choice into the cycle. Perhaps mindfulness or a third-person perspective can be used to gain some distance. For example, "How would your best friend comment on this affair?" Then try behavior pattern breaking targeted at choices to continue or stop the affair.

Understanding schemas and mode work sets ST-C apart from other therapies. It is different in conceptualizing what "caused" the affair and how the healing process unfolds. The cause in our minds is important from three aspects:

- How can this understanding assist to "affair-proof" a relationship?
- How can a change in relevant modes provide more security to the traumatized partner?
- How can the recognition of the mode cycle facilitate an earlier foundation of insight, a reduction of blame, the taking of responsibility, and a layer of hope?

In this way, outcomes change. Mode therapy can effectively address the many challenges of a couple with one partner in an affair. In this sense, we are able to stress the experiential and interpersonal behavioral aspects of this therapy, making it truly a third-wave therapy and setting it apart from its cognitive origins. Generally, the shift to working with modes is now central in ST. Unfortunately, critics of ST continue to characterize it as a type of cognitive therapy. Now ST notes cognitions, but tends to bypass negative thoughts or assign them to a parent mode, and then address the dynamic experientially.

Shirley Glass has stated:, "The fact is, sometimes an affair can be understood by exploring the deficiencies in the marriage, but often it cannot" (2003, p. 40). She described the "prevention myth": that a loving partner and a good marriage will prevent affairs. While we agree that a loving partner does not prevent affairs, a good marriage is a barrier. ST defines "good" as a relationship in which partners shift from maladaptive coping modes to a healthier coping by the Healthy Adult. As pointed out above in the typology of affairs, we can usually trace the occurrence of an affair to a mode clash or an activated schema. The ideal of ST is supporting a couple to move from getting stuck in a mode cycle or flipping between mode cycles to an encounter of two more or less Healthy Adults aware of their full spectrum of needs and able to negotiate their mutual fulfillment. Since the emotional activation in an affair is extremely high, the externalizing tools (such as the mode cycle clash-card or standing up together, looking down on the scene) are very helpful in getting the couple to return and process difficult emotions. Healthy couples work at confronting or getting help with unhealthy modes to the point where the unhealthy mode eruptions are minor and not a threat to the relationship. We aspire to this vision of a healthy relationship.

Sometimes mode clashes are hidden, but eventually they emerge, and the key to ongoing relapse prevention lies in being able to conceptualize and heal the clash. The risk of rupture in the relationship is lessened with greater awareness of mode dynamics.

We often first see the parent modes directed at the betraying partner. This may come through the injured person from Punitive Parent, with harsh moral standards or attempts at revenge. Another way this might be expressed is out of Demanding Parent mode, with demands for complete disclosure of all past betrayals. This can be unrealistic and even impossible to satisfy no matter how much effort is given to the rehashing (think about the task of raking leaves in the back yard, which can never be complete). Instead, aim for a "good enough" disclosure, which might be best contained in a single session.

At some level, the determination of "character" will settle the question of reinvesting after an affair or, indeed, after any series of "bad behaviors." Watch when it comes from a parent mode, rather than Healthy Adult. It is, in a sense, an inequality, and any relationship that allows for one person to go into an unequal position of analysis and judgment has flaws that are bound to undermine connection. Connection must always be between two equal and accepting partners, even though both may disagree about their own or the other's bad behavior. Encourage the couple to turn away from such a coping mode of behavior with the recognition that it is injurious to the self and others, and to deliberately embrace the other more positively through Healthy Adult.

> Nikki was devastated at Mark's "slip" at the office Christmas party. She obsessed about it and demanded that he show "evidence" of a change in "character." While some of this might be considered sensible and even potentially good self-care, the onus was on Mark to prove himself—with Nikki as the prosecutor and judge. The relationship was stuck for a while in this unhelpful dynamic.

Room must be given to acknowledge that we are all flawed. We all engage at times in various sorts of bad behavior that can challenge intimacy. We also need to allow for the possibility of repentance and a lasting change in behavior.

The way to protect both the person who perpetrated the bad behavior and the hurt partner is to help each to understand which modes were involved and the path of healing for such modes.

> Minh had an affair with her work colleague. Her de facto partner, Barry, was prepared to enter counseling: "I don't want to leave. I want to fix things." In therapy, it was found that the affair came from Detached Self-soother mode, and progress was made with weakening that mode and discovering what it was detaching from. Minh also had a self-directed parental voice telling her that she was defective, and in individual sessions discovered the origins of that voice (basically, her mother).
>
> Then she started to unlearn it, block it, and ignore it. Memories were readily at hand of abusive messages in that Punitive Parent voice, and imagery work was carried out to re-parent her Vulnerable Child and impeach the parent. There was further couple work with identifying the triggers.
>
> What triggered the parental voice? This involved looking at the cycle between the couple. Turning to the cycle does not take the unfaithful party "off the hook," but it is less blaming and allows more of a

redistribution of responsibility for the state of the relationship when the affair began.

ST-C aims to make both partners in the couple relationship fully responsible, individually and jointly, for more effectively meeting their own needs. Often, it is understanding where my feelings and needs come from that allows me to be more effective in Healthy Adult mode.

10.1.11   Ground Rules

Shirley Glass (2003) has recommended some ground rules for the disclosure of details, including sexual details. This can be important in handling situations where contact with the third person cannot be avoided. Many of the concepts in her *Not just Friends* (2003) and Janis Spring's *After the Affair* (2012) are presented with clear reasoning. However, there is a drawback. Just telling partners what they should do, and why, is like telling a smoker to stop. Understanding modes, especially compensating modes, can help the couple to address more entrenched emotional issues.

Therapy Tip: Mode therapy is different in its approach to healing a couple ruptured by an affair, be it emotional, sexual, or both. Consider the following:

- Use chair-work to heal the individual mode of the perpetrator (Betrayer) in front of the partner. You can put the mode wanting the affair in a coping mode chair, since we usually regard an affair as a self-soothing behavior. What mode is it? Give it a label and then see how Vulnerable Child feels with what they are doing. Place the Vulnerable Child behind the coping mode chair so it is covered by the coping mode. Start differentiating between the self-asserting part of the affair and balance it with the long-term effects for the attachment-seeking system. Offer two child mode chairs, one for each pole. Is this (the self-soothing coping mode) giving Vulnerable Child what is really needed in the long run? Getting in touch with the vulnerable and attachment-directed child mode helps reconciling.
- Have a dialog between these two child modes. Enter in Healthy Adult to talk to the modes. Can Healthy Adult better fulfill the underlying needs of the assertiveness pole, represented by the Impulsive Child chair? Does Healthy Adult need to teach the Impulsive Child that, just because you feel attraction and approval, it does not mean that you have to act?

10.1.12   When do you Forgive?

There is a chorus of voices in relation to forgiveness. Robert Enright has established the Forgiveness Institute,[13] and there are resources in the work of Richard Fitzgibbons, Shirley P. Glass, and Janis Abrahms Spring (2004). This discussion also belongs in ST-C.

It is often valuable to think about the words we use. Reconciliation implies repeatedly talking something over. *Re* means *to repeat* and *conciliation* means *dialog*. But the word *forgiveness* does not include dialog. It is an action. It is an initiative that comes from a single person. It is a gift to another person. The other person does not have to "deserve" it. If there is a condition ("I'll forgive you if …"), it is not forgiveness. In Christian tradition, to forgive your "enemy" means to forgive as a gift, with no conditions. The enemy does not have to become your "friend" to be forgiven.

Forgiveness is never possible without fully experiencing the injury. It is a process leading to a place of greater acceptance. This is a journey for the betrayed partner. Make sure that it is not pseudo-forgiveness, offered to retain the relationship.

> Alice had a one-night stand at a conference. She was so paralyzed by guilt that she returned home and confessed immediately. Bob was shocked and confused, and only came to some clarity about how he felt when he felt surges of anger. But this was an unfamiliar emotion to him, anger being a taboo emotion when he was raised in a very rigid family. He went to see his parish priest, who encouraged him to grant "forgiveness." He was ready to forgive because he wanted to "wipe the slate clean." Two months later, his family doctor encouraged him to enter therapy because he was waking every morning at 2 am. In therapy, he realized that he still had plenty of feelings about the affair.

A Subjugation schema and a Compliant Surrender mode will sometimes motivate a person to "forgive," but this has little to do with forgiveness no matter how sincerely it is felt: it is a type of avoidance and fear of disconnection. Such forgiveness will further undermine the relationship. A simple test to discover whether a person is forgiving in haste is to set up a dialog between Healthy Adult and Vulnerable Child. Can Healthy Adult validate how the Vulnerable Child is feeling? Validate that an affair is a betrayal, and that betrayal is never OK, no matter how "bad" a partner may have acted? One bad deed does not justify another.

If the betrayed partner can embrace without excuses that they were victimized by this betrayal and that it was not justified, then forgiveness is an

---

[13]   www.internationalforgiveness.com.

option for them. If there is hedging and a strong self-accusatory parent mode causing doubt and question, then hold off the partner from forgiving until the parent voice is completely ignored, or at least much weakened and out of the picture. Forgiving too soon disempowers the injured party and causes more undermining by avoidance and fear.

The betraying party also needs to be treated as an equal. They will feel relieved when their partner stands as an equal and holds them accountable ("on the hook") first, before letting them off the hook. *After the Affair* (Spring, 2012) has a good explanation of the concept. This makes the eventual forgiveness an act between equals.

> Bob had a number of sessions to explore how injured he felt about the affair. He said, "Both Alice and I saved sex until our wedding night. It was something we had together, and now this is uniqueness is lost." In couple sessions, Bob was able to say how he felt. Alice was relieved that he was moving out of a role of subjugation: "I can relate to you as more of an adult I respect. I know I've hurt you ... well, us ... terribly, but your strength is attractive to me."

Forgiveness can and must be given freely as a gift if the couple is ever going to connect and heal again. Forgiveness means you accept the wrong-doing as not being right or justified, acknowledge that the other person is in your debt, voluntarily choose to reinvest in them, not punish them, and raise them up from being in your debt to being an equal again. It does not mean that the process of rebuilding trust has been completed. It does mean, though, that you are giving up your right to punish and keep the other person beneath your feet for what they have done.

Forgiveness, if properly applied, comes from a Healthy Adult mode. It should be a "free" decision, not driven from a desperate need for attachment, as in a Compliant Surrender coping mode, to avoid a conflict. In Healthy Adult mode, a person makes a personal choice to not exact revenge, to not go into Punitive Parent mode and overcompensate towards the offender, but to seek a new beginning in the relationship.

Reconciliation takes a minimum of two people. Usually, it means that relationship hurts have been specifically acknowledged and understood. Dialog is needed so the harmed individual feels sufficiently understood. Note that the dialog should continue to the point where the victim of the hurt feels reconciled, not merely to the point where the offender feels that enough has been said (which is usually about three seconds!).

Sometimes, if a hurt person's schemas are involved, they may never get to the point of saying "I've finished talking about it." Neither party can force reconciliation. It can only be accomplished if both parties can stay in their Healthy Adult mode. An offender can ask forgiveness, but that does not accomplish reconciliation. A victim may be willing to forgive, but an offender might never truly acknowledge the damage done. In both cases reconciliation does not happen, because it is only one-sided.

The liberating news for the Healthy Adult is that a person can always forgive or ask forgiveness without the other person's cooperation. Forgiveness does not require the victim to re-expose their vulnerable self to the perpetrator. True reconciliation, however, almost always does require a mutual coming to an understanding, a sense of repentance and empathy for the hurt caused, and a re-exposing of vulnerability towards each other in order not to keep a wall up.

In true schema mode fashion, it requires some of the understanding that the mode maps and mode cycle clash-card can bring. At the most basic level, what part did each of us play? What do we each really need here? And let us at least mutually care enough to try to act in a Healthy Adult way to fill our own needs without harm to each other. This can build and progress to deeper reconciliation by a commitment to re-parenting and assisting in correcting the damage done by making ongoing positive efforts to offset the specific damage and fill the opposing need, rather than continuing to cause hurt or pain.

Therapy Tip: Simeone-DiFrancesco and Simeone (2016a,b) have listed the steps towards reconciliation.[14]

10.1.13   Healing the Affair with a Ritual

Farrell and Shaw (2012) have written about group exercises to remind members of the group that "us" has a corporate identity. So, too, with couples. We can be sensitive to what might enhance the couple work. The marriage ceremony is full of symbolism. Why not mark relationship recovery with some suitable symbols? The following is a good example:

> Scott and Diana had repaired their relationship after a brief affair. Diana said, "I know I've forgiven Scott and I need to work towards trying to forget. The difficulty is that our marriage was damaged. I wonder if we might re-say our marriage vows? That would help me to get a sense of a fresh start based on a renewed commitment." Scott was happy to make a fresh start in this way. They arranged for a civil celebrant to have a private ceremony in which they repeated their vows.

---

[14]   See www.healinginternational.org.

There are many other potential rituals of relationship renewal. Perhaps the richest resource is the creativity of the couple and knowing what feels right for them.

10.1.14 A Caution

There is a potential difficulty with confidentiality. The disclosure of an affair in individual therapy is not an ethical dilemma, but things can be different if you are the couple therapist as well. There is no golden rule to deal with this challenge, and we are well aware that different therapists deal with it in different ways. Even we three authors have different perspectives! You might think about working towards the revelation of a present-tense affair in a reasonable time span, such as four weeks. An affair does not mean that the couple therapy is over. It might bring the therapy to another level.

We offer the following advice on working with couples when an affair is, or might, be involved:

1. *Suspicion.* If you suspect that one partner might be having an affair, it is best to address this issue in an individual session. If the client denies the affair, accept it and refocus on overt behavior (we are not detectives). If a client manages to behave in a "normal" way while having a secret affair, the affair is eventually part of the balance of this relationship.
2. *Past affair.* If you gain information of a past affair and it is not obvious that this has present-tense consequences, then it is best to leave it confidential. It is more problematic if the betrayed partner expresses a suspicion about the affair or about infidelity in general. The problem is that to encourage keeping an affair secret is to deny the "reality testing" of the injured party. It is preferable to encourage disclosure and deal with the consequences.
3. *Present-tense affair.* If one of the couple is currently in an affair, it is inevitable that this will have an impact on the couple and adversely affect any therapy you offer. At the very least, you should try to get the erring spouse to stop for a period and cease *all* contact with their lover. This will give you some chance to work with the couple. If the client accepts, you might continue working with the couple but also look out very carefully for signs of Detached Protector behavior from the betraying partner. If you perceive this, then it has to be addressed to avoid becoming part of a false game. We believe that affairs are destructive in a relationship, but they happen and it is not up to us to judge our clients' behavior. An undisclosed affair is not a target for therapy.

4. *Not keeping agreement.* If the betraying partner shows signs of not keeping to the commitment they have given you, you will have to empathically confront this behavior. This does not mean the end of couple therapy, but it changes the game. You might work with the affair as a third party, putting it on an extra chair. Our goal is to work on solid ground. Sometimes it is surprising what a couple can deal with, but no one can work on a slippery slope. It is our role to build a solid foundation for working with the couple.

10.1.15 Summary of Affairs

Affairs are painfully common. Often an affair is the reason a couple comes for help, but an affair might be undisclosed and underlie current problems. Perhaps surprisingly, an affair is not the most common reason for a relationship ending. Some research indicates that close to 80 percent of people leaving a marriage say that the reason for getting divorced is "gradually growing apart." Affairs are cited as the reason by about 20–27 percent.[15] An affair is usually a symptom and not the true cause of the breakdown in the relationship.

We think ST can help us and couples to understand when a person "goes outside" the relationship to meet emotional needs. Our mode approach holds promise in healing both parties and the relationship itself after an affair. An adjunct book for couples to use themselves is Janis Spring's *After the Affair* (2012).

In the end, an affair may not be completely destructive. Sometimes the relationship survives and grows stronger—although usually both partners hurt terribly, the affair may indicate that they want something more in the relationship. The perfect dream for the relationship may feel marred, but reality can still be satisfying and rewarding, and may even wind up being better than the untested love of the perfect dream. Even in the wake of a broken relationship, there is the possibility of insight and being wiser the next time around.

10.2 Preparing for Marriage or a Committed Relationship

ST can provide useful material for marriage preparation. Working with a therapist can lead to a map of each partner's core memories and unmet needs (possibly from childhood), and create clear goals for the relationship.

---

[15] Research of L. Gigy and J. Kelly of the California Divorce Mediation Project, cited by Gottman (1999, p. 23).

It is easy to see how much it would benefit a couple to enter a relationship with such knowledge!

Couples can learn relationship skills that are highly targeted and not limited to communication skills. Having clear individual mode maps and a clash-card while they are still in the "in love" stage can go a long way towards helping a couple remain in a satisfying relationship.

Reflect: Think about using the "goodwill" of a couple to deal with potentially sensitive issues in their relationship.

Using the "love target-practice" sheet for couples (Figure 18 in Section 11.5) can help each partner begin to share at a level where empathy for the childhood origins of modes can be established from the beginning. The tools of empathic confrontation, empathic resonance, and empathic self-assertion of needs can help partners lessen blame and begin to meet their needs. This heads off the Avoidance and Angry Child modes that often fuel later disconnection.

Reflect: Think about using a genogram to track intergenerational themes. What modes are most obvious in the decades of family life?

10.3   Domestic Violence[16]

Violence is common, but we must avoid making assumptions about it. Ask the couple whether their conflict has ever involved domestic violence: emotional or psychological abuse, physical intimidation or aggression, or social isolation. Usually, but not always, it is the female partner who is the victim of abuse and, given the usual differences in physical size, more at risk (Barnish, 2004; Hamel, 2005). Therapy does not always work, so you will need to be cautious with what you advise couples (Gottman & Jacobsen, 1998).

> Frank was ashamed to admit it, but "Mandy loses it and hits me. I feel scared most of the time." He continued, "I know I could hit her back but that's not right—it's never right for a man to hit a woman. My parents taught me that. I want it to work between us but I can't relax. I don't feel safe at all."

Assess the level of risk. Barnish (2004) and Heru (2007) listed the risk factors: a previous history of violent partner behavior, uncontrolled and continuous use of drugs or alcohol, fear of serious injury from the partner, past violence that required medical treatment, previous use of or threat of

---

[16]   We would like to acknowledge the contribution of Dr. Malise Arnstein, from her chapter in *Happy ever After?* (Stevens & Arnstein, 2011).

use of a weapon, death threats, stalking or other obsessional behavior, sadistic behavior, a man's history of being in an abusive family as a child, narcissistic or inflated and fragile self-esteem, and patriarchal sense of entitlement.

Gottman and Jacobsen (1998) differentiated perpetrators into three groups:

1. *Low risk of abuse:* couples between which there is rare and low-risk abuse who do not require medical intervention.
2. *Cobras:* estimated as 20 percent of high-risk abusers; often with criminal, sadistic and antisocial characteristics; are deliberate and calculating in their violence; the men, with typically very low heart rate, engage in cold, controlled instances of violence.
3. *Pit Bulls:* estimated to be 80 percent of high-risk abusers; have elevated heart rates; men are more insecure, but also dangerous.

Typically, those in a relationship with a Cobra are more afraid of their partners than those in relationships with Pit Bulls. Barnish (2004), in her excellent review of the literature, found support for a general classification of this type.

> Nancy was terrified to leave Bazza. "He said he would kill me if I left. You know, I believe he'd do it. How can I protect our children? I need to be here. Since he got out of jail he's been worse, and he hangs around with dangerous people. I'm really terrified." Eventually, she was able to leave after she was admitted to hospital following an assault. Bazza was arrested and returned to jail because it was a breach of his conditions of bail.

Reflect: Would Bazza be more likely to be a Cobra or a Pit Bull?

Treatment outcomes studies are not generally optimistic, although David Bernstein and fellow researchers are finding significant advances in using ST to treat psychopaths and in developing empathy in them (Bernstein et al., 2012a). This gives great hope for our ST-C approach of a combination of significant individual work with couples where there are these more difficult psychopathic-type abusive behaviors.

Simeone-DiFrancesco has experienced helping a couple in just such a manner with a co-schema-therapist, with individual healing for the traumatized female and the abusive Pit Bull male. The capacity to heal and actually develop a wonderful mutually re-parenting and empathic connection took much coordination between therapists and careful but non-judgmental openness to "what could be." Many therapists are themselves so triggered by the horror of the abuse that they are not able to form sufficient optimism to bring a couple to this good new beginning.

As both a couple therapist and a forensic psychologist working with offenders, Simeone-DiFrancesco states that it takes a careful, mature, and balanced commitment to the rights, needs and wishes of the victim, along with optimism for change for some of the most wounded offenders. Barnish found that there are some approaches that seem promising (Barnish, 2004; Heru, 2007; Meichenbaum, 2007). The best results in the USA often involve a combination of individual therapy for both partners, gender-specific groups (often court-mandated for the abusers), telephone support for the victims, couple therapy and, later, couples group therapy (Stith et al., 2004; Hamel, 2005; Capaldi & Kim, 2007; Meichenbaum, 2007).

Gottman and Jacobsen (1998) have been very cautious about the merits of couple therapy when there is violence. We tend to disagree with such a blanket statement, seeing the effect of ST with severe personality disorders. If people with such disorders can be helped, violently behaving individuals can be helped, but the careful construction of limits and rights, and the availability of co-therapists as needed, are called for. Gottman and Jacobsen make an exception for couples with low-level or family-only intimate violence and, as others would emphasize, voluntary participation in treatment (Bograd & Mederos, 2004).

The focus of treatment is always the violent behavior, which is regarded as a severe overcompensatory mode. There is no way of gaining "attachment" by violence. There are no excuses. In fact, the overcompensating behavior is driven less by the attachment system than by the assertiveness system striving for control. While over-controlling, you cannot expect to be loved. Control creates dependency, not attachment! The responsibility to abstain from violent behavior always lies with the perpetrator. Self-responsibility or agency-for-self is emphasized with men who behave violently, but understanding the underlying motives helps. Going back to childhood injuries in imagery can reveal the backstage scene and the roots of the overcompensation and helps to implement adult assertive behavior.

Goldner (1998) emphasized the need for women to pay attention to the messages of their internal fear responses to their partners (no matter how sincere, romantic, or hopeful the promises of the partner). Some women, who have lost their ability to think in terms of self-care, may need coaching. Watch out for submissive coping behavior in the past as a personal trait. Domestic violence is a mode cycle, too, maintained by submissive behavior! It is better to seek support by stepping out of the silence and improving your autonomy step by step.

Dottie had been subject to occasional violence over the years: "It wasn't every week or even every month, but I stayed on edge. I think it kept me in my place."

Her husband, Todd, had a conversion experience, but their pastor rightly insisted that he attend a domestic violence course run through a church agency. Todd later said, "I had some ingrained patterns I had to change. I really appreciate Dottie hanging in there, but I was the one who had to change. I had a new faith, but I really needed to understand how my violence has affected the family and make necessary changes in how I behaved."

Heru (2007) and Hamel (2005) offer a very useful checklist for women who feel unsafe and may need to separate and seek refuge:

- Memorize important and emergency phone numbers.
- Teach children these numbers and how to dial the local emergency number.
- Keep information about domestic violence in a safe and private place.
- Keep a cellphone or change for a payphone handy.
- If possible, open a separate bank account.
- Set up support—friends, neighbors, family—and keep in touch.
- Rehearse the escape plan.
- Leave spare keys, money, clothes, copies of important identification, financial, health, insurance documents, and anything needed with a trusted person.

Dr. Arnstein added:

- Know your rights, your legal situation, and where alternative accommodation can be found, including refuges, because staying with people unknown to the abuser may be important for safety.

Goldner (1998) advised that joint couple therapy is only appropriate after the man has demonstrated that he has taken full responsibility for his behavior, shows remorse, understanding of and empathy for his partner's position and reactions, and is on a path of non-violence for a few weeks (Gottman and Jacobsen would say six months). We concur with these admonitions, and perhaps it is best to continue individual therapy until both are stronger in Healthy Adult.

It should be clear to all that any relapse of the male partner into violence at any stage of the therapeutic involvement—during the single-gender group phase, the assessment, the couple therapy or couples group—will lead to the involvement of police, legal intervention and the couple's permanent separation.

Research indicates that the incidence of violent episodes is likely to increase during the six months after separation (Barnish, 2004). Both partners can be involved in separation counseling sessions, but with a paramount concern for the woman's safety. Couples mediation within the context of the family court can be of benefit (Kelly & Johnson, 2008). Understanding the underlying motives of the (ex-) partner helps in cooling down emotions and seeing the separation as the result of a "misfit," rather than as the fault of one partner or the other. Support groups for women can help to empower the woman in this transition. The involvement of other agencies and professionals is important during this phase.

There may be strong schema vulnerability for the couple in a violent relationship. This should be carefully assessed along the lines suggested above for affairs. ST with violent partners can become more effective by working with modes. Anger is not simply anger. You can make distinctions between the child states of Angry Child and Enraged Child, the intimidation of Bully and Attack or the defensiveness of an Angry Protector. This helps us to recognize not only the cues but the "anger sequence" and how it relates to personality dynamics. Finally, all forms of anger expressions are fueled by the Angry Child mode, indicating the activation of the assertiveness system. This anger is potentially functional but needs to be directed by the Healthy Adult mode, which includes respecting the personal needs/rights of others. Otherwise, attachment-based relations cannot be gained in the long run.

Reflect: Punitive Parent directs anger, but is not the source of the anger.

The first goal is to disconnect the anger as a basic emotion from its over-compensatory "mantle." The method is similar to that described in Section 8.2. First place the overcompensatory anger in a chair and ask questions of the mode. The core question is: What are the long-term consequences of the expression of the anger? If the person is in the chair, responses might include either turning away or counter-attack.

In the next step, you might add a chair for the Vulnerable Child beside the Angry Child chair and ask the client to sit down on the Vulnerable Child chair. Ask them, "What do you think about the result of this anger expression? What do you essentially need?" The idea is to validate the anger as an attempt to gain control and assertiveness, but to realize that a price is paid in the rupture of intimate connection.

In the final step, therapist and client reason about a more balanced expression of anger. Eventually, an "extension" technique is needed for some creative input, from, say a "best friend" perspective.

Ned was chronically angry and at times had been violent to his de facto partner, Suzzie. He was disinhibited by alcohol intoxication (Detached Self-soother), but what was most problematic was his intimidating use of anger (Bully and Attack). Ned was also very entitled, with a Self-aggrandizer mode. Ned's therapist wanted to teach him anger management techniques when he was "hot" and could put the skills into practice, especially while under some stress. And it was helpful to work out how to manage the modes that contributed strongly to Ned's "losing it."

Suzzie contributed to the problem as well. She spent most of the time in Detached Protector and Compliant Surrender modes, but she also had a hidden Enraged Child that delighted in provoking Ned in subtle ways.

While you will need time to address the childhood origins of schemas and modes, this is the work that needs to be done to establish stability in the couple relationship. This can be done with individual treatment as well as couple sessions. But take time, rather than rushing the couple back together before it is safe.

Therapy Tip: Think about violence from a mode perspective. Is the violence coming from Bully and Attack, or Angry or Enraged Child, justified by Punitive Parent? In Bernstein et al.'s work (2012b), they investigated what might be called "forensic" modes, which are associated with antisocial attitudes (Conning-Manipulative, Predator, etc.).[17] Think about whether you feel you are able to balance the committed care to a psychopath with the same level of commitment to the domestic violence victim.

10.4   Substance Abuse Related Problems

A lot has been written about substance abuse. It is often an issue in couple therapy, so we want to bring a schema model perspective. Samuel Ball (1998) outlined an integrative approach to treating addiction problems with a possible underlying personality disorder in his "Dual focus schema therapy." His approach is primarily based on the schema model but has not incorporated contemporary work with modes.

In this section, we use alcohol abuse as an example, but the general principles are applicable to the abuse of other drugs and to other impulsive or addictive behaviors, such as gambling, overeating or excessive internet use.

In ST-C, it is important to shift the focus to the interactional process of the couple rather than its content. If you see latent aggression or

---

[17]   See his presentation on change with psychopaths on the ISST website (www.schema therapy.com).

manipulative traits in the non-drinking partner, there will need to be a very soft empathic confrontation based on the here-and-now situation. Sometimes the parent modes in the non-drinking partner can express an Unrelenting Standards schema.

Therapy Tip: A bridge of reconnection can be built. It may be established through mutually enjoyable activities. This may also help the drinking partner feel that you care about more than the problematic drinking and are trying to provide some immediate benefits through therapy.

Be careful about an alliance against the drinking partner. The alliance is against the drinking behavior. In the mode model, this is conceptualized as Detached Self-soother. Note that most people with substance abuse problems simply have no better solution for coping with their emotional discomfort. Given certain traumatic experiences, escaping with alcohol (or other addictive behavior) seems like the least of many evils. The challenge in therapy is to access the underlying triggers of the avoided emotions while re-parenting and affirming the drinking partner as a person.

Address the drinking pattern as a Detached Self-soother mode. You can do chair-work. Place it in a separate chair (the "drinking chair"). Here the mode can be engaged (as formerly described for a Detached Protector):

- When did you show up first?
- What was that situation like?
- In which way were you helpful?
- What do you prevent?
- What purpose do you serve?
- What would happen if you disappeared?

This inquiry reveals both the hidden emotions of the child modes—the vulnerable emotions as well as the blocked anger—and the "commandments" of the internalized parent modes. Chairs for the two child modes and the parent modes are added in the order of the mode map. Take care not to be too static, and do not oversimplify: there are probably as many reasons to drink as there are drinkers. Following the internal dynamic through the use of chairs reveals typical internal mode cycles, with flips between two or more coping modes. One of them is described in the following case vignette and in Figure 15:

> Mary accused Bob of drinking too much. He claimed that his level of drinking was normal in his social circle. The first step was to examine his drinking. But at the end of the session there was no agreement about how

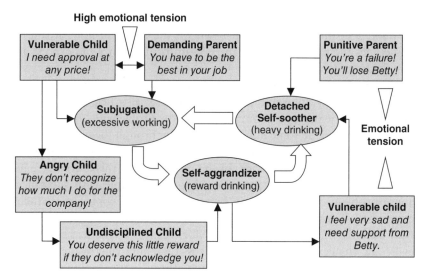

Figure 15   A typical internal drinking mode cycle. Source: Based on Roediger and Jacob (2010)

much was consumed, so the therapist assigned the couple the homework of separately monitoring his drinking.

In the next sessions, the two protocols were compared. While there was considerable overlap, some differences remained. For example, one night Mary smelled alcohol on Bob after work. Bob, however, denied touching alcohol.

Establishing the "facts" is almost impossible and should be avoided. Instead, the therapist noted such differences, without attempting to establish who was right, and took the opportunity to establish a controlled drinking experiment.

Bob chose the drinking rules from Table 5 that he wanted to follow, and the therapist made a protocol that included an initial blood check followed by a second in the month after the end of the experiment. There was an agreement that if he failed the test he was committed to enrolling in an outpatient alcohol addiction program. If he did not follow through on this agreement, Mary stated that she had no choice but to ask him to leave. All this was recorded. All three had a copy of the contract.

In the following session, a typical drinking situation was examined in terms of modes:

One night, Bob became highly intoxicated. He drank alone in the living room after Mary went to bed. He described his sequence of feelings. He felt

Table 5 Social drinking guidelines

Drinking situations	Drinking behavior
Never drink alone. Don't drink with people you don't know. No drinking before 6 pm. No hard liquor. Only drink while taking a meal. Not more than one glass of wine or beer with a meal. Don't drink when you're feeling bad. Two sober days each week. Don't drink alcohol when you're thirsty.	One glass should last at least 1 hour. Sip at least 10 times from one glass. Not more than 2 glasses within 1 hour, even when you're celebrating. One alcohol-free drink between two glasses with alcohol. Don't party more than twice a week. Train to refuse drinks when someone offers you one.

guilty because he had broken his social drinking rules during the day. His Punitive Parent voice said, "You can forget about passing the test! You'll fail and Mary will leave you anyway!" The Vulnerable Child felt hopeless and desperate, so he started drinking.

Perhaps surprisingly, when the steps that led to the drinking were analyzed, it was revealed that he had had a very successful day: he had made a big sale for his company. The voice in his head said, "Those bastards in my company don't acknowledge that I'm the No. 1 seller!" He felt anger, which led him to drink a glass of wine with lunch. Later, he felt guilty and could not enjoy his success. This feeling spoiled the rest of his day and he returned home sad, wanting to talk with Mary about his mistake. But Mary was watching TV and he did not feel confident enough to interrupt her. After the program, she was tired and wanted to go to bed. He felt rejected, even though he had not expressed any needs, and his sadness turned into a kind of frustrated anger.

The therapist did not stop with the successful sale, but asked the parent modes what they expected from Bob in his job. This revealed that Bob had strong Demanding Parent voices pushing him to always to be the best. He devoted an excessive amount of each week to his job (Surrender mode). On the child chair, he admitted that he needed the approval of his boss so much that he would do almost anything to gain it. Mary's sexual withdrawal increased his need. Bob's excessive work was an expression of Detached Self-soother mode. In the following days, this overwork resulted in a building tension. It was a vicious circle.

10.5   Returning to Couple Therapy

It is a trap to look only at the drinking pattern. This case illustrates the need to acknowledge the underlying sadness of the Vulnerable Child. Bob needed support. His Angry Child was not obvious. He needed to approach Mary and find more connection. His need for approval through his job undermined the emotional bond between the couple. The therapist coached Bob to express his needs to Mary openly and to find effective ways to combine sex with caressing (making sex more appealing to Mary). When he readjusted his work–life balance, the urge to drink diminished.

Working with the internal mode cycle requires that you deal with the whole person. This can be done in individual sessions and the results presented in a following couple session. Usually, the internal dynamic and conflicts within the drinking partner, between the hidden Angry Child and Demanding or Punitive Parent modes, have to be addressed and processed in individual sessions. Try to find a good balance between dealing with the past and current functioning.

Therapy Tip: You might find that a 3:1 ratio of individual and couple sessions helps the non-drinking partner to feel sufficiently included in the process.

If there is a relapse, in the next session draw the mode cycle preceding the drinking behavior. The drinking is usually just the tip of the iceberg—the chain starts much earlier, so the therapist and the couple have to trace it back to the initial situation in which the drinking partner felt uncomfortable.

This constellation can be explored with a chair-work session for the couple. The coping mode here is typically a surrendering behavior. The involved child modes and parental voices are placed on the chairs backstage. Then both partners and the therapist can stand and look down on the chairs, as if looking down on a mode map. The function of the coping mode is validated and acknowledged as possibly the best previous solution, but now we can see that the Self-soother schema is a consequence of an exaggerated (Surrender) coping mode. Thus, the goal of therapy is a better balance between the acknowledgment-seeking and a truly self-assertive behavior.

Being concrete this way helps to break the cycle. It can reduce feelings of guilt and shame. You might also explore the disadvantages of the drinking behavior for attachment. Encourage assertiveness rather than surrender. Create mutual understanding. The final step is to share ideas for a better coping.

Reflect: There are many ways of being supportive. Think about the assistance of "best friends" or "wise minds," or using religious texts, a support group, an Alcoholics Anonymous 12-step program, or anything potentially helpful.

Sometimes life circumstances need to change before anything can be accomplished. Once the drinking partner understands more about the hidden motives for drinking (such as blocked anger) and can find ways to meet child needs, this can result in more control over the drinking behavior. Then the couple therapy with a drinking partner returns to "normal" couple therapy. If not, a specialist or residential program might be necessary.

The 12-steps of Alcoholics Anonymous are very useful. However, we have some reservations. There is no clear strategy for becoming aware of the modes, so the group can become a substitute soothing entity for the drinker. The drinking partner can attach to this accepting group and continue to avoid their own underlying tensions in life. We appreciate the successes this program brings in helping people become and stay abstinent, but it might not deal with the psychological difficulties associated with the "dry alcoholic." This is not to diminish the very real gains in helping sobriety and keeping people alive, but this is only the first step to a full psychological recovery. So it is important to keep a now dry alcoholic in couple therapy to address their underlying issues. There is a risk that the Alcoholics Anonymous group can be used by the drinking partner to collude against the non-drinking partner, with the group and sobriety becoming the only priority. How can the partner complain? In such cases, the therapist needs to help the non-drinking partner raise couple needs that are not swept aside. The goal is not only abstinence, but mutual growth in the Healthy Adult.

10.6   The Resistant Partner

There is the familiar problem of dealing with a resistant partner. What do you do when one of the couple has minimal commitment to working on issues? They may express a desire to "deal with the marriage," but lack willingness to examine problems in any depth. The schema therapist needs to confront this without losing connection with the more reluctant spouse. Of course, it is difficult if you have doubts about the stated motive.

We suggest conceptualizing the problem using modes and mode maps. This can be very useful because the therapist can avoid adopting an accusing parental voice, but can address the mode as being the cause of difficulties, perhaps for reasons not yet fully understood. The therapist and the resistant client can examine the mode map. This gives a joint perspective for speculating about what some of the resistant parts (modes) are doing. Or you can map this out with chairs to show the day-to-day struggle in the self and the relationship. Standing together may help to gain an "above" perspective. Sometimes, you must work individually with the resistant partner before any ST-C work can be done jointly. It is important to recover a willingness to be vulnerable in order for therapy to gain traction. The standard ST approach of modes in the "here and now" is highly relevant.

We emphasize understanding the mode dialog. While ST conceptualizations go back to childhood, our approach is often in the here and now, especially when one of the couple resists any exploration of the past with strong denial and Detached Protector avoidance. Then a focus on the mode dialog is relevant.

> Frances was a computer programmer and tended to be "hyper-rational" (her own words). Her partner, Barry, was more emotionally aware but also at times emotionally driven. Naturally, both dynamics caused a mismatch in their relationship. This was understood in terms of Detached Protector for Frances and alternating between Angry and Vulnerable Child for Barry.
>
> Their therapist decided that he needed Frances to be emotionally present before he could address Barry's child mode needs. He used some visual imagery relating to Happy Child (the ice-cream visualization), which seemed to help her to be more emotionally present. She was not as resistant to experiences of sensual happiness.

Reflect: What techniques have you found most useful for bypassing Detached Protector mode?

Emotion-focused therapy for couples (EFT-C) is being more "here and now." An experienced ST-C therapist also knows how to work in the present tense. Slow down the process so that it allows the resistant individual to have a chance to succeed. At some level, they want the relationship to work. This provides leverage. You do need a good conceptualization of why the client is resistant to looking at their past, to seeing any problems in their family of origin, to doing anything experiential, or to filling out inventories. All this needs to be quickly addressed.

Therapy Tip: Intervene with empathic confrontation to meet the resistance. Put the Detached Protector on a coping mode chair (as described in Section 10.4 for the drinking behavior) and start investigating them. Perhaps use some self-disclosure, revealing that the detached coping keeps you away, too, leaving the lonely child backstage, unseen, and abandoned again as in childhood. But now it could be different if the Detached Protector would only give you a chance! It will help to appreciate the lack of willingness to fully engage in therapy. Be aware of your own schema activations (i.e., Unrelenting Standards) as a guide to what is happening with the client's blocked and hidden modes.

The partner's guardedness and mistrust may be so great that a referral is needed to another ST colleague to prepare the partner for ST-C. It may be useful to pass on to the other therapist the case conceptualization you have obtained thus far.

To Do: Consider the metaconceptualization of what makes relationships and marriages clash. Usually, it is the rough edges of the personality displayed by unhealthy coping mechanisms that trigger the partner. This results in escalating reactions and unhealthy coping mechanisms. All of this is driven by unmet needs and painful schema-patterned memories.

ST-C is designed to achieve personality change and emotional healing. Other therapies tend to be more solution-focused, but ST-C is change-focused: me change first, and then the relationship. This can give hope for couples—even those with traits of personality disorder. However, the skill of therapy is in how we deal with the oppositional and controlling modes that obstruct the relational part of therapy. ST-C is best done with a combination of art and science.

10.7 The More Personality Disordered

The great strength of ST is that it has been designed to help lower functioning personality-disordered clients. It has been established through rigorous research that ST is highly effective in treating borderline personality disorder (Farrell & Shaw, 2012). This group of clients exhibits emotional disturbance and often highly destructive patterns of interaction. They present some of the greatest challenges to therapists in treatment. There has also been growing support for ST in treating incarcerated prisoners. This is associated with the antisocial personality disorder (Bernstein et al., 2012b). More recently, the results of a large randomized controlled trial were published (Bamelis et al., 2014). The study demonstrated the effectiveness of ST in treating paranoid, histrionic, and narcissistic personality-disordered clients. It is reasonable to conclude that ST has a good clinical understanding of these disorders and uses effective interventions to assist change among the most disturbed of client groups. It would seem that the foundation of a couple therapy needs to be robust enough to handle personality-disordered individuals. It needs to be a therapy that normally takes such cases in stride, and then some!

There is still a further step to proving the effectiveness of ST-C. We know that even the severely personality-disordered enter intimate relationships, and the result is rarely mutual bliss! So how do we approach this?

We advise using a mode approach to treating the couple. The area of prominent dysfunction is conceptualized in terms of coping modes.

> Andrew was a highly successful businessman. He was aloof and contemptuous. He had seen a psychoanalytically oriented psychiatrist, who made a diagnosis of narcissistic personality disorder. With his de facto partner, Andrew saw an ST-C therapist, who conceptualized his narcissistic personality disorder in terms of a Self-aggrandizer mode. Andrew's partner was highly dependent, although this had not been diagnosed. The therapist understood her constant surrender to maintain attachment as a Compliant Surrender mode. This informed the mode map that guided therapy.

This can be done with all the personality disorders. For example, the schizoid might be seen in terms of Detached Protector or Fantasy modes. The avoidant might be similar, but a careful evaluation of the withdrawal mechanism should be carried out. The borderline is well mapped out with Bully and Attack, Detached Self-soother and other modes, depending on the specific case. Others typically include Suspicious Overcontroller and possibly Angry Protector for the paranoid. The schizotypal personality disorder is moving towards a classification on the schizophrenia spectrum, but it could still be conceived with a Magical Thinking mode.[18] The antisocial personality disorder is best treated with Bernstein's forensic modes:

> Sally was charged again for fraud-related offences, to the exasperation of her partner, Dolly. The ST-C therapist understood the fraud as indicating a Conning-Manipulative mode, and this was addressed in therapy with chairwork.

There is no easy way forward in dealing with the severely personality disordered. ST offers a way of understanding such personality traits and provides a dynamic model for understanding relational patterns. A range of highly effective interventions have been demonstrated to effect lasting change in personality. We recommend using a mode case conceptualization.

---

[18]   DSM-5 still includes schizotypal in the list of personality disorders, but it is an uneasy fit and it should properly be considered with schizophrenia.

To Do: Think about the most difficult couple you have treated. First identify any traits of personality disorder. Identify the most prominent modes. Now map out a characteristic couple interaction using a mode map or mode cycle clash-cards. What interventions would be most appropriate? Does this help you to think about the couple in a different way?

Reflect: Even though ST has proven techniques, the severely disordered client will have traits of personality that are difficult to change. Sometimes it is tempting to conclude that nothing works with an individual. Instead, it is better to think that it will simply take more time. We know that ST interventions work *in time*. The challenge is to persist! Working with the personality-disordered in couple therapy gives certain advantages and leverage at times when partner and therapist can co-parent together.

10.8 Separation and Divorce

Naturally, some couples will eventually separate. Can ST-C add a unique perspective on this process?

ST was developed to work with complex and rather intractable cases, including chronic affective disorders and personality disorders. It makes sense that we will see plenty of relationship failure—as well as, we hope, many successes. ST-C can also help us to better appreciate the dynamics of separation. The despair and hopelessness can be understood in terms of schema dynamics. At times, separation or separation on probation is a much-needed lever to heal a relationship. At other times, it can be the first step towards a permanent parting. The separation issue for the couple needs to be examined within the entire couple mode cycle as well as the individual schema/mode healing plan.

To Do: Think about schema vulnerability and how this is expressed in modes. Consider which modes seem to be driving the separation. Is it an Angry Overcompensator? Is there a lonely, abandoned, or terrorized Vulnerable Child? We usually see Detached Protector or Detached Self-soother at some point. What memories from childhood or dynamics identified in the family genogram play into the momentum towards separation? Were there positive models? Did the couple see commitment, perseverance, and endurance in their family systems? Are there high levels of intolerance or sensitivity about minor issues? What about impulsive acting-out?

Also consider the possible reasons for ending the relationship.

- What has the couple tried, to fix their relationship?
- How are the modes clashing?

- Have you adequately informed them of the possibilities of personality healing and change?
- Do you, as the therapist, have schemas activated from your own personal or family experience that have resulted in a lessened sense of hope? If so, think about peer or individual supervision.

To Do: Think about a couple whom you are treating but who are on the verge of ending their relationship:

- Can you imagine working with each of the couple on an individual basis to try to change their "rough edges"?
- Do you think there is any chance of success with that person?
- Would you be willing to try?
- Have you laid this out as an option to both? If not, why not?

Note that most couples who give up do so because they cannot envision the other person ever meeting their needs. They have lost hope and often look to the therapist to confirm their perspective. The road may be rough, long, and hard, but in our view it is the person in treatment, not the therapist, who decides when enough is enough. This is an ethical question with many ramifications, especially if there are children. We can clearly inform the couple of what therapy will require. Can we call it self-destructive if one partner keeps trying when there is "no hope"? These are hard questions.

Our job in ST-C is to tell them there is a road and what it looks like. Whether they wish to travel on it is their individual choice and not for us to judge. But we can probe a bit to be sure the desire to work on the relationship is from the person and not from a Punitive or Demanding Parent mode (or a misguided sense of guilt). Understanding this may help a person realize that they can put a limit on suffering. There may also be cultural issues, since leaving might not be considered an option. We believe that this is where psychology ends and respect for the individual's values becomes paramount.

Consider also:

- *Risk.* Are both partners physically safe? Is the relationship putting someone in danger?
- *Abuse.* Is the person enabling intolerable abuse by staying?
- *Giving up.* Is separation really about moving out and exerting leverage, or about giving up and shutting the door?
- *Remorse.* Does the offending partner show genuine remorse and an ability for empathy?

In these situations, to reduce the loudness and strength of the judgmental Punitive or Demanding Parent voice, the therapist can explain to the couple that their mode cycle, not each other, may be the problem. It is helpful to see the difficulties in "soluble" terms, rather than as a reason for the couple to give up. If you can get a mutual commitment to work on repair, you are no longer counseling for separation but working with a very distressed couple. That is progress!

Reflect: It is helpful for the therapist to continue to advocate for the relationship until one or both decide that it is over. At times, a couple will separate despite all your attempts to help them.

It is best if both can decide to separate and be confident that they are in Healthy Adult mode. But often one—not two—wants to separate, and the other will feel abandoned. Then the agenda changes to post-separation issues, such as limiting destructive interactions, especially those that might affect children, keeping issues out of the legal arena, and mediating on financial matters and the division of property. These provide an important continuing role for the therapist, but the focus has shifted.

Advanced Therapy Tip: Simeone-DiFrancesco has linked a child mode to influencing the decision to divorce. It is a type of Protector Child (Edwards, ISST Special Interest Group). There is a sense of helplessness that is not cognitively mediated. It is not simply being in the Vulnerable Child mode. Protector Child is reinforced by the internalized parent mode commentary, which makes the child feel totally stuck and that they have "tried everything, without anything working." This can lead to abandoning the relationship early in therapy. This individual does not have an open and mature judgment. They have only this Protector Child mode. The child wants to escape the situation, and at the same time protect himself or herself from recrimination from internal guilt, or from judgment from outside others. Since it is a child mode, there will be restricted alternatives, and it requires Healthy Adult redirection.

> Gerry had a desperate wish to leave Emilia. This justified his romantic interest in a co-worker. But the couple therapist empathically confronted him: "Gerry, you need to slow down. There are some issues here in your marriage that need to be faced. If you run from your wife, you'll carry the baggage into any future relationship." The therapist saw that Gerry was acting in Protector Child mode from a "fed-up place," as he expressed it.
>
> The therapist helped Gerry see that his Vulnerable Child did not need to be "protected" by another "child" who lacks wisdom, experience, and coping options. This mode felt like a way of taking care of what Gerry really

needed, but this was only a self-justification. In individual and couple sessions, the therapist provided re-parenting and emotional support, validation of hurts, and eventually soothing attachment, which helped to stabilize a frantic child ready to abandon the marriage.

We can look at this developmentally. Children are often helpless and feel trapped in the face of parental choices. The child mode trying to meet childhood needs can feel like an accurate appraisal, but it is developmentally arrested. It is set at the maturation level of the age of the Protector Child, and hence lacks adult creativity, knowledge, life experience, independence, and assertiveness. It seldom has an accurate appraisal of what is or is not changeable.

Parental and maladaptive coping modes generally lack any ability for negotiation, adult influencing ability, assertive limits, and seeing consequences. There are many that choose to surrender (a coping mechanism) in terribly destructive marriages because of their moral or spiritual commitments, while at the same time they may have an activated parent mode. The Demanding Parent reinforces their Vulnerable Child mode, who feels helpless. It tells the child that this is how life is and that they should not to expect anything different, or some other variation of invalidation. Hence, Protector Child mode may be fear-driven by the Vulnerable Child mode, and lacking the assertive quality of a healthy Angry Child or of being validated by Healthy Adult to absolutely push for the necessary change.

> Claire was raised in a very "traditional" home. Her father was domineering and rigid, and allowed no expression of any dissenting opinion. Claire later experienced three decades of emotional abuse from her husband. Finally, when her youngest daughter finished college, she was able to take a step back from all her family responsibilities and ask some painful questions about herself in the relationship. After some sessions of ST, she saw that in a relationship dominated by Demanding and Punitive Parent she had mostly remained in Compliant Surrender mode: "I can see my role now. I danced the same dance."

ST case conceptualization is an important early priority. There may be only limited openness to what might be achieved in therapy. Paradoxically, it is often people with strong Punitive and Demanding Parent modes who stay in the situation long enough to experience something new and better from ST-C, yet they have their own "sack of rocks to let go of." Also paradoxically, sometimes the unhealthy parent modes can help! Such modes can sometimes be left as an "ally" for a while.

In therapy, it is important to employ Healthy Adult to find appropriate explanations, create opportunities for future change, and develop kind and empathic but, nonetheless, firm boundaries.

To Do: Try to see the modes in play both in the partner choosing to leave and in the partner choosing to stay. Imagine the complex interplay of the modes and their joint triggering in the couple interaction leading to key decision-making.

> Nick was very anxious at the prospect of the coming separation. He became highly controlling in his behavior, which Tracey labeled "stalking." Tracey was reactively trying to get some distance but, paradoxically, what she felt most acutely was abandonment. This drove her "push–pull" behavior that was becoming so disruptive.

It is helpful if the couple has enough stability so that neither reacts with a non-repairable action, or unsafe and precipitous behaviors. Of course, this is not easy with emotionally driven people, but the therapist can explain that a productive time-out might help both to settle down. It might also de-escalate emotions and create some productive space to look at matters from a Healthy Adult perspective. Equally, there are other reasons that may drive an agenda of separation. See whether there are underlying reasons, such as:

- "To see if I miss you"
- "To make you appreciate and miss me"
- "To prepare you to live on your own, because I'm too afraid to tell you straight that I've decided to divorce"
- "To see if I can financially make it on my own."

It is inevitable that these purposes will be recognized as manipulative or destructive.

The decision to separate and end a relationship needs to be made from Healthy Adult mode. When the other modes push leaving, that reflects immaturity and unhealthy avoidance.

> Sally asked her therapist, "I want to check you out on a few things. Do you ever recommend separation?" Her therapist thought for a moment and said, "For you, now, I can hear that something is intolerable for you. Am I right? Help me understand what you feel on this matter."

A skillful schema therapist will try to redirect the client to understanding how their modes operate. There are ditches on both sides of the road. They may want you to support an action they will take to the partner, quote you, and act with even more justification. On the other side of the road, they may leave therapy prematurely because you did not fit into their plan.

Finally, it comes to balancing the need for assertiveness and self-realization with the need for attachment and belonging. If autonomy is more attractive then remaining connected, a separation on probation for a month (or three) provides the couple with new impressions and experiences that can be reappraised in a following conjoint session. Sometimes the absence of the partner reveals his or her attraction. Maybe the time spent apart leads to a sense of relief for one of them. However, the therapist does not have to know the outcome. The therapist tries to unblock the road, allowing the client to try to gain new experiences instead of dealing with expectations. The ultimate goal is reinforcing the Healthy Adult, looking for a balanced need fulfillment together, in well-balanced distance ("living apart together") or in separate lives.

Summary

ST-C echoes the sentiment of "When I was a child, I used to talk like a child, and think like a child, and argue like a child, but now I am a man, all childish ways are put behind me" (1 Corinthians 13:11). It does not judge a person in terms of where they are "at," but tries to value the person—regardless of "bad behavior." It is a therapy for the most broken of individuals. We try to hope in all things.

This chapter has addressed a range of issues that can influence a romantic relationship. We have considered the emotional damage resulting from an affair, violence, or substance abuse. We have also discussed some treatment issues, such as the resistant partner. The beginning and the end have been addressed through our discussion of the role of ST in relationship preparation and in approaching separation. Finally, we have considered how ST-C can address the more severe traits of personality disorder.

11

Differentiating Needs from Wants, and the Challenge of Integration

In ST, the key to a satisfying couple relationship is for the Healthy Adult mode to fulfill the emotional needs of the child modes in the best way. One aspect of this is distinguishing *needs* from *wants*. This skill is useful for both the couple and the therapist. You can think about it as a tool to differentiate what is negotiable and what is not in a relationship. All this leads naturally to an inner "dialog" about what the child is really looking for, which may be quite different from the child's expression of wants. This chapter outlines how to make this distinction. There is also a focus on "bringing it all together."

11.1 Needs

What constitutes a need? There is only limited research to establish a definitive list of needs; "Needs have a long history in psychology and psychiatry, and various writers have offered lists of what they considered to be the most important needs" (Flanagan, 2010). This is also relevant to the ST model. In 1980, Simeone-DiFrancesco reviewed a compendium of existing value inventories (unpublished) with her professor Dr. Gary Bridge of Columbia University. There were many definitions but, almost universally, there was some distinction between needs and wants.

In ST, early maladaptive schemas are formed by needs not being met in a consistent way. Clearly, neglect and abuse do not eradicate a person's needs. Resulting basic emotions indicate that core needs are not being met.

Schema Therapy with Couples: A Practitioner's Guide to Healing Relationships, First Edition.
Chiara Simeone-DiFrancesco, Eckhard Roediger, and Bruce A. Stevens.
© 2015 John Wiley & Sons, Ltd. Published 2015 by John Wiley & Sons, Ltd.
Companion website: www.wiley.com/go/difrancesco/schematherapywithcouples

Needs are universal. They belong to the essence of being human. This includes the basic need to think, choose, and act. Needs are so fundamental that we connect them to the concept of "rights." To dispute the right of a partner to have a basic need fulfilled is abuse or bullying. This understanding can help an individual to claim this and to know that to go into Compliant Surrender coping mode is never going to be healthy when it contradicts a need (and hence a right). It helps to understand the universal and hence non-negotiable nature of needs.

Therapy Tip: Depression may be thought as a reaction to a "vacuum of unmet needs."

11.2 The Difference between Needs and Wants

At best, a want seeks a way for a need to be met. Many wants are neutral. For example, I have a need for recreation as a human being, and I choose to ride my bicycle. The need is for recreation; the want is a choice—to ride a bicycle. I am not dehumanized if I cannot ride my bike. I may choose you to be my friend as a way to fulfill my human need for friendship, but you may or may not be available. My human need for friendship remains as an essential part of me, even if the friendship with you (my specific choice) does not. If there is a problem with you becoming my friend, for whatever reason, I am not dehumanized. However, if this experience makes me so fear abandonment and hurt that I deny myself the openness to ever make another friend, then I contradict my own essential human need, and hence dehumanize myself. In other words, I am acting in a schema-driven way, which keeps me from meeting my human need. To abstain from striving for my own human needs militates against attaining human happiness (see Table 6 for more examples). We can also make the following distinctions:

- *Needs.* One criterion of a need is that it is universal. Does it apply to all human beings of all nationalities, cultures, and times? Does an individual need it to be fulfilled to be human? These questions quickly sort out needs from wants. For example, do all humans need to think for themselves? If yes, then reflective reasoning is a basic human need. Ultimately, needs are not subject to personal awareness.
- *Wants.* Wants denote negotiable, personal choices. They may arise from one's culture, context, and individuality. Wants are individually chosen. Sometimes, to assist comprehension or application of this topic, we refer to wants as *wishes*. In this text and in our tables, the

Table 6 Needs versus wants

Needs	*Wants*	*Couple Connect-Talk™*
Understanding, support, Healthy Adult limits, strength in not listening to my gut and parent voice in my head.	To go visit my Mom with me weekly, or not complain if I go.	Dialog over my parent mode and my not knowing how to handle Mom's demands. You helping me to not cater and support in ignoring Punitive Parent mode.
Acceptance and ongoing connection.	Buying to have the best clothes.	Your affirmation that you see me as beautiful and feel devoted to me, allaying my fears.
Belonging; concern for needs of children and my role. Acceptance.	Running around taking the kids to soccer games three times a week with unquestioned expectation that you agree.	Identifying our family values. Weighing our family time loss against the advantages of team sport, and looking for alternatives that provide local involvements and no drain on family time. Strengthening family dialog and acceptance.
Partnership, equality. Recreation to look forward to. Connection.	"Me" time, so I don't feel used. Going out with the girls or the guys. More sex / making love.	Talking about how we, together, can invest in the home work and chores and then take off together for an even better result! Associating my Neglected Infant mode for soothing with learning how to soothe by our emotional connection, which in turn leads to more mutual love-making.
Respect.	Demanding you work outside the home and bring in income.	Sharing my pressures and stresses and us learning to put limits on spending so we can share a life together, versus work all the time.
Love.	Getting attention from others, especially the opposite sex. Allowing myself to get into personal conversations.	Discussing my lonely feelings and need to feel treated special. Allowing you a chance to meet that need and accepting your enthusiasm, versus knocking it off.

(Continued)

Table 6   (*Continued*)

Security.	Being at the beck and call of my boss. Working 70 hours a week.	Talking to you about my parent voice and you helping me to ignore and calm my Vulnerable Child, and reassuring me that all will be well with my putting limits. You being willing to be adaptable and not thinking ill of me.
Equality.	Making contemptuous comments and joking at you.	Letting you know when I feel hurt by your lack of affirmation and corrections.

Source: Adapted from Simeone-DiFrancesco and Simeone (2016b)

terms are interchangeable in meaning. The chosen wants depend for fulfillment on opportunity and availability. Wants are expendable, flexible, and variable, even when connected to life's rock-solid underlying needs. As an example, the need for food, which is a necessity of life, can be satisfied with any selection of foods and in any social ambience.

Many human conflicts can potentially be clarified by making such a distinction. Schema clashes are often based on one person suppressing or actively setting aside another person's needs or mistakenly holding to their own wants, believing that peace would require their surrender or the subjugation of their own needs to a specific set of wants.

Bella wanted Mark to appreciate her cooking. She came from an Italian family in which good food was at the center of family life. Mark was a busy executive, and for him food was "fuel" for the task at hand. This led to frequent clashes.

Distinguishing needs from wants helped Bella to recognize that food is a basic need, but that how that need is expressed is a want. She also came to understand that having quality family time was also a need, and she began to find creative ways to organize this within Mark's busy schedule. Mark acknowledged this: "It's great, the way you organize us to go on picnics."

Basic human needs are not threatening to others who, as humans, have the same needs. It is only in the area of wants that personal self-interest gets threatened. Wants are negotiable. That which is desired, useful, even urgently and intently wished for is often connected to, and almost substituted for, a need, but it is not essential for existence in a particular form, quality, or amount. Wants are countless and of every possible type, unlimited and never-ending, interchangeable. They may also be abusive, punitive, arbitrary, and totally disconnected from universal human needs. For example, a tyrant who rules a country follows his wants at the expense of the people's needs.

Therapy Tip: Wants may be an expression of the Punitive Parent mode, such as when someone feels the "need" to yell at their partner who just banged up the family auto in the parking lot. So separating needs (as part of a child mode) and wants (as socially distorted expressions of parent modes) is important in ST.

The distinction can be seen in this example:

> Lance is attracted to a co-worker, Betty. He has a need for human relationship. This connection is intrinsic to all humanity. Lance has the want of getting to know Betty better. However, if this interest is not reciprocal, Lance's want could easily become stalking!

Jeffrey Young's conceptualization of "domains" is essentially a list of core needs: connection and acceptance; autonomy and performance; realistic limits; inner-directedness and self-expression; and spontaneity and pleasure. Those domains link up with the 18 identified early maladaptive schemas. The first five schemas belong to the domain of connection and acceptance. Below is a partial list of needs that deal with the overall need for relationship.

Reflect: The needs we refer to in this chapter are defined a bit more broadly than the core needs we listed in Chapter 1, as the concept was developed by Simeone-DiFrancesco and Simeone (2016a,b) before we began to write this book together. Nevertheless, there is a significant overlap. The following is adapted from Simeone-DiFrancesco and Simeone's (2016a,b) "Non-negotiable Needs". Do you agree? Would you disagree on any point? What would you add to your list?

1. *empathy:* to be heard or listened to with attitudes of respect and openness when I speak about things that matter, including my values and goals
2. *trusted connection:* to depend on my partner and not be abandoned; to have confidence that he or she will always be faithful and not betray the relationship

3. *companionship:* to be and to have a best friend, including being confident that our conversations are private
4. *intimacy:* a unique sharing of union of mind and heart between a couple who love each other
5. *service:* to have a positive attitude of giving help to others
6. *self-actualization:* to know oneself; to discover one's inner reality of preferences, goals, and ideas, and to experience that one is a valued human being
7. *belonging:* to have a place in the world, in life, and to be in a relationship, including being part of an accepting community
8. *safety:* to not be harmed; to lead a peaceful existence without fear and threat
9. *love:* to give love and be loved, including its aspects of affirmation, affection, enthusiasm, openness and tested acceptance, and involving a certain sense of belonging to another
10. *meaning in life:* to know that my life has meaning and value
11. *dialog:* to experience caring and connecting communication of mutual self-disclosure, openness, and vulnerability
12. *acceptance:* to have a place of refuge where faults are forgiven, where we receive the benefit of the doubt, where I can be myself without question, criticism, or opposition.

Reflect: What do you think are the results of unmet needs? Does it matter at what age that the needs went unmet? Can you think about times in your life when your needs went unmet? What legacy did this produce for you? When your needs were met, did that help to overcome previous experiences? Can you identify frustrated wants in your life right now? What needs might be indicated? Use the list above to help you work this out.

11.3　Practical Application

The therapeutic utility of distinguishing needs and wants is that it differentiates what is universal and non-negotiable from what is subject to compromise. It helps to have a clear boundary of self-assertive respect when couples try to deal with areas of clash and disagreement. It also provides a litmus test for abuse: "Go against my needs and you are 'de-humanizing' me. That means abuse!"

> Sally knows that her husband, Jim, has the same needs as she does, even if he is unaware of it. This leads to her being confident that there is a win–win

approach for them as a couple. If this can be clarified, she can be certain that it will benefit him as well. As she learns how to differentiate the need from the want, she becomes more confident in her judgment. Then she can approach him to clarify areas of self-interest, work out a mode map, and begin a negotiation process about how each might like to fulfill their respective wants.

This can provide a way out of gridlock (Gottman, 1999). It is much easier to develop resonance with someone's needs, because needs are by definition universal, so we can all "relate." To be human is to have the same set of needs.

Here is an extended case example.

> Paul wanted to move to Alaska for a job promotion, but Carina wanted to be with her family in Arizona. His underlying need was to feel safe. Her underlying need was also safety.
>
> Simeone-DiFrancesco was able to bring some perspective to the clash by using her "needs vs. wants tool." It became apparent that the couple was in gridlock because they were focused on their wants; neither was able to identify their needs (on which they might find agreement). Tension was so high that neither could talk about the issue, but Carina persevered and came to appreciate that Paul defined safety in terms of financial security. When he felt financially secure, he was able to sleep at night and relax. This feeling of security offset the parental voice in his head telling him that he would fail if he was not careful. It helped to picture Little Paul and how he always felt that he would fail (Failure schema, Vulnerable Child mode).
>
> Carina was able to argue that his coping mode was inflexible and that his feeling of being unsafe was not realistic in their situation. They both realized that his feeling of lack of safety was connected to the father-like parent voice in his head. They had been working on their own mode maps, so he was able to recall this understanding when she came to him softly and confidently. She knew she could reach him (after all, they had the same core needs), so she was not prepared to give up her belief that they could work their way out of gridlock to a healthy outcome.
>
> Before gaining an assertive stance, she would have become defensive, and that would have resulted in a win–lose decision for them as a couple. The resulting misery and resentment would have undermined their relationship. No matter who "won," the result would be that their relationship lost. It was clear that there could be no realistic progress if they both remained stuck in their wants. In Healthy Adult mode, she could clarify both her and Paul's needs, so their wants became flexible and ultimately they could find a solution *for their relationship*.

Carina learned from her therapist that the reason we cling to a want is connected to either being in one or more child or parent modes, and often to associated misattributions. These can push an individual into an unhealthy coping mode.

Reflect: These types of clashes lie in the area of choices, which present something of a difficulty in ST. It can feel like being in Healthy Adult mode to stick to a choice (versus surrendering). It can be hard to recognize that such a choice is emotionally in a child mode or following a script from a parent mode. It is equally difficult to recognize that reactions from schema chemistry follow from the comfort and familiarity of past schema patterns.

In this case, because Carina and Paul had done mode mapping, they had placed some "emotional deposits" into their friendship bank account. Carina remained calm and positive in the face of Paul's closed mind on the subject. She had a path to take, and she knew how to get there.

First, Carina suggested they both do mode maps and try to work out what were the unmet needs. They were able to see how the parent mode gave Paul the message that nothing was more important than the priority of financially improving themselves, and how his Vulnerable Child mode felt nausea at the thought of turning down such an opportunity. Eventually, he was able to recognize how safe they actually were, using his sense of reality while at the same time empathizing with how bad it felt to be unsafe. Together, they linked back to the memory that he had of his father screaming at him at age 9. The father said that he would never amount to much, and naturally he felt a complete failure.

Then she shared her mode map, which showed how she felt overwhelmed because she feared his abandonment, seeing him putting his job first, ahead of her, so she also felt unsafe. She heard the voice of her mother complaining that she could never rely on her father. She recalled the example of her mother, who had to take charge and handle things herself. So, as Little Carina imaged her Vulnerable Child, she remembered how scary it felt in identifying with her mother, and how determined she became to never have to rely on a man.

Carina opened up and shared this with Paul. She knew that she needed to stop acting in this overcompensating mode, and not demand that they move close to her family for help with the children, but instead allow herself to trust and open up to Paul. Paul was amazed—he never had anyone put such trust in him. He realized that Carina really did love him, which was a realization that helped to re-parent his Vulnerable Child. He moved towards her emotionally and affirmed a commitment to be safe for her, that he would not put his job before her, and that he only wanted what was best for them both. Carina cried in his arms and finally felt safe.

Paul realized that he had almost made the most foolish decision of his life. He felt good about himself because he had a wife who needed and depended on him. He knew this was better than anything his father had, so he ignored the paternal voice in his head and the feeling in his gut predicting financial doom. He felt confident0 that together they would make it, and he liked this new experience of feeling safe and connected to someone who thought the world of him.

In the end, after bringing all options to the table, they moved somewhere that they both felt was a great place to bring up children. It was neither Alaska nor Arizona.

In summary, Carina was able to see that the gridlock was due to being stuck in wants and not being able to identify or speak about their true underlying needs. This opened up a path to mode mapping and the belief that, once the components were identified and put in the right boxes, they could both get into Healthy Adult mode, where they could agree on their needs. This enabled them to become creative and flexible; now they could discuss and negotiate their wants. In the end, neither overpowered the other, and a seemingly gridlocked issue became the forum for significant emotional growth, re-parenting, and connection together.

Had Carina been inappropriately advised to use an acceptance strategy for this seemingly gridlocked issue, or had the therapist looked at it from as a "gridlocked perpetual problem" (Gottman, 1999), it is highly likely that the outcome would have been worse. Jeff Young, when he found that cognitive therapy was not resolving his backlog of cases, did not "accept" that those emotionally disabled people and relationships simply had to stay that way. This creativity and optimism about what is therapeutically possible had a formative role in developing ST.

We believe that what ST has done for personality disorders is also possible with difficult couples using a mode map, a mode cycle clash-card, and the needs vs. wants sorting tool. Maybe this provides a way out of the idea that a "perpetual gridlock" requires acceptance and tolerance. This may be a path to higher levels of resolution and potentially to a new level of intimacy.

The example of Paul and Carina demonstrates the use of the ST-C needs vs. wants tool. It leads the way to insightful mode mapping, helps calm the Vulnerable Child, and gives the healthy parenting guidance of the Healthy Adult.

11.4   Advantages of Distinguishing Needs and Wants

The ST-C needs vs. wants tool assists in schema and mode healing because it helps to identify the basic or core need. Healthy Adult is then able to:

- use communication skills to effectively communicate the need to their partner and others
- stay on track, because of their confident knowledge that the need is a fundamental one
- fulfill the need.

This leads to an important assurance. An individual in Healthy Adult mode is able to distinguish between needs and wants. Wants are negotiable and needs are non-negotiable. Healthy Adult can address needs, and re-parent and co-parent the self (with partner or therapist, or even God), so that the needs are considered and ultimately receive "good enough" responses by the self or others through appropriately assertive action plans. The modes turn up unhealthy rough edges when the "needs" seek fulfillment by demanding inflexibility, rigid thinking, and fear-restricted choices, which are actually wants. Figure 16 shows a needs vs. wants tool diagrammed for Kurt and Sylvia, while Figure 17 is a blank one for your use. The tool helps to separate wants from needs after you analyze a clash with the mode cycle clash-card.

11.5   An Exercise to focus on Unmet Needs

Exercise: Think about a particular need:

- Why is this need important to you?
- What is your personal history with respect to this need?
- Can you imagine a "dream come true" in relation to it?
- What wish (i.e., want) or desire could you realistically ask of your partner in relation to it?
- How can you, on occasion, come together to evaluate any changes in what either of you might need or want?
- How would your partner like this need to be filled reciprocally?

Then go through the same questions with the partner. Consider filling this information into the love target-practice sheet (Figure 18). No two people are ever the same: we are all a little off center, and the bull's-eye is never where you expect it to be. Practice means trying to do it now. Have fun with it!

Needs vs. Wants"Tool"Diagrammed

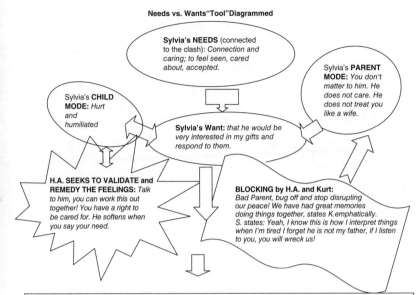

Figure 16   Needs vs. wants tool for Sylvia and Kurt. Source: Simeone-DiFrancesco and Simeone (2016a,b)

Unfortunately, unhealthy rough-edged aspects of modes are often passed on over the generations. As Giuffra (ISST Couples Special Interest Group) noted:

Experiences are heralds of other people from other times, young and old, internal and intergenerational, loving and hateful, protecting and punishing. Their shadowy forms transform the couple's present experience with fear, demand, yearning, a need to fight, flee or perhaps freeze, or an unconscious

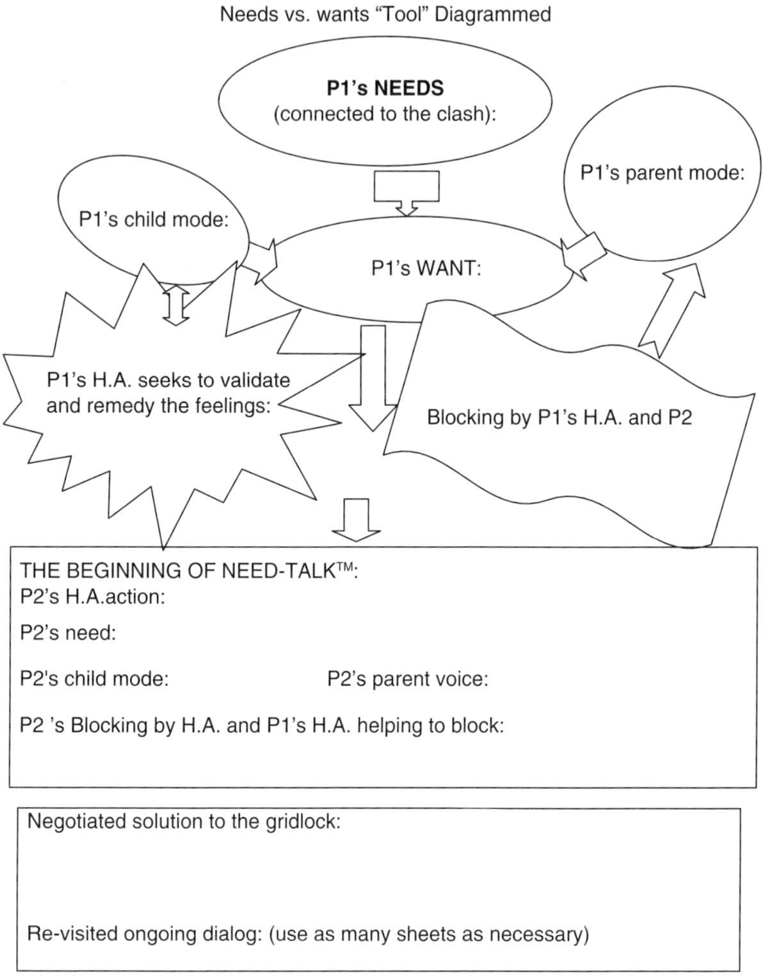

Needs vs. wants "Tool" Diagrammed

Figure 17 Blank needs vs. wants tool. Source: Simeone-DiFrancesco and Simeone (2016a,b)

call to halt the current experience that has been subtly awakened by a sound, a smell, a touch, an expression or even a request ...

The Healthy Adult self learns to recognize when the Vulnerable or Angry Child is getting triggered and learns to parent and protect the modes. Healthy Adults use space, solitude, and/or meditation (a mindfulness practice) to sense and differentiate child modes within the self and within their partner. They provide space to express and transform child or protector modes instead of trying to control, deny, lecture or react to them.

Love "target-practice" ST for marriage and couples

Write in your circle a core memory that typifies what you felt as a child and summarizes the chronic unmet need you had. Under your name, specify the memory, the unmet need and the wish (want) that would help make it better now.

After you write this, try practicing with Cupid's arrow and see it you can hit your partner's wish on target! Rate each of three attempts on a scale 1 (needs a lot of practice) to 10 (perfect). The partner who gets the most points for being close to the bull's eye wins.

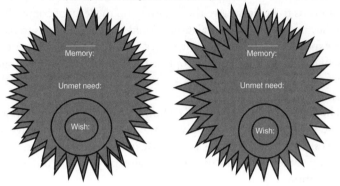

Figure 18   Love target-practice. Source: Simeone-DiFrancesco and Simeone (2016a,b)

11.6   Bringing it all Together

The task is now to turn to integration. We now try to bring together the distinctive elements of ST. This includes using mode mapping and mode cycle clash-cards, together with imagery and chair-work. These experiential techniques give ST-C a multidimensional quality. This approach works through both experience and cognitive understanding. Its integration results in greater effectiveness.

To Do: As you read this section, try to get a feel for the practical sequencing and application of these tools. It is not offered as an inflexible recipe, but as an opportunity to "look over the therapist's shoulder." It shows the process of working with couples.

Couples often present with a recent clash:

Sally and Brett came in with signs of distress. Sally moved her chair further away from Brett and closer to the therapist. Both began to talk about a clash that had not been resolved. The therapist affirmed this: "You are still raw from that experience. We can work with it right here and now." There was a deliberate attempt to affirm hope and simultaneously deepen the feelings. It felt safe to express them. The therapist then encouraged the couple to do a mode map to identify the modes involved in the encounter.

You might consider giving each of them a blank mode map to fill out. What was the trigger for each of them? You can create the master proto- type of the mode map on a whiteboard and have a mode cycle clash-card handy. If possible, underline that both have made decisions that have affected their relationship, and perhaps the couple will see for themselves what needs to be done. Are they clashing on the level of coping behaviors? Do they need slower de-escalation? Could they be oblivious to past forma- tive experiences and the parent voices involved? If the influence is from parental modes, then you can opt to do two individual mode maps, and then combine the results into a mode cycle clash-card in a follow-up session.

The bigger the legacy of one or both partners, the more important it is to use mode maps in working with the couple. With more dysfunctional couples, additional work has to be done in individual sessions. The level of listening, validation, and re-parenting also plays a part in any analysis of the situation.

Here are more examples of experiential techniques in which ST-C inte- grates the use of mode maps and mode cycle clash-cards:

Sylvia, a 26-year-old professional photographer working in a large metrop- olis, felt deeply hurt after a few years of marriage because she believed that her 35-year-old husband, Kurt, was still treating her like an add-on in his life, rather than a wife. As an accountant he was not too spontaneous … she had to initiate doing special things together, and he would normally ignore this or act uninterested, or only want to do them together with their chil- dren. She had a list of hurts and felt humiliated. This included her observa- tion (the presenting major trigger) that she had given Kurt gifts that he did not focus on or respond to. She concluded that she would never be impor- tant to him and wondered why he married her. However, she kept trying to please him. The therapist identified her Compliant Surrender mode—a pri- mary coping mechanism. This could shift to Detached Self-soother, in which she tried to take care of herself and be happy doing things by herself or with the kids.

Kurt was used to acting like a bachelor and relating mostly as a buddy to his fellow accountants. Over the years, he felt that anyone he was attracted to would eventually leave him. He recognized a pattern of emotional aban- donment with his father, who could be crude and punitive to him, giving him long lists of chores to "make up" for what he did not do "right." His father was abusive, calling him names as a child, exploding over small things without warning, and then, as he did his chores, he would watch his dad and his sister go off to the ball games or other fun activities together. When Sylvia would withdraw or get upset over things, it was not surprising that he felt worthless to her.

Sylvia had had a different experience. Her generally abusive father would put a lot of thought into a gift for his daughter on her birthday or at Christmas. She would travel to her father's home 500 miles away, but she never minded. It was the only time Sylvia ever felt special to her father. Sylvia had a schema activation related to gift-giving, not in a typically negative fashion, but rather because it was such a unique and positive experience of caring from her father. Hence, Kurt's lack of interest in her gifts was hurtful. A gift was more than a thing; it was a gift of herself. It was her intention to please him with a gift to get his interest, and hopefully he might want to make love more often. Love making and gifts were ways that made her feel more connected and caring.

Until this was explored in terms of meaning for Little Sylvia, Kurt was totally unaware of why gifts were such a big deal. Seeing the individual mode map for Sylvia moved Kurt to tears. He regretted how his actions, which were innocent and not malicious, had caused Little Sylvia such pain. He wanted to repair this legacy and give the responses she needed.

As holidays approached, the therapist and the couple set about doing a mode cycle clash-card (Figure 19). Initially, it was difficult for Kurt and Sylvia to hear what the parental voices were saying to each of them. They did

Mode Cycle Clashcard

P.1: Trigger (Schemas / core memories): *Sylvia*		P.2: Trigger (Schemas / core memories): *Kurt*	
Emotional Deprivation, Mistrust / abuse. The only time my father showed caring was in buying me gifts.		*Abandonment and Subjugation. Dad expected me to do things his way, and punished me by long lists of chores, while he doted on my sister.*	
Internalized Parent Voice: You don't matter to him. He does not care. He does not treat you like a wife.	**Coping Mode:** *Complaining he doesn't like my gift (Overcomp.) (Later shifting to self-soothing & distancing)*	**Coping Mode:** *Ignoring Sylvia's gifts and working out at gym with my brother (Detached Protector)*	**Internalized Parent Voice:** *You'll fail in making her happy. She is so demanding. Better ignore her gifts also to feel less guilty.*
Child Mode: (blocked / active):		**Child Mode:** (active / blocked):	
Vulnerable Child (hurt, helpless, rejected)	Angry Child (resentful, humiliated)	Vulnerable Child: (insufficient, helpless)	Angry Child: (unfairly punished and controlled)
Neglected core need: Connection and caring To feel seen, cared about, accepted **Wish:** That he would be very interested in my gifts, focus on them, and respond to them.		**Neglected core need** : Reliable Attachment Given the benefit of the doubt and not mischaracterized. **Wish:** That she stop criticizing what I am not doing. Being more important than her gifts.	
Healthy Adult solution: Sharing my childhood experiences with him. Asking directly for some attention. Making plans for what I want to do with him. Seeing Kurt as the victim of his childhood. Calm my VC myself when I feel hurt again.		**Healthy Adult solution:** You (talking to VC) are OK! Don't hide, show my feelings and needs. Ask Sylvia to accept me the way I am. Offer her time to enjoy herself in a way that is pleasing to us both, be creative. Tell her how I have been manipulated by my father with expectations, and ask her what she really needs and wants from me.	
Result: We are both feeling closer and happier. We negotiate more openly and assertively any and all plans that are being made. Sylvia is taking pains to seek out Kurt's opinion on them and to affirm her pleasure with whatever Kurt's initiative is. Kurt expresses excitement and deliberate enthusiasm over Sylvia's gifts, but then re-focuses her that the gift he wanted was she, and he would ask for that gift, have her put a bow on herself, ask her to just spend time with him, and do other things which would affirm he felt she was special.			

Figure 19   Sylvia and Kurt's mode cycle clash-card. Source: Roediger, modified by Simeone-DiFrancesco

not readily link their past memories to the gift-giving trigger. However, the connection was very clear to the therapist, who understood the impact of the punitive and abandoning father on Kurt and the severe emotional and physical abuse by her father on Sylvia. The only exception was the care shown in gift giving. Until this was seen, both Kurt and Sylvia were convinced that their thoughts were accurate.

Kurt maintained, "She's being just a little too demanding, don't you think, about what she wants me to do with her gifts?"

Sylvia thought, "He doesn't care about me. I'm not important to him."

It was the mode cycle clash-card and externalizing the voices with chairwork that helped them to objectify the messages that had been repeatedly given to them as children (hence the development of dysfunctional schemas). The schema therapist explained how the brain assesses and categorizes current situations in terms of past learning. So, for each, there was simply no evidence to dispute long-held assumptions.

When each put these conclusions (parent voices) together with the intensity of emotions (child modes) that they were experiencing, it pushed them into their predictable clashing behavioral coping patterns. Kurt became avoidant, detached, confused, and emotionally inhibited; Sylvia became detached, anxious, and self-soothed. When she went off to self-soothe, he saw it in terms of anger and punitive withdrawal, recalling his experience of his mother. Equally, his non-responsiveness when Sylvia would give him gifts felt as though she did not count in his world.

Here is how they mapped it out:

Completing the mode cycle clash-card, with the assistance of the therapist, helped to clarify the story for each. In the next session, the modes were put in chairs. The mode interactions were mapped out.

The focused sharing of Healthy Adult and Vulnerable Child modes was a new experience for both Kurt and Sylvia. It led to a new sense of hope in their marriage. Identifying and encouraging the modes led to directed sharing and provided a structure to their feelings. Previously, what they talked about was filled with negative experiences, complaints, expressions of hurt and frustration, or detachment. The result was a sense of despair. The therapist modeled empathy and emotional exploration—it all felt much safer and more hopeful.

The techniques used with a couple in going through their individual mode maps, mapping the dialogs between the modes, and putting the modes in chairs are used in the same way with the mode cycle clash-card. Note coping modes when they clash. This can lead to a sense of relief and empowerment. The couple can finally see that they each have the ability to modify their coping mode, especially they begin to "get" that this was the way that they coped, and that to continue in this way is not in the best interests of either of them. Remember to include key sentences in the Healthy Adult area.

After working through the interfering clashes, the couple will usually calm down and the way is clear for an emotional reconnection (provided by the Vulnerable Child modes longing for attachment). The key is in helping both to be in touch with their own emotional needs. Schema clashes often arise if one does not fulfill the *wishes* of the other. Bridging the gaps is like getting out of a dead-end street: whether you like it or not, you have to drive back to the main road. We have to find the way from a concrete want to the more general need, which in turn gives more space and flexibility for two Healthy Adults to negotiate a possible solution.

11.7   Reconnecting the Vulnerable Children

In ST, the focus is on meeting identified childhood needs. The most effective way to introduce change in the adult is to meet those needs: "The new experiences, interactions and implicit attitudes that make up the process of meeting core emotional needs become the building blocks for the Healthy Adult mode" (Farrell & Shaw, 2012, pp. 38–39).

Importantly, the schema therapist will address such needs. And, eventually, the couple can be coached to re-parent each other by learning to address each other's needs. It is amazing, but the couple can learn that their reciprocal rough edges can be smoothed and their original hopes, trust, and love can be reignited. This is enhanced when the couple can connect through their Vulnerable Child modes. This is a potentially important resource in the couple relationship. At some level, most couples actually believe that their love can be mutually healing … but it is not easy.

While our specific tools, such as the mode map or clash-card, may change and evolve over time, the concepts are quite stable and connected to the theory of healing. Note that our use of these techniques is not "eclectic." ST-C theory and conceptualization lead to a directed use of tools. While we think that therapists may gain from eclectically utilizing the concepts of schemas and modes, and a technique here or there, they could potentially miss the strength of ST-C. In ST-C, the conceptualization drives a pretty standard intervention, which is set out in Table 7. The model allows for individual creativity and differences between schema

Table 7 Essential elements of ST-C

- Giving the couple a map conceptualizing their problem
- Working with the form of the clashes, not the content
- Inducing perspective changes (by standing up)
- Remitting the unmet need
- Healing trauma experientially in imagery re-scripting
- ... and through the attachment of the therapist
- Using the therapist relationship in a re-parenting way
- Teaching the couple talking in a healthy adult way
- Engaging the need-focused, re-parenting, inner positive healing power of each partner.

---

therapists, but for therapy to be ST-C it has to be essentially based on the elements listed in the figure.

Nor is it clear that ST-C tools will be effective when extracted from the whole program. It is conceivably possible that they can be used in less than optimal ways without the comprehensive package of principles, attitudes, goals, and conceptualization found in ST-C. We stress this point in an effort to prevent misapplication and the therapy disasters possible with an approach of "I'll pick and choose which aspect of ST-C I want to apply." We liken the power of ST-C to the productive and positive power inherent in some uses of well-trained hypnotherapy, such as in the applications of Milton Erikson. Placed in the hands of an untrained person who thinks they know hypnosis, hypnotherapy, like ST-C, may well have less than optimal results!

Mutual re-parenting can be achieved through imagery work. If the therapist can soothe the Vulnerable Child, then the observing partner can see how the therapist acts in that situation. This models how Healthy Adult can respond to a personal need. This can be used as a transition for the witnessing partner to learn to soothe the Vulnerable Child of the other, perhaps initially holding their hand at the time of the intervention.

A good example of this in action is demonstrated by Jeff Young in a training DVD, *Schema Therapy with Couples* (Young, 2012). He worked with a couple, Christine and Chris, to identify individual needs, again showing the essential quality of this focus in our ST-C work. He demonstrated how to raise up what is wanted from the partner. He coached them to be sensitive and empathic, rather than angry and frustrated ("This is like a child who needs love and respect"). He assumed that both people in the relationship have a child inside, and that it is up to each to re-parent the other.

> He focused on a recent incident they reported, involving their daughter, Alex, and her boyfriend. He began by exploring both the issue and their emotional responses (very much in the vein of EFT-C). He then used imagery with a childhood memory: "Picture as if it's happening and you can see it. Can you say it the way they would have said it?" He then shifted to the recent image of the argument: "Now tell him, as Little Christine to Adult Chris, what you need."
>
> Young expertly linked the emotions of childhood events to present issues, and then explained the activation of Subjugation and Defectiveness-Shame schemas. He used re-parenting (to the inner-child): "I know that you feel that you're never being heard, but I ..." The wife then could say to her husband, "I know that when I say a criticism it adds to a load, but I know you're a great dad. I am concerned about this ..."
>
> Then Young coached the husband: "It feels like ... (from Little Chris), and what I need is ... (try not to be critical). I want to see that you don't feel I'm terrible." Then he asked the wife to respond as a caring parent, "You are a good person, you do nice things." He also encouraged the husband: "Try to visualize little Christine believing that her opinions mean nothing. Tell her, 'I do value your opinions ...'"

The Vulnerable Child is seen by the partner, and this leads to emotional reconnection. While working with one partner, the therapist has to be aware of not losing the other partner and to include them when possible. In individual sessions, the therapist cannot remain neutral, but can balance their involvement in the next conjoint session, including by using self-disclosure techniques. By that means, the therapist serves as a role model for how to be involved on an emotional level and become balanced again by changing perspectives to a Healthy Adult level. This may feel safer for some vulnerable people.

Couples can learn to use their Vulnerable Child mode to soften a partner or engage their empathy. This can take the heat out of an interaction.

> Nicholas came home irritable because of some disappointments at his business. He walked in, noticing some children's toys on the floor, and said, "Three suppliers let me down today, and now I can't even come home to a tidy house!"
>
> Naturally, Britta heard the accusation and blame in this comment, but she went to Vulnerable Child mode to respond: "When I hear your words it crushes me. I've been working in therapy to not be subject to my father's condemnation, but your irritation leads me to believe that my father was

right all along. [Shifting to Healthy Adult.] Can we talk about this more reasonably? I've had a challenging day as well."

ST will show persevering partners how and what it means to develop or stay in Healthy Adult mode, to productively use the Vulnerable Child mode to bring out the empathic resonance in their partner, to eventually re-parent their own inner Vulnerable Child, and in a limited way to re-parent their partner. An ST case conceptualization and treatment plan will indicate how to pass on this re-parenting technique to the couple. The goal is to assist them to mutually heal themselves and each other by de-escalating their recurring clashes.

Therapy Tip: You may find it useful when doing emotional work to have a "transitional object" (Winnicott, 1958), such as a soft toy or a teddy, for the person to hold. Some people find this very comforting.

One ongoing source of re-parenting for some couples can be spirituality. Christian couples have found that a personal prayerful application (quite different from cognitive Bible study) of a verse or two of scripture (also called *Lectio Divina*) serves as an ongoing highly experiential re-parenting intervention. See the work of Simeone-DiFrancesco and Simeone (2016ab) for an in-depth development of this concept.

11.8   Tone of Voice

Another way to achieve re-parenting in the couple relationship is to focus on language and tone. Young advised the couple in the video, "Speak to each other in not-like-enemies [language] or scolding parents, but try to speak to the child in the other." This is the key to an important use of language in the couple relationship. Both are encouraged to recognize schema activation, especially child modes, and then to speak gently to the child and, if possible, meet any expected needs. Bringing the Vulnerable Child to the attention of the couple allows sensitive parenting behavior by the partner. This provides a way out of negative cycles in the relationship and, importantly, offers a way forward.

> Tina speaks to Harry, who never got affirmed by his father: "Darling, just relax and be here with me on the couch. I don't want you to work all the time. It's you who I value. Just being my best friend is the most important thing."
> Stan says to Judith, who always feels she is never doing enough to make everyone happy, "Come on now, leave the dishes in the sink and go throw

this Frisbee with me. You deserve to 'play', you know, it's not all work ...
We've got to have some fun, every day! You work very hard every day, and
you really do deserve time just relaxing."

The priority in ST is to get the relationship emotionally close, rather than
being right in an argument. This is supported by Gottman's research
about the need for more positive than negative interactions (1999).

Therapy Tip: In an ISST Marital/Couples Subcommittee meeting,
Wendy Behary said that there is a sense in which she will see a couple
as "two of her children." Her job is to re-parent them both. She has
developed some creative ways to do this, including using childhood
photos.

Couples can also use voice-mediated messages and flashcards. Such
audio messages can be taken away from a session to be easily accessed
through their iPod or smartphone. Audio flashcards preserve the therapist's voice and transfer the solution-oriented atmosphere of the sessions
into everyday life. This is an important resource that can be used in clashes,
supporting the shift into a Healthy Adult mode. The therapist's voice
moves the clients much more than memories or written notes can. As the
busy ST therapist knows, it is sometimes a challenge to be able to stay sufficiently connected to those who need us, and, of course, even when we
are present in a session we can "miss a beat."

While such misses are grist for the therapeutic mill, we also seek to provide more reliable sources of re-parenting that can continue to help the
couple not only when we are not available, but in future years once therapy
has decreased its pace or ended. Brief email exchanges serve as a lifeline
between sessions, allowing the therapist to adjust the process exactly when
needed. Small effort, large effect! When clients use this option excessively,
it needs empathic confrontation, such as revealing personal limits from the
therapist's side, to force the river into its bed again. Most clients do not
abuse this option: in a study in the Netherlands, borderline patients had
the chance to phone the therapists between sessions. Only 5 percent made
excessive calls, and they reacted compliantly to empathic confrontation
(Nadort et al., 2009).

The role of a schema therapist is very demanding. In our experience,
many do not prepare for couple sessions or do not articulate a clear
case conceptualization, and as a result do not have a comprehensive
road map of where to take the couple. In ST-C, the expectation is to
keep refining the case conceptualization through tools such as mode
maps and mode cycle clash-cards. Making use of the model and the
techniques listed in Table 7 sets a clear course for therapy, keeping

therapist and client on track. In this way, a joint reference perspective provides both with a safe harbor when the emotional tide is high. They reconnect in regard to the mode cycle on an emotional level to mutually better fulfill each other's needs.

11.9   Preparing for Termination

Dale Hurst, a psychologist in Cairns, Australia, encourages couples to bring their "A game" to conflict resolution: "Bring your best capacity to communicate, negotiate, compromise and resolve conflict in a win–win way." It is easy to forget this and go into automatic mode cycle reactions. Typically, this is dysfunction reacting to dysfunction.

The role of the therapist in the final stages of therapy is to help the couple master the new skills, to slow down, to be mindful and to respond respectfully to each other. Encouraging a new skill such as this is an example of behavioral pattern breaking.

The final item on the agenda is to work towards the exit of the therapist. How therapy ends is best brought up at the beginning of ST-C. This advanced preparation provides a positive understanding of termination, and decreases the chances of abrupt endings. It can include an agreement about how this will take place for the particular couple. There are times when a couple will refuse to consider how it might take place, in which case the question can be brought up again as the therapy unfolds. But, eventually, therapy sessions will taper off in frequency as termination approaches. Helpful questions might include: "What do we need to achieve for you to be more confident in managing your relationship without our regular sessions?"

The final sessions can be understood in terms of relapse prevention. Help the couple to identify early warning signs of deterioration.

Inge and Bobby had recovered a sense of stability and connection in their relationship. They were able to articulate a narrative of what had taken their marriage off the rails. Bobby was a house husband with three young children. Inge's job as a medical registrar had taken up 80 hours a week.

She said, "I think a warning sign is when I feel overburdened and resentful. I tend to take the stress home and I can't 'give' to Bobby. I tend to resent all demands and miss the importance of connection."

Bobby responded, "Yes, it really is about a balance. We can handle the bad week, but when it becomes a bad month or two, then we're sacrificing too much for the hospital."

Then develop a strategy for relapse prevention:

> The therapist asked about the best way to avoid deterioration in the rela-
> tionship. Bobby said, "I think having a regular time, like date night, is
> important. This also provides a marker for us: if it keeps getting canceled, we
> know something's wrong." Inge agreed: "This is important to recognize.
> Also, I need to listen to Bobby when he raises the 'us' in our relationship."

It is also very useful, approaching the end of therapy, to help the couple
articulate a relationship story. This will include an account of what went
wrong. It will also include a narrative of relationship recovery through
therapy, what both learned and how to avoid a repeat of the original crisis
in the future.

Some couples will want to add "check-up" sessions, perhaps every three
to six months. Once the couple can recognize their mode vulnerability,
revealed in mode clashes, it is possible to anticipate times of vulnerability
and perhaps take extra precautions. Of course, all of this is part of relapse
prevention.

Finally, a couple contract can be useful:

> The therapist recommended to Inge and Bobby that they "contract" around
> a mutual agreement: "What I'd suggest, Inge and Bobby, is that you agree
> that it only takes one of you to ask for a return for a single session of cou-
> ple therapy. For example, if at some point in the future, say, Bobby thinks
> that things have become stuck again, he can ask that you both return to
> therapy. And because of today's agreement, Inge will have already agreed.
> This allows you to talk about the problem, get some feedback from me or
> another therapist and think about whether a few sessions might be helpful.
> This is a mutual commitment: to return for a session at the request of the
> other."

Gottman and Silver also recommended that couples find a shared meaning
for their relationship "that has to do with creating an inner life together—
a culture rich with symbols and rituals, and an appreciation for ... roles
and goals that link" (Gottman & Silver, 1999, pp. 243–244). Shared
meanings renew and enrich a relationship.

Not all therapy has to "work." There are other therapeutic outcomes
besides the restoration of the relationship. For example, identifying and
resolving dysfunctional modes can lead to a less reactive relationship. This
can help a separated couple to better carry out parenting responsibilities.
Indeed, it is a good outcome if a couple learns to distance in a functional
way, respect each other, and share remaining responsibilities.

But some couples learn to refresh their relationship and start a new phase of growing together. This is the best result, of course, but not always possible. It is worth adding that any personal growth will increase the chances of a more successful relationship with another person in the future.

Summary

In this chapter we introduced the important needs vs. wants tool. This is a good way to introduce Healthy Adult functioning in couple therapy. We also emphasized the importance of integrating the use of the various interventions, including mode maps, mode cycle clash-cards and chair-work, illustrated with a number of case examples. The importance of the couple learning to re-parent each other was set out as a goal of ST-C work, along with how attention to tone of voice can be helpful. The natural result of a successful therapy is ending it in a healthy way. We can think in terms of "relapse prevention" in the final sessions of therapy with a couple. Realistically, though, some relationships will fail and our role is then to facilitate the couple's choice for separation in a healthy way, if possible. In Chapter 12 we look at the more positive aspects of relationships and how they can be encouraged.

12

Building Friendship, Building the Healthy Adult

Relationships have become all-important. The positive is sought, but not always achieved. How can we become better at bringing this to couples?

12.1 Payments into a Relationship

An intimate relationship is like a bank account. It is easy to run into "the red," and making deposits is the only way to keep a healthy balance. One way to do this is to have mutually enjoyable activities—an investment in the couple relationship.

It is an obvious but important point that couples who stay in a relationship and are happy tend to like each other! Gottman said that "happy marriages are based on a deep friendship" (1999, p. 19). This protects the relationship from negative emotions that could otherwise easily overwhelm it, so we try to add positive interactions. Eventually, positive feelings can become the norm, so after an ambiguous exchange one partner does not jump to a negative conclusion.

Gottman (1999) emphasized the importance of building friendship. This involves two aspects: having a connection that embodies certain key elements of a growing friendship, and having bonding experiences. The latter can be experiences of enjoyment together, or, as Smalley (1988) described, they can be adventures that have an element of potential disaster to be endured and overcome! Gottman also suggested a range of useful couple exercises to build friendship. Simeone-DiFrancesco and Simeone (2016ab) list attitudes that are a litmus test of Healthy Adult mode, which builds friendship (see Table 8).

Schema Therapy with Couples: A Practitioner's Guide to Healing Relationships, First Edition.
Chiara Simeone-DiFrancesco, Eckhard Roediger, and Bruce A. Stevens.
© 2015 John Wiley & Sons, Ltd. Published 2015 by John Wiley & Sons, Ltd.
Companion website: www.wiley.com/go/difrancesco/schematherapywithcouples

Table 8 Building friendship or turning into enemies

An enemy:	Modes	A friend (all Healthy Adult):
Treats you unequally; acts the teacher/controller	OC	Treats you equally: same rights, same considerations
Talks in conclusions: is not open, does not let you in	DP/OC	Details what is on his/her mind and is open to your influence
Does not make self vulnerable: does not expose Vulnerable Child	DP/OC	Makes self vulnerable; allows your self to "need" you and shows Vulnerable Child
Hurts, harms, hates	OC	Loves, offsets hurts
Negatively interprets words and actions	OC	Automatically gives benefit of the doubt
Puts self first. Constantly.	OC	Puts friend first. Normally.
Neglects to fulfill needs	OC/DP/CS	Seeks to fulfill needs, finding them out
Resents and opposes	OC	Affirms and assists
Excuses self	OC	Apologizes sincerely and makes effort to discuss and empathize
Denies damage was done	OC/CS/DP	Recognizes and corrects damage
Non-protective and disloyal	OC/CS/DP	Loyal and protective
Damages reputation	OC	Defends reputation
Knocks your efforts	OC	Affirms your efforts
Brings out the worst in me	OC/DP/DS/CS	Brings out my best side
Discourages	OC	Encourages
Expects failure	OC	Lifts me up when I fail
Freely ridicules, criticizes	OC	Comments cautiously, helpfully
Immediately corrects	OC	Corrects only with permission
Automatically takes other's side	DP/OC	Automatically on my side
Tells the truth harshly	OC	Tells the truth with sensitivity
Disagreement includes rejection	OC	Can disagree without rejection
Silent treatment when disagree	OC	Open and accepting although disagree
Throws my weaknesses in my face	OC	Doesn't rehash past mistakes
Intimidates	OC	Doesn't overpower
Threatens abandonment	OC	No abandonment; is a "safe place"

CS = Compliant Surrender; DP = Detached Protector; DS = Defectiveness-Shame; OC = Overcompensator

Source: Adapted from Simeone-DiFrancesco and Simeone (2016b)

ST-C not only trains people to shift into Healthy Adult mode, but encourages the couple to use their Healthy Adult capacity to "loan" it to the partner. This will help that person to escape their life-traps. The first step is to stop mode (or schema) clashes. The one who first realizes that they are in the early stages of a mode clash can give a sign to the partner to interrupt the cycle and possibly suggest a temporary separation into different rooms. In this way, Healthy Adult, even if limited to one person, can prevent unnecessary conflict. The next step is to see the partner's Vulnerable Child behind their overcompensating, surrendering, or detaching behavior, to give the partner time to cool down, take the first step towards reconciliation, when possible, and, finally to forgive. This is enabled by applying the schema–mode model to better understand unconscious motives.

It is important that clinicians have a comprehensive picture of what Healthy Adult mode looks like. Only in that way can we put it forward as a model for couples. Usually, this is built up over a number of sessions.

To Do: Write out a full description of Healthy Adult functioning. You might begin with a description of a person who modeled it for you. Then add what might be more generally applied to everyone. Finally, describe your experience of being in Healthy Adult mode.

Therapy Tip: When therapy gets stuck, ask the person or couple to shift to Healthy Adult and analyze the situation together (Arntz & Jacob, 2013).

12.2   Communicating as Healthy Adults

Distressed couples usually come in with a "bad culture" of communication. After they understand their dysfunctional interaction, their communication style may need to change.

You can enhance this with a couple by teaching the principle that one "owns" the sent message. If I own it, I am responsible for it. This clarifies the responsibility for communication. It helps to escape the trap of a spouse complaining or implying, "You don't understand. What's wrong with you?" It is the role of the therapist to insist that the sender of the message continues to work at what is said, until the message sent is the message received. This is usually a relief to the listener, who stops feeling blamed and judged for any inadequacy in failing to understand. And it helps the sender of the message to learn new communication techniques. Naturally, all this is a challenge for couples and a part of their communication skills training that is specific to their communications with each other.

Couples usually discover in their journey together a range of idiosyncratic meanings and give quite different "weights" to words. Assumptions are usually problematic for both therapist and couple.

Gottman (1999) also gave attention to styles of communication. He encouraged a "soft start-up" and the elimination of highly negative or personal criticism (his "Four Horsemen of the Apocalypse"). He offered a de-escalation technique that decreases emotional arousal. In ST-C, we also incorporate this appreciation of the need for physiological de-escalation and self-soothing.

There is also a need for a specific mode focus in communication. After the couple have managed to stop frequent mode clashes and better understand their cycles, they will still need skills to talk to each other in a healthy and constructive way. This will involve bypassing coping modes and mutually reconnecting with the Vulnerable Child of the partner.

Therapy Tip: One of John and Julie Gottman's techniques (2009) is coaching to agree with "one point" to de-escalate conflict. Encourage one partner to find and validate at least one point or part of a point that the other is making, saying "I agree that …" This is effective even if the person does not agree with *all* the points being made.

12.3   Build the Positives

Friendship deepens with positive experiences. There is a history of encouraging positive behaviors in couple work. Hendrix's (1988) "care behaviors" exercise is a very effective one. It involves getting each to list (with the therapist's encouragement) five small things that their partner has done in the past that made them feel loved. With distressed couples, it might not be easy for them to remember any positive interactions, but persist even if it means going back to when they first dated. Smalley (1988) has an excellent list of "101 ways" of enhancing love in a relationship (instead of Paul Simon's "50 ways to leave your lover"). Couples can use Smalley's list to check off their own personal choices.

> Carly did not find it easy to list five things Mark had done, but eventually came up with the following:
>
> - Brought home flowers.
> - Sometimes a kiss on the cheek before leaving for work.
> - Noticing when she was wearing something different.
> - Going for a walk and chatting.
> - Gave a compliment on a meal that she prepared.

Mark was then given the homework of choosing one thing from the list to do at least five days a week. The key to this is that the list comprised what Carly had previously found to be affirming for her. It was not based on what Mark believed to be loving actions (which could miss what she wanted from him). Mark made a similar list, which was given to Carly so she could respond in a similar way.

This is a simple behavioral strategy to rebuild positive experiences in the relationship. It helps rebuild attachment.

Reflect: There has also been some writing about "love languages" that can assist couples in understanding of how to convey love in the way that will be most appreciated by the partner (Chapman, 2010). Do you use this insight with couples?

A variation on "care behaviors" is "surprise behaviors," in which both think of something really nice to do for the other (about once a month). This is something new and different, not done before, and not included on the list of care behaviors.

Brent thought about what might really surprise and please Casey. He bought tickets to a Beatles tribute concert, knowing the Fab Four were Casey's favorite group as a teenager. They both had a wonderful night, and it gave Casey hope: "Maybe Brent can meet my needs." The well thought-out surprise added spice to their relationship.

You might suggest that the couple have a date night to go out and simply enjoy being together (Fertel, 2004). Also consider the following:

Frank gave Belinda a four-hour beauty package at a health resort as part of a romantic weekend away.

Belinda made a leather bookmark to be a gift for Frank, but not for a birthday or an anniversary—just as an appreciation.

Therapy Tip: Another suggestion is face painting (Solomon & Takin, 2011, pp. 28–29). This encourages emotional attunement. The couple are encouraged to sit facing each other and look silently into each other's eyes: "Look closely at your partner's eyes and imagine you're going to paint the eye. What would you notice to do that well?" Then follow up with face painting. Encourage one to lightly touch the partner's face with their index and middle fingers: "With the tips of your fingers, lightly outline their face and the neck, and 'paint' around the eyes, nose, cheeks, mouth …" The two aspects of this exercise—eye contact and touch—both reinforce the couple connection. Of course, use your therapeutic judgment to assess when the couple might use this technique productively.

You can think about this as building blocks for a "secure base" in sessions (Johnson, 2005). Positive experiences function as times of connection and hope for a better future. There is a sense of security in meeting deeply felt needs. Also, through positive experiences a couple can confront the ways in which mode dysfunction has previously defined their relationship. Incorporating this emphasis on experiencing their friendship together is a great balance to working with the difficult material of clashes.

Therapy Tip: You can have the couple rate their friendship on a rating scale. How do they rate it today? How was it at the start of therapy? What is good about it now? What parts of the friendship do each most enjoy? What parts would each like to improve on? What would deepen it most to become a "best-friend" type of friendship?

12.4   Out-of-Session Trust Building

It is also important to assist the couple to establish a secure base in their day-to-day life, not just in therapy.

> Lance had an affair with a work colleague. After a month or so, she became very demanding and made threats about what would happen if he did not leave his wife, Claire. Finally, in desperation, the woman rang Claire, who was shocked to be informed of her husband's infidelity. Lance ended the affair, and both came for couple counseling.
>
> The infidelity was experienced as traumatic by both Lance and Claire. This can be understood in terms of an attachment injury. There was a lot of emotional turbulence (naturally!) in the first eight sessions of counseling, but slowly progress was made. Claire was able to tentatively trust Lance enough to believe him when he said he was not with someone.

The therapist introduced a technique from Mort Fertel's Marriage Fitness program:

> "Lance, I want you to make one promise a day and keep it. It needs to be a small promise, such as 'I'll bring home a carton of milk tonight', or 'I'll pay that bill today.' Do this each day, at least five days per week, and this dependability will begin to build trust in your relationship."

This is pure behaviorism, but any experienced therapist knows how long it takes for trust to build after a betrayal. This speeds up the process.

Gradually, Lance and Claire began to cooperate better on daily tasks. There were periods of relative normality, although it did not take much to bring on a cycle of blame and recrimination.

They worked on "issue-free zones." They set aside times for them to just talk, show some affection, and enjoy some activity together. Both wanted to get more exercise, drop some weight, and become more fit. They decided to go for a 30-minute walk each day, "come rain, hail, or snow." (Having a dog can be helpful.) They found that this was a time to connect.

The therapist explained it to them in terms of attachment: "Your relationship was given a 'body blow'. We call that an attachment injury, and for your marriage to recover you need to have some experiences of safety and connection. It's good that you've made your walks an issue-free zone. Naturally, you have to have robust talks at other times, in order to work through conflicted issues, but equally you need times just to connect—it's what makes being a couple worthwhile."

Smalley and Trent (1990) articulated the "hidden key" to friendship: there is a need for both strength and gentleness. This includes the "lion" personality and also the "soft-side of love." It takes self-control combined with empathy to not to follow one's natural inclinations (to get annoyed or angry or to lecture, especially when feeling justified). Meeting for a *jour fixe* each week (e.g., on Sundays for half an hour), strictly following the communication rules outlined in Section 7.8 of this book, guarantees both partners a safe space to talk about difficult issues. This prevents gridlock caused by postponed unspoken problems. In family life, there are always testing moments. The "masters" of relationship make conscious decisions to place their love, relationship, and friendship as a higher value. There is also the wisdom that embodies "adding hard-side love in a healthy way" (Smalley & Trent, 1990).

12.5 The Sexual Relationship

Sexuality embodies us. It brings a range of emotional attachment issues, needs for self-calming, and body memories. There are many connected triggering components.

Of course, sexual intimacy is relevant to overall satisfaction in the relationship. Schnarch (1998) talked about it as a "window" into the relationship. He also had practical advice, such as encouraging couples to hug until relaxed. This is one way an intervention can be designed to provide secure base experiences. Attachment is used for both care-eliciting and pair-bonding (Del Giudice, 2009).

We believe that ST-C can bring a distinct approach to sex therapy. It is obvious that schema and mode clashes can adversely affect a couple's intimate relationship, and that positive bonding experiences will make deposits in the emotional bank account. While some sexual experiences are ugly, there is also a great potential for the peak human experiences—or even better peak couple experiences!

When the gift of self is not mutual, it is easy for one or the other to be used as an object.[19] Partners easily and commonly develop "negative radar" for being the instrument of someone's self-pleasure rather than a cherished person to whom the lover is attached. This might mimic how Detached Self-soother coping mode uses an object. The partner who wants more sex may want relief from anxiety or feelings of being unloved or unwanted (mode map their unmet need and remember possible infant modes playing into psychosexual awareness). A skillful schema therapist can bring the expression of sexuality from the deadlocked issue of "sex" to a very fruitful appreciation of inner unmet emotional needs.

12.6   Schemas and Modes in Sexual Therapy

The issue of self-giving is emotionally laden, even schema-laden! It easily gets burdened with Self-sacrificing and Entitlement schemas in a couple relationship. ST in the area of couple sex therapy needs to be able to intercept an entitled coping mode coming from the little child chronically frustrated in the attachment area (the Emotional Deprivation schema), as well as the subjugated or even overcompensating abuse victim. Identify unhealthy coping mechanisms.

The schema of Emotional Deprivation is commonly associated with sexual issues. It can be placed on a continuum of severity. On the mild side is a lack of affirmation, and the extreme side includes broken parental boundaries from sexual abuse. Somewhere in mid-range are bad memories of relationships that included sexually activity. Sexuality can become disconnected from self-giving, friendship, and lasting emotional connection. It can become a means for self-satisfaction and devoid of any spiritual meaning.

Therapy Tip: The presence of entitlement is a good marker for an unhealthy coping mode.

---

[19]   See www.mindfulness.org.au/URGE%SURFING.htm#TeachingUrgeSurfingToClients.

Approaching sexuality from the aspect of the modes allows for the Healthy Adult to provide comfort to the child modes, and to be able to tolerate certain emotions with empathy and mindfulness. This creates new layers of friendship that allow the partners to build ever-growing emotional connection and provide a satisfying gift of self in all areas, including their sexuality.

> Norma needed the support of her therapist to stop submitting with Compliant Surrender because she feared David's anger. She also could hear her mother say, "Do your duty" through her Demanding Parent mode. Norma took some time to identify what she needed to change in their relationship so she could feel more connected and become more aroused. David noted the change in her willingness, and it was more satisfying for him as well. There was more shared friendship in their Healthy Adult modes. David also realized that he needed to become more aware of his emotions to get out of Detached Protector mode. He saw that couple clashes led to him shutting down emotionally. He could only connect through sexual intimacy— although it was devoid of real intimacy. This was an area the couple schema therapist decided to work on with him individually.

The mode cycle clash-card is a helpful tool for looking at a couple's underlying sexual dynamics. The card appears as a third party in the game. This displaces the problem to the couple's interaction rather than remaining with one of the partners! It also avoids guilt.

At some level, each can surrender aspects of their ultimate independence and self-interest to the interest of the other. There is a free choice in the Healthy Adult self to meet this need for connection, love, and intimacy in the personhood of the other. The partner reciprocally determines to offer their friendship-based intimacy. Wojtyla (1993, pp. 134–135) commented:

> The strength of such a [mature] love emerges most clearly when the beloved stumbles, when his or her weaknesses ... come into the open. One who truly loves does not then withdraw love, but loves all the more, loves in full consciousness of the other's shortcomings and faults, and without in the least approving of them. For the person as such never loses his/her essential value. The emotion which attaches to the value of the person is loyal.

In ST, this acceptance is made manifest as a couple mutually re-parents each other, and this in turn creates a fertile soil for the development of loyalty, devotion, and an intimate and tender sexual life together. In this "law of *ekstasis*" or the law of self-giving, "The lover 'goes outside' the self to find a fuller existence in another" (Wojtyla, 1993, p. 126).

ST-C strives to add an awareness of the personhood and fragile inner child. There is a dedication to the welfare of the other at a deep level. We hope that this will provide some safety for the relationship to grow in intimacy. Emotional resonance can be brought to each person's inner needs. In other words, this concern and respect of the other is not put aside by the physical aspects of sexual desire, for it serves their loving connection. The erotic dimension is just one form of love.

It is rarely the physical dimension that drives a sexual clash between couples (no matter how adamant a couple is on this point!). With each couple, the schema therapist must patiently help them uncover their hidden emotional needs, anxieties, and especially their attachment and intimacy fears.

Reflect: Do you think that sexual expression might best be considered a want or a need? One might argue that the underlying need is to be loved.

Sexual activity is part of the interplay of mutual sensitivity and negotiation in a romantic relationship. The couple are guided to increase their awareness of their inner personal emotional needs, and how those needs translate into wishes—something both partners can empathize with.

> Maggie was frustrated with her partner's lack of interest in sex. She said, "Bobbie has recently just lost interest. I have a healthy desire for intimacy, but all I get is 'Not tonight.'" Both were willing to discuss this in therapy, and the impasse was understood in terms of them both using Detached Self-soother to escape work stress. Maggie was using sex to self-soothe, and Bobbie was binge eating. It was helpful to bring their Vulnerable Child needs into therapy.

The mode map can be used to track interactions. Therapeutically intervene to lift sexual experiences from Detached Self-soother into the realm of Happy Child (play) and Healthy Adult sensitivity to the partner. There is a risk for the couple, if they are anxiously attached, that moments of disconnection will lead to the attachment system being hyper-activated. Additionally, a partner who is avoidant will shut out the partner.

When there is secure attachment in the couple relationship, it will facilitate relaxed and confident engagement. Couples with a distressed relationship tend to be caught in cycles of critical demanding and defensive withdrawal, both in general and in sexual interactions. The therapist can place sexual experiences in the overall context of attachment patterns; for example, lack of desire can be due to a preoccupation with safety (Johnson & Zuccarini, 2010).

As progress is made in ST-C, the focus is increasingly on creating positive cycles of emotional responsiveness. Partners are encouraged to risk, confide attachment needs and fears, and reach and respond to each other. The therapist extends this to their sexual relationship.

> Brad and Nancy had been married for over 30 years. The past few years, after the children left home, were a strain. Nancy felt the absence and was troubled by the emptiness of her marriage. They entered couple counseling when Nancy raised the question of separation.
>
> They responded well to the process, and eventually the therapist suggested they do something together that they had found enjoyable in the past. They joined an old-time dancing group at their local golf club. This provided enjoyable "together" times. The therapist described these dancing nights as providing the building blocks of a more secure attachment.
>
> Then Brad raised the question of some kind of sexual interaction: "I know we haven't been intimate in years, but I really miss it and I still find you attractive. I've liked the touch side of dancing together." Since Nancy had also been enjoying dancing again, she was willing to work towards physical intimacy. Their therapist recommended that they begin slowly, with affectionate touch and then limited massage. Gradually, sexual intimacy resumed and provided some of the glue their relationship needed.

12.7   To Strengthen the Healthy Adult

One goal in ST-C is to strengthen the Healthy Adult mode. Kellogg and Young (2006, p. 449) noted that the Healthy Adult serves as an "executive function" in relation to the other modes. It helps to meet the child's basic emotional needs. This includes three functions:

- It nurtures, affirms and protects the Vulnerable Child.
- It sets limits for the Angry Child and Undisciplined Child in accord with principles of reciprocity and self-discipline.
- It battles or moderates the maladaptive coping and dysfunctional parent modes.

The Healthy Adult mode becomes the basis for more mature relating as a couple. It is the best way to encourage effective communication. The Healthy Adult "takes a mature integration of limits, often a moral compass, the ability to act on conviction versus pure emotion, the ability to self-calm, and the mature integration of effective social skills" (Roediger, 2012b).

> Nikki had three young children with Bobby, who had a gambling problem. For years she fumed about his losses, but through many sessions of individual ST she learned to change her patterns of behavior. This ultimately strengthened her Healthy Adult. She was able to confront Bobby: "You actually need

a residential program to deal with your problem. If you do go, I'll be waiting with the children when you get out; if you don't, we'll leave now."

Healthy Adult represents reasonable thoughts and self-reflection, enabling functional problem solving. This includes mindful "here and now" perceptions, an interruption of spontaneous, dysfunctional coping behavior, an emotionally detached reappraisal of internalized parent mode cognitions, the impeachment of the parent modes, and supportive self-instructions to induce and maintain functional coping (Roediger, 2012b). This is close to acceptance and commitment therapy and third-wave therapies. It helps to become mindful of the trigger to schema or mode activation. Encourage the client to get out of the trap of automatic responding. Imagery work is very helpful to detect and accept current mode activations as the result of childhood wounds. Mindfulness is a counter-balance against the powerful impact of our schema activations that allows us to switch into a more distanced, self-reflective level of functioning.

Therapy Tip: It is also helpful to use "urge surfing," which encourages a person to pay attention to the urge while "surfing" on top of it, rather than being drawn into the behavior. Simply observe the urge and watch how it increases with time and diminishes after peaking.[20]

Sometimes beliefs are so deeply entrenched in the brain that they cannot be deleted or fundamentally changed. In those cases, the goal is not so much to change the beliefs but to identify them and interrupt dysfunctional coping modes. Urge surfing is helpful for resisting impulsive reactions as part of behavior pattern breaking. ST, like dialectical behavior therapy, can combine Eastern acceptance strategies with Western change strategies in a balanced way (Roediger, 2012b).

Developing a Healthy Adult is important in couple relationships. This basic awareness can foster a solid and determined adult judgment on how to handle the relationship in a way that will best benefit both. This will inspire perseverance in attaining true and lasting change.

12.8   Values as Strengthening the Healthy Adult

Acceptance and commitment therapy has emphasized the central role of values in guiding our life choices. What do we put first in our lives? Values may have a connection to schemas; for example, an individual may overvalue money because a schema of mistrust taught him to not trust others, so financial security becomes a prime focus in life.

---

[20]   Available at www.contextualpsychology.org.

Healthy Adult mode includes the "wise mind." Wisdom includes seeing things with clarity. In schema terms, this includes gathering evidence against schema-driven "values" and against "mode exaggerations." It is also important to watch reactions to triggers. How do we bring maturity to bear on issues? As the Healthy Adult mode matures, it is like a growth in wisdom: "Be open with the wise, he grows wiser still, teach a virtuous man, he will learn yet more … are you wise? It is to your advantage" (Proverbs 9:9, 12). In Healthy Adult, there is an inner moral compass that we should not ignore.

ST-C is also about discovering these great qualities of the human being and affirming them as basic principles of our interactions. We believe that lasting connections in families and couple relationships happen when these principles are respected. All this is even more important than any rules of communication; it is a question of the fundamentals by which we become safe for one another.

Couple Exercise: Download a values questionnaire. Simply Google this and choose what appeals, or download Stephen Hayes's Personal Values Questionnaire.[21] Fill one out and discuss.

12.9   Happy Child as Well

It is easy to forget about Happy Child when facing potentially serious problems in adult relationships, but it is essential to regain a sense of playful spontaneity while dealing with the serious business of fulfilling inner needs. Think about how you might encourage a return to playfulness in the couples you treat. The couple will not reconnect through our clever words, but because they become able to share some "happy child time" again.

What do happy children have? Enthusiasm is part of the answer. This is a wonderful relationship quality. Often, it goes counter to instinctive schema-driven reactionary modes.

Using deliberate enthusiasm, even when one's feelings are lagging, is a very effective way to de-escalate the intensity of one's own triggered feelings, to create what Dr. Giuffra called a moment of stillness and space, to pause and go up to Healthy Adult mode (we call it "floating up," using the mode map plus the idea of some limited mindfulness and distancing from the immediate trigger). This deliberately applied enthusiasm forces one out of unhealthy overcompensating, detached, or surrendered modes. Of course, couples will sometimes complain if what you ask is out of their comfort zone. That is the point. Getting healthy is usually out of our comfort zone when we are triggered!

21   Available at www.contextualpsychology.org.

Fulfilling needs creates human happiness. Happy Child mode is more than an ephemeral state. It has a solid foundation that is deeper than the ever-shifting emotions of the Vulnerable and Angry Child mode states. Happy Child comes from *satisfaction*. The stem of this concept comes from two Latin words, *satis*, meaning enough, and *facere*, meaning *to do* or *to make*. Hence, satisfaction means the "fulfillment or gratification of a desire, need, or appetite" (Morris, 1969). The resulting state is the Happy Child mode.

The Gottmans (2009) encourage couples, in building their friendship system, to create rituals of connection that become familiar to the relationship. These can be listed on cards. Many couples find daily greeting and parting rituals important. A lack of enthusiasm in greeting can be connected to "failed bids for connection." The emotional bank account will drain away with failed bids. There is value in adding Happy Child playfulness to such rituals.

Reflect: Think about a couple you recently had in treatment. Can they laugh in a spontaneous and healthy way? This includes seeing and enjoying the fun of a situation. It is sabotaged by hostile or cutting humor. Happy Child is best a mutual experience.

> Marjorie and Cyril had made good progress in therapy. There was a new lightness in the room, with less of the former power struggle, and they reported mutually enjoyable activities on date nights. The therapist raised the possibility of more Happy Child states in their relationship. She did an ice cream visualization, as recommended by Farrell and Shaw (2012). At the end of the session, she recommended homework in relation to thinking together how they could have Happy Child as part of the sensual pleasure of their sexual foreplay.

There is a healthy mode cycle in a relationship when both partners can flexibly shift between Healthy Adult, Vulnerable Child, and Happy Child modes. There is open communication, especially about individual and couple needs. The Healthy Adult mode can take risks, learn new ideas, and update models of the self and world, with an enhanced ability to reflect on schemas (Atkinson, 2012).

Summary

Potentially, with couples, $1 + 1 = 3$. There is something *more* about a satisfying relationship. That extra is what draws people together, and keeps them together through experiences of disappointment and pain. In this chapter, to round out our exploration of ST-C, we explored the goal of friendship and what can be achieved by using ST-C and by strengthening the Healthy Adult.

Appendix A

Self-care for the Couple Therapist

There is a lot of wear and tear in doing couple therapy. This is accentuated when dealing with personality-disordered people, which multiplies complexity and risk. This appendix sets out some guidelines for protecting yourself during therapy.

A.1 The Risk of Working with Severe Personality Disorders

Therapy is an intimate relationship, but we do not usually select who we work with. Couples simply come through the door. Those in difficult relationships will suddenly include us. There is a wake-up realization: "If this individual treats their partner badly, and that's pretty much a given, why would I expect them to treat me any differently?"

Inevitably, we enter a helping relationship with our clients, and at times we suffer "friendly fire." Sometimes a person will enter couple counseling with a fixed agenda, such as getting the partner diagnosed or ruled an unfit parent, or getting custody of the children, and when that does not happen they blame the therapist. They may even make a complaint to the registration board. Some people do not know how to treat anyone well. There can be a risk of violence, even potentially murder, so self-care involves a good "relationship alarm system." It is foolish to deny our vulnerability.

There are in-session concerns. Emotional volatility can be confronting and go well beyond our comfort zone as therapists. It is easy to become

Schema Therapy with Couples: A Practitioner's Guide to Healing Relationships, First Edition.
Chiara Simeone-DiFrancesco, Eckhard Roediger, and Bruce A. Stevens.
© 2015 John Wiley & Sons, Ltd. Published 2015 by John Wiley & Sons, Ltd.
Companion website: www.wiley.com/go/difrancesco/schematherapywithcouples

too involved when trying to assist couples in distress, so the danger of enmeshment is always present. We are not immune from what Figley (1995) called "compassion fatigue." In containing couples, it is helpful to focus on the here and now in session using mode cycle clash-cards, which helps to re-channel overwhelming expectations and emotional reactions into more manageable ways.

A.2   The Psychopath

There are two kinds of personality disorder in which the risk is especially high. First, think about antisocial personality-disordered people with psychopathic traits. The psychopath might be reasonably easy to pick out when incarcerated (think in terms of 25 percent of that population), but is less obvious in a normal clinical setting. Their charm tends to be initially quite persuasive. It helps to know some give-away signs. The life-motto of a psychopath is "A sucker is born every minute." Everything is said with spin. There is an ever-present coercive or manipulative element.

To Do: Think about how you can recognize the Conning-Manipulative mode, which has been repeatedly seen in forensic populations. This may be your first indication of psychopathy.

Reflect: When you encounter psychopathic anger, it is highly revealing. It tends to be coldly instrumental and efficient—just enough is "let out" to intimidate you into doing what they want, but no more.

Examine possible counter-transference reactions to the psychopath. Do you feel that you are being "played"? Usually, they will use gentle persuasion (until you resist, when it can get ugly).

Robert Hare developed the Hare Psychopathy Checklist, and has since revised it (Hare, 2003). It is the best psychological instrument for identifying this personality. He has also written *Without Conscience* (1993), which provides a good introduction to the disorder. Note that not every spouse who thinks their partner is a psychopath is correct—but some are!

The self-care issues in treating the psychopath are numerous. How do we protect ourselves? The most important step is early identification. Too often, a therapist will wake up too late. It is helpful to understand that our normal therapeutic style is risky with this kind of person. We tend to lead with empathy and emotional openness, but this will be read as being vulnerable and weak. It is seen as an open invitation to be taken advantage of in some way. Therapeutic rationalizations, such as "I should be able to help anyone" (Unrelenting Standards schema or Demanding Parent mode), are potentially dangerous.

It is foolish to think that our clinical skills will protect us. Robert Hare has admitted that he has been taken in by psychopaths, and he is the world expert. Never assume that you are in the clear. And, finally, to actually treat the psychopath, the essential ingredient is respect—their respect for you! It helps in ST to be able to quickly identify and label modes. You can then determine how to deal with them productively. Only in this way can you make any therapeutic progress.

There is something within us that recoils from the psychopath, especially when we recognize who we are dealing with. It can help to distinguish the person from what has been done, even when the actions are callous and hurtful to others. They still need the respect that is due to everyone we treat.

Therapy Tips: It will not be easy to get a psychopath into a Vulnerable Child mode. One of the best ways is to use guided imagery in which your client focuses on past hurts from others, and then makes a link to what in their current adult life feels similar. It is also important to be honest and frank. If you cannot find something to like about them, this will be sensed and the work cannot be done.

It is important to confront contradictions or histories that you do not think are accurate (this might include accounts by police of a crime), perhaps as a tentative inquiry: "I don't see how this fits, but I'm sure there are some emotional reasons why you put it out there like this … Can you help me understand them? It's hard to help you when I don't know the real you."

Use your empathic confrontation skills and also the therapy relationship itself to give feedback on how their behaviors affect you. You can use chair dialogs between that part of them that wants to be controlling, bullying and hostile, and the part underneath that is terrifically scared to be vulnerable. Let each side express itself. You also can reframe the issue of self-control and limits as something that is also in their self-interest, as it increases their ability to sustain a healthy relationship with another human being and ward off their own loneliness.

Another Tip: You might think about having two therapist chairs. One is for Healthy Adult, and the other provides a place for angry feelings and manipulative coping impulses. This can enable you to express intense negative feelings while keeping an exit free to return to Happy Adult and maintain the therapeutic relationship.

> "When you treat me this way, there is one part of me that really hates you and would like to kick you out of therapy. But returning to Happy Adult chair I can see that your Bully mode is just a way to protect your Vulnerable Child. This helps me to stay in touch and not take Bully and Attack personally."

A.3 The Borderline Patient

Every therapist has a story about treating someone with borderline personality disorder, and it is usually a tale of woe. There is no need to repeat the DSM-5 criteria, which are well known, but think about some common characteristics. The borderline is always "high-maintenance"—a bottomless well of need. The therapist has no better chance than the borderline's partner of fully meeting this need.

There are often difficulties with explosive anger. It is like being at the foot of a volcano, waiting for an eruption. But borderline anger is unlike that of the psychopath: it is unprocessed and spills everywhere, like raw sewage spilling from a sump! Rage can be external, with personal attacks against the therapist or anyone at hand, or internalized, with self-injury or suicide attempts. Note whether Punitive Parent modes are generally outward or inward. The borderline generally lacks internal anchors for identity and Healthy Adult skills. Moods are unstable, and therapy can be like being on a roller coaster. In some instances, there can be a lack of reality testing, but this is usually stress-related and somewhat transient.

While borderlines tend to "like" therapy, they present difficulties for anyone trying to help them. It is easy to be drawn into a kind of "emotional psychosis," which can be overwhelmingly confusing and even present problems with contagion and unforeseeable flips into a distanced Detached Protector, even in a "good" session. There are practical difficulties in finding a therapeutic connection without reactively distancing or being fused with them.

Therapy Warning: It can be alarming to experience the therapist's schemas getting triggered by the client's fragments of early states. You might even experience an infant mode response, with a possibly frightening fantasy of being an infant in the care of a borderline mother! This can be quite disturbing, so it is important to process your schema activations in a healthy way.

There are a lot of practical problems in managing borderline individuals. This includes the stress of dealing with someone who can become acutely suicidal. There is a range of potentially bad behavior, such as stalking, aggressive lashing out, threats, and even violence. Needless to say, the need for boundaries cannot be overemphasized.

The psychoanalytic concept of "primitive emotional communication" can be useful in understanding bad behavior from borderline people. This acknowledges that some individuals will experience great distress but will not be able to put that distress into words (even though that is the point of therapy). Borderline people are very poor at mentalization

(Fonagy et al., 2004), so teaching them by being a good model is crucial for building the Healthy Adult. Standing up may help the person to reflect on what was going on in both their and the therapist's chair below. This third-person perspective can train them to adopt a more realistic perspective.

Infants who are pre-verbal can only cry, which distresses people but does effectively convey the internal state of the infant. This is, of course, an expression of an infant mode. It will evoke the same internal state in the carer. It is a form of non-verbal communication of mode to mode, but this helps us to understand the non-conscious rationale for bad behavior. Infants simply have no idea how to behave better. There is no need to take it personally. Wendy Behary (ISST Couples Special Interest Group) has suggested picturing the child mode next to the Overcompensator mode while people are acting out. It may also be a marker for someone in an infant mode.

> Amanda "exploded" at Mary, her therapist. She said some very unkind words, and Mary was tempted to end therapy. However, she took the incident to her supervisor, who discussed the concept of primitive emotional communication.
>
> Mary was able to say in the following session, "Amanda I know you were very angry in our last session. I felt hurt by some of the things you said. I believe that you were trying to make me feel as bad as you felt at the time, so I can understand more about what you experience. Does that make sense? I just wanted to tell you that I think I get how you feel so abused."

Reflect: Can you identify Amanda's primitive communication to Mary?

A.4 The Sexual Boundary

There are boundary considerations in treating very difficult couples. Realistically, there is some risk of crossing sexual boundaries, and therapists have to be on guard about this. Reflect on your relationship history. Have you ever dated a psychopath or borderline partner, or had to deal with a partner with such traits? If you recognize this in your relationship history, you may have some unhealthy patterns of attraction.

The psychopath might be considered an example of hyper-masculine sexuality, and the borderline has some hyper-feminine attributes. Some may be drawn to those aspects, despite the danger. While this risks stereotyping, if you identify any vulnerability it is best to acknowledge and manage the risk.

Therapy Tip: It useful to develop a 10-point scale to assess your level of attraction in a given situation. Rate 9/10 as "Run off with the person you are treating," 8/10 as losing control, and so on up the scale. Once you have the scale, assign management strategies to each stage: tell my supervisor; share in peer supervision group; raise with my romantic partner; go into therapy; refer the individual (without telling them the reason!); and so on. It is useful to have a two-point buffer between going beyond an acceptable boundary and more comfortable management. And remember, brinkmanship is risky.

A.5   Positive Behaviors for Self-care

Norcross and Guy (2007) wrote a useful book on self-care titled *Leaving it at the Office*. Their advice includes some of the following:

- Think about your values on a regular basis. Perhaps do a values questionnaire (from acceptance and commitment therapy). Maybe write a personal mission statement (Covey, 1990).
- Promote the positive in your life. Stevens reflected, "I discipline myself to do good things such as going to a favorite art gallery, attending a concert or finding a new restaurant. Nothing beats spending quality time with friends." Overseas trips may become part of your annual calendar. As therapists, we deal with a lot of ugliness, so we need to balance this with an emphasis on the beautiful.
- Debrief as soon as possible after a critical therapeutic incident. Identify someone among your close colleagues whom can you ring immediately.
- Have a peer supervision group. It is a good additional support to have individual supervision on an ongoing basis.
- Consider personal psychotherapy. At times, this is an absolute need for any practicing therapist. In a time of stress, going into therapy should be our first response, not a reluctant last resort!
- Foster healthy escapes, exercise and maintain your physical health. Do not forget what you tell people in treatment about exercise.
- Do an environmental audit of your office. How pleasant is it as a workplace? Have a colleague look it over and give you feedback. One idea is to have a refresh center, with fresh fruit, drinks, and maybe some energy food for that low point in the afternoon.
- Track your self-care, including by recording what you do for a month. Sometimes it useful to have a "decompression ritual," such as listening to music in the car driving from the office to home.

- Use spiritual resources, such as meditation, mindfulness, retreats, prayer, *Lectio Divina* or devotional reading.

Paul MacLean (1990) proposed the triune brain. This is a helpful way to think about what needs to be addressed through relaxation and self-care. Broadly, a distinction is made between the reptile, mammal, and human brain (which evolved in stages, according to evolutionary theory!). How do reptiles relax? One man answered this with, "Flat out on a rock in the sun." Mammals tend to groom each other and use a lot of touching for affiliation. Humans can uniquely enjoy beauty, creativity, and spirituality. To cover all parts of the brain, have a glass of wine in a spa bath, while listening to a symphony by Beethoven, with your spouse giving you a foot massage!

Summary

Couple therapy is both a challenge and a joy. Even in a day full of appointments, couples tend to be energizing. And sometimes a couple will return, years later, to tell you about the difference your counseling made to their relationship. It is a rare privilege to know that you have made a lasting difference—possibly the difference that saved a loving relationship.

As therapists, we get to live a thousand lives. Of course, this is sometimes ugly and even damaging to us. But, equally, we often see the courage of people who take risks and fashion a better relationship. We are there when much of it happens, and we can glimpse the potential of love to "always protect, always trust, always hope, always persevere" (1 Corinthians 13:7).

ST-C is a new therapy; it is in the early stages of development. Eventually, ST-C research will include careful evaluation, beginning with single-case experimental studies and eventually randomized controlled trials.

We invite you to practice ST-C with couples, to make discoveries and to share with colleagues in professional settings to further develop this work.

We wish you all the best as you practice and contribute to the development of ST-C.

References

Abrahms-Spring, J. (2004). *How can I forgive you?* New York, NY: Harper–Collins Publishers Inc.

American Psychological Association (APA). (2002). Criteria for evaluating treatment guidelines. *American Psychologist, 57,* 1052–1059.

Anderson, T. (1990). The reflecting team: Dialog and meta-dialog in clinical work. *Family Process, 26*(4), 415–428.

Australian Psychological Society (APS). (2010). *Evidence-based psychological interventions in the treatment of mental disorders: A literature review.* Melbourne, Australia: Australian Psychological Society.

Arntz, A. (2008). Schema-focused therapy for borderline personality disorder: Effectiveness and cost-effectiveness, evidence from a multicenter trial. *European Psychiatry, 23*(2), S65–S66.

Arntz, A. (2012a). A systematic review of Schema Therapy for BPD. In J. Farrell & I. Shaw (Eds.), *Group Schema Therapy for borderline personality disorder: A step-by-step treatment manual with patient workbook* (pp. 286–2940). Chichester, UK: Wiley-Blackwell.

Arntz, A. (2012b). Schema therapy for cluster C personality disorders. In M. van Vreeswijk, J. Broersen, & M. Nadort (Eds.), *The Wiley-Blackwell handbook of Schema Therapy: Theory, research and practice* (pp. 397–414). Oxford, UK: Wiley-Blackwell.

Arntz, A., & Jacob, G. (2013). *Schema Therapy in practice: An introductory guide to the schema mode approach.* Oxford, UK: Wiley-Blackwell.

Arntz, A., & van Genderen, H. (2010). *Schema Therapy for borderline personality disorder.* Chichester, UK: Wiley-Blackwell.

Arntz, A., & Weertman, A. (1999). Treatment of childhood memories: Theory and practice. *Behavior Research and Therapy, 37,* 715–740.

Schema Therapy with Couples: A Practitioner's Guide to Healing Relationships, First Edition.
Chiara Simeone-DiFrancesco, Eckhard Roediger, and Bruce A. Stevens.
© 2015 John Wiley & Sons, Ltd. Published 2015 by John Wiley & Sons, Ltd.
Companion website: www.wiley.com/go/difrancesco/schematherapywithcouples

Atkinson, T. (2012). Schema therapy for couples: Healing partners in a relationship. In M. van Vreeswijk, J. Broersen, & M. Nadort (Eds.), *The Wiley-Blackwell handbook of Schema Therapy: Theory, research and practice* (pp. 323–335). Oxford, UK: Wiley-Blackwell.

Ball, S. A. (1998). Manualized treatment for substance abusers with personality disorders: dual focus schema therapy. *Addictive Behaviors, 23*(6), 883–891.

Bamelis, L., Bloo, J., Bernstein, D., & Arntz, A. (2012). Effectiveness Studies. In M. van Vreeswijk, J. Broersen, & M. Nardort, M. (Eds.), *The Wiley-Blackwell handbook of Schema Therapy* (S. 495–510). Oxford, UK: Wiley-Blackwell.

Bamelis, L., Evers, S., Spinhoven, P., & Arntz, A. (2014). Results of a multicenter randomized controlled trial of the clinical effectiveness of schema therapy for personality disorders. *American Journal of Psychiatry, 171*, 305–322. doi: 10.1176/appi.ajp.2013.12040518

Barnish, M. (2004). *Domestic violence: A literature review.* London, UK: HM Inspectorate of Probation. Retrieved from www.homeoffice.gov.uk/justice/probation/inspprob/index.html.

Basch, M. F. (1980). *Doing psychotherapy.* New York, NY: Basic Books.

Bateson, G. (1972). *Steps to an ecology of mind: Collected essays in anthropology, psychiatry, evolution and epistemology.* Chicago, IL: University of Chicago Press.

Baucom, D. H., & Epstein, N. (1990). *Cognitive-behavioral marital therapy.* Levittown, PA: Brunner/Mazel.

Beck, A. (1963). Thinking and depression. *Archives of General Psychiatry, 9*, 324–333.

Bennett-Levy, J., Butler, G., Fennell, M., Hackman, A., Mueller, M., & Westbrook, D. (Eds.) (2004). *Oxford guide to behavioral experiments in cognitive therapy.* Oxford, UK: Oxford University Press.

Berman, P. S. (2010). *Case conceptualization and treatment planning: Integrating theory with clinical practice.* Los Angeles, CA: Sage.

Bernstein, D., Vos, M. K., Jonkers, P., de Jonge, E., & Arntz, A. (2012a). Schema therapy in forensic settings. In M. van Vreeswijk, J. Broersen, & M. Nadort (Eds.), *The Wiley-Blackwell handbook of Schema Therapy: Theory, research and practice* (pp. 425–438). Oxford, UK: Wiley-Blackwell.

Bernstein, D. P., Nijman, H., Karos, K., Keulen-de Vos, M., de Vogel, V., & Lucker, T. (2012b). Schema therapy for forensic patients with personality disorders: Design and preliminary findings of multicenter randomized clinical trial in the Netherlands. *International Journal of Forensic Mental Health, 11*, 312–324.

Bograd, M., & Mederos, F. (1999). Battering and couples therapy: Universal screening and selection of treatment modality. *Journal of Marital and Family Therapy, 25*(3), 291–312.

Boszormenyi-Nagy, I., & Krasner, B. (1986). *Between give and take.* New York, NY: Brunner/Mazel.

Botvinick, M. M., Braver, T. S., Barch, D. M., Carter, C. S., & Cohen, J. D. (2001). Conflict monitoring and cognitive control. *Psychological Review, 108*, 624–652.

Brown, E. M. (1991). *Patterns of infidelity and their treatment.* New York, NY: Brunner/Mazel.

Capaldi, D. M., & Kim, H. K. (2007). Typological approaches to violence in couples: A critique and alternative conceptual approach. *Clinical Psychology Review, 27*(3), 253–265.

Chapman, G. (2010). *The five love languages: The secret to a love that lasts.* Chicago, IL: Northfield Publishing.

Covey, S. (1990). *The seven habits of highly effective people.* Melbourne, Australia: The Business Library.

Covey, S. (1997). *The seven habits of highly effective families.* New York, NY: Golden Books.

Creamer, M., Forbes, D., Phelps A., & Humphreys, L. (2007). *Treating traumatic stress: Conducting imaginal exposure in PTSD* (2nd ed.). Melbourne, Australia: Australian Centre for Posttraumatic Health.

Crittendon, P. M. (2000). A dynamic-maturational approach to continuity and change in pattern of attachment. In P. Crittenden & A. Claussen (Eds.), *The organization of attachment relationships: Maturation, culture and context* (pp. 343–357). Cambridge, UK: Cambridge University Press.

Damasio, A. R. (1999). *The feeling of what happens: Body and emotion in the making of consciousness.* New York, NY: Harcourt Brace.

Del Giudice, M. (2009). Sex, attachment, and the development of reproductive strategies. *Behavioral and Brain Sciences, 32*, 1–67.

Simeone-DiFrancesco, C. (2010). *Schema therapy for couples and marriages.* ISST website, linked to the original web publication by Wisconsin Family Growth and Reconciliation Center, LLC. Retrieved from www.wisconsinfamily.org

Simeone-DiFrancesco, C. (2011). *Stages in marital or couples schema therapy.* Unpublished paper, ISST Couples/Marital Subcommittee.

Simeone-DiFrancesco, C. (2012). *Re-defining the modes in the service of couples/marital work.* Unpublished paper, ISST Couples/Marital Subcommittee.

Simeone-DiFrancesco, C., & Simeone, R. (2016a, in press). *Evangelizing-doctors, a triadic model for catholic medical facilities: Healing the body, evangelizing the soul, Jesus-centered schema and mode healing for the person and marriage.* Malibu, CA: Healing International, Inc.

Simeone-DiFrancesco, C., & Simeone, R. (2016b, in press). *Jesus-centered schema therapy handbook for marriage & family.* Malibu, CA: Healing International, Inc.

Doherty, B. (2014). *National registry of marriage and family therapists.* Retrieved from www.marriagefriendlytherapist.com/values/

Edwards, D., & Arntz, A. (2012). Schema therapy in historical perspective. In M. van Vreeswijk, J. Broersen, & M. Nadort (Eds.), *The Wiley-Blackwell handbook of Schema Therapy: Theory, research and practice* (pp. 3–26). Oxford, UK: Wiley-Blackwell.

Ekman, P. (1993). Facial expression and emotion. *American Psychologist, 48*, 384–392.

Farrell, J., & Shaw, I. (2012). *Group Schema Therapy for borderline personality disorder: A step-by-step treatment manual with patient workbook.* Chichester, UK: Wiley-Blackwell.

Fertel, M. (2004). *Marriage fitness: An alternative to counseling.* Baltimore, MD: MarriageMax Inc. Retrieved from www.marriagemax.com

Figley, C. (1995). *Treating compassion fatigue.* New York, NY: Routledge.

Fitzgibbons, R. (2005–2011). *Institute for marital healing.* Conshohocken, Pennsylvania. Retrieved from www.maritalhealing.com

Flanagan, C. (2010). The case for needs in psychotherapy. *Journal of Psychotherapy Integration, 20*(1), 1–36.

Fonagy, P., Gergely, G., Jurist, E., & Target, M. (2004). *Affect regulation, mentalization and the development of the self.* London, UK: Karnac.

Frederickson, B. L. (2003). The value of positive emotions. *American Scientist, 91,* 330–335.

Freud, S. (1893–1895). Studies on hysteria. *Standard Edition of the Complete Psychological Works of Sigmund Freud, 2,* 1–305.

Freud, S. (1905/1963). *Dora: An analysis of a case of hysteria.* New York, NY: Collier.

Freud, S. (1917). Mourning and melancholia. *Standard Edition of the Complete Psychological Works of Sigmund Freud, 14,* 237–260.

Gasiewski, J. F. (2012). *The origins of punitiveness: Beyond the punitive parent.* Unpublished paper.

Giuffra, M. J. (2012). The crowded therapy room: The shadow land. *Somatic Therapy Today, 2*(3), 30–34.

Glass, S. (2003). *Not just friends: Rebuilding trust and recovering your sanity after infidelity.* New York, NY: Free Press.

Goldner, V. (1998). The treatment of violence and victimization in intimate relationships. *Family Process, 37*(3), 263–286.

Gordon, K. C., & Baucom, D. H. (1988). Understanding betrayal in marriage: A synthesised model of forgiveness. *Family Process, 37*(4), 425–449.

Gottman, J. (1999). *The marriage clinic: A scientifically based marital therapy.* New York, NY: W.W. Norton & Co.

Gottman, J. (2011). *The science of trust: Emotional attunement for couples.* New York, NY: W.W. Norton & Co.

Gottman, J., & Jacobsen, N. (1998). *Breaking the cycle: New insights into violent relationships.* London, UK: Bloomsbury.

Gottman, J., & Schwartz Gottman, J. (2009). *Level 1: Bridging the couple chasm, Gottman couples therapy: A new research-based approach.* Washington, DC: The Gottman Institute.

Gottman, J., & Silver, N. (1999). *The seven principles for making a marriage work.* New York, NY: Three Rivers Press.

Grant, A., Townend, M., Mills, J., & Cockx, A. (2009). *Assessment and case formulation in cognitive behavioral therapy.* London, UK: Sage.

Grawe, K. (2004). *Psychological therapy.* Goettingen–Bern, Switzerland: Hogrefe & Huber.

Greenberg, L. (2002). *Emotion-focused therapy: Coaching clients to work through feelings.* Washington, DC: American Psychological Association Press.

Greenberg, L. S., & Goldman, R. N. (2008). *Emotion-focused couples therapy: The dynamics of emotion, love and power.* Washington, DC: American Psychological Association.

Hackmann, A., Bennett-Levy, J., & Holmes, E. (2011). *Imagery in cognitive therapy.* Oxford, UK: Oxford University Press.

Hamel, J. (2005). *Gender inclusive treatment of intimate partner abuse: A comprehensive approach.* New York, NY: Springer.

Hare, R. (1993). *Without conscience: The disturbing world of the psychopaths among us.* New York, NY: Guilford Press.

Hare, R. (2003). *The psychopathy checklist—Revised* (2nd ed.). Toronto, ON, Canada: Multi-Health Systems.

Hargrave, T. D. (2000). *The essential humility of marriage.* Phoenix, AZ: Zeig, Tucker & Theisen, Inc.

Hayes, S. C. (2004). Acceptance and commitment therapy, relational frame theory, and the third wave of behavioral and cognitive therapies. *Behavioral Therapy, 35,* 639–665.

Hayes, S. C., Strohsal, K. D., & Wilson, K. G. (1999). *Acceptance and commitment therapy: An experiential approach to behavior change.* New York, NY: Guilford Press.

Heimann, P. (1950). On counter-transference. *International Journal of Psycho-Analysis, 31,* 81–84.

Hendrix, H. (1988). *Getting the love you want.* Melbourne, Australia: Schwartz & Wilkinson.

Heru, A. M. (2007). Intimate partner violence: Treating abuser and abused. *Advances in Psychiatric Treatment, 13,* 376–383.

Hubble, M. A., Duncan, B. L., & Miller, S. D. (1999). *The heart and soul of change.* Washington, DC: American Psychological Association.

Jacobson, N. S., & Christensen, A. (1996). *Integrative couple therapy: Promoting acceptance and change.* New York, NY: Norton.

Jacobson, N. S., & Margolin, G. (1979). *Marital therapy: Strategies based on social learning and behavior exchange principles.* New York, NY: Brunner/Mazel.

Johnson, S. M. (2004). *The practice of emotionally focused couple therapy: Creating connection* (2nd ed.). New York, NY: Brunner–Routledge.

Johnson, S. M. (2005). *Emotionally focused couple therapy with trauma survivors: Strengthening attachment bonds.* New York, NY: Guilford Press.

Johnson, S. M., & Zuccarini, D. (2010). Integrating sex and attachment in EFT-C. *Journal of Marital and Family Therapy, 36*(4), 431–445.

Kanfer, F. H., & Schefft, B. K. (1988). *Guiding the process of therapeutic change.* Ann Arbor, MI: Research Press Publications.

Kellogg, S. H. (2004). Dialogical encounters: Contemporary perspectives on 'chair-work' in psychotherapy. *Psychotherapy: Theory, Research, Practice, Training, 41*(3), 310–320.

Kellogg, S. H. (2012). On speaking one's mind: Using chair-work dialogs in ST. In M. van Vreeswijk, J. Broersen, & M. Nadort (Eds.), *The Wiley-Blackwell handbook of Schema Therapy: Theory, research and practice* (pp. 197–207). Oxford, UK: Wiley-Blackwell.

Kellogg, S. H., & Young, J. E. (2006). Schema therapy for borderline personality disorder. *Journal of Clinical Psychology, 62*(4), 445–458.

Kelly, M. (2010). *Rediscover catholicism: A spiritual guide to living with passion and purpose.* Boston, MD: Beacon Publishing.

Kelly, J., & Johnson, M. (2008). Differentiation among types of intimate partner violence: Research update and implications for treatment. *Family Court Review, 46*(3), 476–499.

Kersten, T. (2012). Schema therapy in personality disorder and addiction. In M. van Vreeswijk, J. Broersen, & M. Nadort (Eds.), *The Wiley-Blackwell handbook of Schema Therapy: Theory, research and practice* (pp. 415–424). Oxford, UK: Wiley-Blackwell.

Kindel, T. L., & Riso, L. P. (2013). *Are schema modes important for relationship functioning in married and dating couples: Implications for schema therapy with couples.* Poster presented at the annual meeting of the American Psychological Association, Washington, DC.

Lawson, A. (1988). *Adultery: An analysis of love and betrayal.* New York, NY: Basic Books.

Leahy, R. L. (2001). *Overcoming resistance in cognitive therapy.* New York, NY: Guilford Press.

Leary, M. R. (2000). Affect, cognition and social emotion: The role of self-reflection in the generation and regulation of affective experience. In R. Davidson, K. Scherer, & H. Goldsmith (Eds.), *Handbook of affective sciences.* New York, NY: Oxford University Press.

Linehan, M. M. (1993). *Cognitive-behavioral treatment of borderline personality disorder.* New York, NY: Guilford Press.

Lobbestael, J., van Vreeswijk, M., & Arntz, A. (2008). An empirical test of schema mode conceptualisations in personality disorders. *Behavior Research and Therapy, 46,* 854–860.

Lockwood, G., & Perris, P. (2012). A new look at core emotional needs. In M. van Vreeswijk, J. Broersen, & M. Nadort (Eds.), *The Wiley-Blackwell handbook of Schema Therapy: Theory, research and practice* (pp. 41–66). Oxford, UK: Wiley-Blackwell.

Lockwood, G., & Shaw, I. (2012). Schema therapy and the role of joy and play. In M. van Vreeswijk, J. Broersen, & M. Nadort (Eds.), *The Wiley-Blackwell handbook of Schema Therapy: Theory, research and practice* (pp. 209–227). Oxford, UK: Wiley-Blackwell.

MacLean, P. (1990). *The triune brain in evolution.* New York, NY: Plenum Press.

Maturana, H., & Varela, F. (1998). *The tree of knowledge: Biological roots of human understanding.* Boston, MA: Shambhala Press.

McDougall, J. (1985). *Theatres of the mind: Illusion and truth on the psychoanalytic stage.* New Yotk, NY: Basic Books.

McGoldrick, M., & Gerson, R. (1985). *Genograms in family assessment.* New York, NY: W.W. Norton.

Meichenbaum, D. H. (2007). *Family violence: Treatment of perpetrators and victims.* Retrieved from www.melissainstitute.org

Meichenbaum, D. H., & Goodman, J. (1971). Training impulsive children to talk to themselves: A means of developing self-control. *Journal of Abnormal Psychology, 77,* 115–126.

Messer, S. B. (2001). Introduction to the special issue of assimilative integration. *Journal of Psychotherapy Integration, 11,* 1–4.

Miller, W. R., & Rollnick, S. (2002). *Motivational interviewing: Preparing people for change* (2nd ed.). New York, NY: Guilford Press.

Millon, T. H. (1990). *Towards a new personology: An evolutionary model.* New York, NY: Wiley.

Morris, W. (1969). *The American heritage dictionary.* New York, NY: American Heritage Publishing Co., Inc./Houghton Mifflin Company.

Nadort, M., Arntz, A., Smit. J. H., Giesen-Bloo, J., Eikelboom, M., Spinhoven, P., ... van Dyck, R. (2009). Implementation of schema therapy for borderline personality disorders with versus without crisis support by the therapist outside office hours: A randomized trial. *Behavior Research and Therapy, 47,* 961–973.

Norcross, J., & Guy, J. (2007). *Leaving it at the office: A guide to psychotherapist self-care.* New York, NY: Guilford Press.

Ogden, P., Minton, M., & Pain, C. (2006). *Trauma and the body: A sensorimotor approach to psychotherapy.* New York, NY: W.W. Norton & Co.

Omaha, J. (2001). *Affect management skills training manual.* Chicago, IL: Chemotion Institute. Retrieved from www.johnomahaenterprises.com/AMSTManual.pdf

Parfy, E. (2012). Schema therapy, mindfulness and ACT: Differences and points of contact. In M. van Vreeswijk, J. Broersen, & M. Nadort (Eds.), *The Wiley-Blackwell handbook of Schema Therapy: Theory, research and practice* (pp. 229–237). Oxford, UK: Wiley-Blackwell.

Rafaeli, E., Bernstein, D., & Young, J. (2011). *Schema Therapy. The CBT distinctive features series.* New York, NY: Routledge.

Roediger, E. (2011). *Praxis der Schematherapie.* Stuttgart, Germany: Schattauer.

Roediger, E. (2012a). *Basics of a dimensional and dynamic mode model.* Retrieved from http://www.isstonline.com/sites/default/files/Roediger,%20E%20-%20 Basics%20of%20a%20dimensional%20and%20dynamic%20Mode%20Model-doc.pdf

Roediger, E. (2012b). Why are mindfulness and acceptance central elements for therapeutic change in schema therapy too? An integrative perspective. In M. van Vreeswijk, J. Broersen, & M. Nadort (Eds.), *The Wiley-Blackwell handbook of Schema Therapy: Theory, research and practice* (pp. 239–247). Oxford, UK: Wiley-Blackwell.

Roediger, E., & Jacob, G. (2010). *Fortschritte der Schematherapie.* Goettingen, Germany: Hogrefe.

Roediger, E., & Laireiter, A. R. (2013). The schema therapeutic mode cycle in behavior therapy supervision. *Verhaltenstherapie, 23,* 91–99. CCC-Code: 1016-6262/13/0232-091$38.00/0.

Roediger, E., Behary, W., & Zarbock, G. (2013). *Passt doch! Paarkonflikte verstehen und lösen mit der Schematherapie.* Weinheim, Germany: Beltz.

Rosner, R., Lyddon, W., & Freeman, A. (2004). *Cognitive therapy and dreams.* New York, NY: Springer.

Sager, C. (1981). Couples therapy and marriage contracts. In A. Gurman & D. Kniskern (Eds.), *Handbook of family therapy* (pp. 85–130). New York, NY: Brunner & Mazel.

Schnarch, D. (1998). *Passionate marriage.* New York, NY: Owl.

Schore, A. N. (2003). *Affect regulation and the repair of the self.* New York, NY: W.W. Norton & Co.

Sexton, T. L., & Coop-Gordon, K. (2009). Science, practice and evidence-based treatments in the clinical practice of family psychology. In J. Bray & M. Stanton (Eds.), *The Wiley-Blackwell handbook of family therapy* (pp. 164–326). Hoboken, NJ: Wiley.

Sheffield, A., & Waller, G. (2012). Clinical use of schema inventories. In M. van Vreeswijk, J. Broersen, & M. Nadort (Eds.), *The Wiley-Blackwell handbook of Schema Therapy: Theory, research and practice* (pp. 111–124). Oxford, UK: Wiley-Blackwell.

Siegel, D. J. (1999). *The developing mind: How relationships and the brain interact to shape who we are.* New York, NY: Guilford Press.

Simpson, S. (2012). Schema therapy for eating disorders: A case study illustration of the mode approach. In M. van Vreeswijk, J. Broersen, & M. Nadort (Eds.), *The Wiley-Blackwell handbook of schema therapy: Theory, research and practice* (pp. 145–171). Oxford, UK: Wiley-Blackwell.

Smalley, G. (1988). *Hidden keys of a loving lasting marriage.* Grand Rapids, MI: Zondervan.

Smalley, G., & Trent, J. (1990). *The two sides of love: Using personality strengths to greatly improve your relationships.* Wheaton, IL: Tyndale House Publishers.

Smucker, M., & Dancu, C. (2005). *Cognitive-behavioral treatment for adult survivors of childhood trauma.* New York, NY: Rowman & Littlefield Publishers, Inc.

Solomon, M., & Siegel, J. (1999). *Countertransference in couple therapy.* New York, NY: W.W. Norton.

Solomon, M., & Tatkin, S. (2011). *Love and war in intimate relationships: Connection, disconnection and mutual regulation.* New York, NY: W.W. Norton & Co.

Spring, J. A. (2012). *After the affair: Healing the pain and rebuilding trust when a partner has been unfaithful* (2nd ed.) New York, NY: Perennial Harper Collins.

Steele, V. R., Staley, C., Fong, T., & Prause, N. (2013). Sexual desire, not hypersexuality, is related to neurophysiological responses elicited by sexual images. *Socioaffective Neuroscience & Psychology, 3,* 20770.

Stern, D. N. (1985). *The interpersonal world of the infant.* New York, NY: Basic Books.

Stevens, B. (2012b). *Infant modes.* Unpublished paper presented to ISST Couples Group.

Stevens, B., & Arnstein, M. (2011). *Happy ever after? A practical guide to relationship counselling for clinical psychologists*. Brisbane, Australia: Australian Academic Press.

Stith, S. M., Rosen, K. H., McCollum, E. E., & Thomsen, C. J. (2004). Treating intimate partner violence within intact couples relationships: Outcomes of multi-couple versus individual couple therapy. *Journal of Marital and Family Therapy*, *30*(3), 305–318.

Stolorow, R. D., & Atwood, G. E. (1992). *Contexts of being: The inter-subjective foundations of psychological life.* , Hillsdale, NJ: The Analytic Press.

Teasdale, J. D., Moore, R. G., Hayhurst, H., Pope, M., Williams, S., & Segal, Z. V. (2002). Metacognitive aware-ness and prevention of relapse in depression: Empirical evidence. *Journal of Consulting and Clinical Psychology*, *70*(2), 275–287.

Tomkins, S. (1962–1963). *Affect, imagery, consciousness* (volumes 1–2). New York, NY: Springer.

van Genderen, H. (2012). Case conceptualization in schema therapy. In M. van Vreeswijk, J. Broersen, & M. Nadort (Eds.), *The Wiley-Blackwell handbook of Schema Therapy: Theory, research and practice* (pp. 27–40). Oxford, UK: Wiley-Blackwell.

van Genderen, H., Rijkeboer, M., & Arntz, A. (2012). Theoretical model: Schemas, coping styles and modes. In M. van Vreeswijk, J. Broersen, & M. Nadort (Eds.), *The Wiley-Blackwell handbook of Schema Therapy: Theory, research and practice* (pp. 27–40). Oxford, UK: Wiley-Blackwell.

van Vreeswijk, M., Broersen, J., & Nadort, M. (Eds.) (2012a). *The Wiley-Blackwell handbook of Schema Therapy: Theory, research and practice*. Oxford, UK: Wiley-Blackwell.

Weeks, G. R., & Treat, S. (1992). *Couples in treatment*. New York, NY: Brunner/ Mazel.

Weertman, A. (2012). The use of experimental techniques for diagnostics. In M. van Vreeswijk, J. Broersen, & M. Nadort (Eds.), *The Wiley-Blackwell handbook of Schema Therapy: Theory, research and practice* (pp. 101–109). Oxford, UK: Wiley-Blackwell.

Winnicott, D. W. (1958). *Collected papers: From paediatrics through psycho-analysis* (1st ed.). London, UK: Tavistock Publications.

Wisman, M., & Uewbelacker, L. (2007). Maladaptive schemas and core beliefs in treatment and research with couples. In L. Riso, P. du Toit, D. Stein, & J. Young (Eds.), *Cognitive schemas and core beliefs in psychological patterns: A scientist-practitioner guide* (pp. 199–220). Washington, DC: American Psychological Association.

Wojtyla, K. (1993). *Love and responsibility* (revised ed.). San Francisco, CA: Ignatius Press.

Wright, J., Basco, M., & Thase, M. (2006). *Learning cognitive-behavior therapy: An illustrated guide*. Washington, DC: American Psychiatric Publishing.

Yang, M., Coid, J., & Tyrer, P. (2010). Personality pathology recorded by severity: National survey. *British Journal of Psychiatry*, *197*, 193–199.

Young, J. (2012). *Schema therapy with couples*, DVD. American Psychological Association Series IV Relationships hosted with Jon Carlson. Retrieved from www.apa.org/pubs/videos/4310895.aspx

Young, J. E., & Gluhoski, V. (1997). A schema focused perspective on satisfaction in close relationships. In R. J. Sternberg & M Hojjat (Eds.), *Satisfaction in close relationships* (pp. 356–381). New York, NY: The Guilford Press.

Young, J. E., Klosko, J. S., & Weishaar, M. E. (2003). *Schema therapy: A practitioner's guide*. New York, NY: Guilford Press.

Young, J., Arntz, A., Atkinson, T., Lobbestael, J., Weishaar, M., van Vreeswijk, M., & Klokman, J. (2007). *Mode inventory SMI 1.1*. New York, NY: Schema Therapy Institute.

Index of Therapy Tools and Interventions

Index

Schema Therapy with Couples: A Practitioner's Guide to Healing Relationships, First Edition.
Chiara Simeone-DiFrancesco, Eckhard Roediger, and Bruce A. Stevens.
© 2015 John Wiley & Sons, Ltd. Published 2015 by John Wiley & Sons, Ltd.
Companion website: www.wiley.com/go/difrancesco/schematherapywithcouples